Nucleoethics:

Ethics in Modern Society

David Tribe

Nucleoethics:

Ethics in Modern Society

MacGibbon & Kee   London

BJ
1012
T72

Granada Publishing Limited
First published in Great Britain 1972 by MacGibbon & Kee Ltd
3 Upper James Street London W1R 4BP

ISBN 0 261 63266 3
Printed in Great Britain by
Richard Clay (The Chaucer Press) Ltd
Bungay, Suffolk

Contents

Glossary of Terms

AMORALITY: absence of a moral code.

CHRISTOETHICS: belief that morality derives from Christianity.

CHRISTOMORALITY: moral codes based on Christianity.

ENDOETHICS: belief that morality derives from individualism; see p. 196.

ENDOMORALITY: moral codes based on individualism.

ETHICIZE: investigate ethics.

ETHICS: study or theory of the origin and nature of right and wrong.

Ethos: group customs, usually of a moral kind.

EVIL: supposititious influence of the devil.

IMMORALITY: *immores* or moromalpractice or persomoromalpractice; see below.

Immores: behaviour opposed to prevailing *ethos*.

IRRELIGIOETHICS: belief that morality derives from freethought.

IRRELIGIOMORALITY: moral codes based on freethought.

MORAL: concerning 'voluntary' behaviour which directly affects others in what they deem important matters of duty; see p. 53.

MORALISM: unwarranted generalization from moral particulars.

MORALITY: moral code or *mores* or moropractice or persomoropractice.

MORALIZE: preach morality.

Mores: *ethos*.

MOROMALPRACTICE: breaking one's own moral code.

MOROPRACTICE: following one's own moral code.

NUCLEOETHICS: a study of the social factors that collectively mould morality; see pp. 205–6, 229, 233 and 247.

PERSOMORALITY: personal moral code in a context of nucleo-ethics without ideological dominance; see pp. 17, 258, 265 and 280.

PERSOMOROMALPRACTICE: breaking this.

PERSOMOROPRACTICE: following this.

POLITICOETHICS: belief that morality derives from politics.

POLITICOMORALITY: moral codes based on politics.

RELIGIOETHICS: belief that morality derives from religion.

RELIGIOMORALITY: moral codes based on religion.

SCIOETHICS: belief that morality derives from science.

SCIOMORALITY: moral codes based on science.

SIN: disobedience to the supposititious will of God.

VICE: sin or *immores* or moromalpractice.

VIRTUE: abstract quality of goodness or *mores* or moropractice.

Introduction

Ethology, which used to mean 'the science of ethics'[1] but now signifies a gloomy mixture of human zoology and the pathology of instincts, is today's fashion. Or perhaps yesterday's. The pendulum of fashion never stops. Indeed it grows shorter and faster. Soon 'ethology' may be recharged with its old meaning. Even 'ethics' may be rehabilitated. It will be none too soon.

One of the more singular of modern trends has been the devaluation of deontology, or the science of duty. 'Moralize', which used to describe the ancient art of the fable-writer, now suggests the tatty artifice of the leader-writer. A 'virtuous woman' conjures up an ageing butch standard-bearer of the Women's Liberation movement frantically burning an exhausted bra. 'Ethical advertising' is a cant phrase for the promotion of pharmaceuticals, an area which, during a brief flirtation with the advertising world, I found to be among the seediest of its sub-continents.

Why has the language of ethics and morality been so degraded? Is it that we live in a more corrupt age? From historical researches I very much doubt it. One looks to the past in vain for the noble savage or the unspoilt Pre-Raphaelite. Is it that goodness has become so abundant that we no longer need accurate language to describe it? Hardly. While the apostles of progress can point triumphantly to man's increasing mastery over the environment – which may be a precondition of the brave new world but is certainly no more – we look in vain for increased mastery over ourselves.

In part the cheapening of moral language has accompanied the decline of religion with which it was so long automatically associated. 'Sermonize' and 'pious' have gone the same way as 'moralize' and 'righteous': down. As traditional religion would

9

seem to be in a permanent decline it will be hard to rescue ethics while it lies in the same pit. In part moral concepts have declined as a reaction against those temporal powers, other than the churches, off whose tongues they tripped most gracefully and most hypocritically. In part there is a turning away from the moral philosophers, traditional guardians of moral language who used to converse at least with other educated classes but now talk only to one another. If an outsider eavesdrops on their conversations he may form the impression that they are so obsessed with relativity theory and linguistic individuality that they have come to believe the Humean paradox a reality: 'If there were *nothing* for which all or most informed people would have a similar approbation, people being temperamentally different in this respect – then *nothing* would be a virtue and *nothing* a vice.'[2]

With the clergy dumb or the laity deaf, our elders no longer deemed our betters or our leaders our moral guides, and the fount of moral learning absorbed within the vales of Academe, it may be wondered how we remain moral at all. Unless, that is, we decide that moral precepts can have little or nothing to do with moral practice. This idea at once raises two further questions. Why, in that case, has ethicizing for so long dominated the mind of man? If ethical theories are all lacking, what is the true architectonics of morality?

At once we can point to the guidance of parents and teachers and peer pressures beginning from the moment toddlers have to accommodate themselves to others at nurseries. But parents, teachers and peers are themselves as diverse as the children they influence. What, if any, are the principles they hold in common? And how does principle become transformed to practice, without which it is devoid of interest to other than scholars? Traditionally authoritarianism has answered both questions. Principles are established by authority (physical or mental or spiritual or usually all combined). Each generation absorbs, preserves or slightly modifies, and passes on authorized information. The technique of instruction is authoritarian. Children are taught morals as they are taught arithmetic lessons or the catechism. What they take in they are expected to regurgitate. If they take nothing in, this is assumed to be the result of a perverse will which has to be broken. As we shall see, however, the theory of authoritarianism has always been suspect; while, whatever its past merits, an entirely new situation has arisen from the growing challenge to it.

The precise date[3] of commencement of this challenge is hard to fix. Any dating of this sort is largely arbitrary as time does not conveniently change gear according to monarchs' reigns or other devices for mapping historical epochs. Yet certain events do seem to be so traumatic in their impact and seminal in their influence that it becomes possible to relate them to philosophical outlook and social change. It is hard, for example, not to agree with Comte that the French Revolution of 1789 symbolizes a challenge to authority, political and ecclesiastical, which has made it a watershed in the intellectual topography of Europe (including the Americas and certain other overseas areas largely within the European tradition). Similarly I would identify the First World War as the trigger for a new release of anti-authoritarianism, social and cultural, whose full implications were not realized till after the Second World War.[4] To some extent I am influenced in the last assessment by my personal experiences. I was brought up, in the thirties and forties, in Australia, a land which was classless in everything but money, influence, examination passes and whatever else ensured success in life. Democracy and meritocracy were no doubt already more than theoretical ideals in Britain; but as late as the fifties I was surprised on my arrival by the patronizing snobbery of the upper classes, the forelock-touching of the lower, and the extreme conservatism, within their several traditions, of appearance and *mores* of the various groups that formed the richly textured British society. In the 'swinging Britain' of the sixties a lot of attitudes broke loose and stayed adrift or slipped into new pigeon-holes. Like trends can be observed throughout the world.

Another change has come since my own youth. This has a familiar sound, as ancient as history. Let me therefore hasten to add that I do not recall a golden childhood. Quite the contrary. I was immensely relieved to outgrow my youthful fears and persecutors. My personal experiences belie the rising statistics of delinquency, notably of violence. Measured by a yardstick that many deem important, playground anecdotes or toilet walls, 'impure thoughts' do not seem to be in the ascendant. What I have in mind is a more fundamental matter. It was widely believed in my youth, even by those who affected to doubt it and defied its implications, that there were in society sources of authority, conferring their own status, that not only safeguarded its traditions – which were in many cases sheer bric-à-brac not worth preserving – but filtered out real knowledge from the perennial flood of purported information and provided an orderly pattern for the development of the individual. They were the equivalent of the elders of the tribe who passed on its ritual secrets and traditional skills through a long programme of training and degrees of initiation. It was assumed that children had less wisdom and teenagers less earning capacity, as distinct from intellect or potential, than their parents; that pupils and students on the whole knew less about academic subjects and administration than their teachers and professors; that artistic and other attainments came at the end of a long apprenticeship of study, practice and humility before one's craft. (There had already been Dada but it was a passing craze.) All this has changed,[5] and I am old-fashioned enough – or old enough – to regret it.

What traditionalists describe as 'the descent to decadence'[6] usually involves a number of overdue reforms in the fields of abortion, sex and divorce laws, contraception, censorship and the like. The contemporary world is seen as 'a moral vacuum where moral views and judgements no longer motivate people'.[7] And we are urged to return to religion as the source of moral values. It is noteworthy that most of those who promote alternatives to religion – humanistic, political, scientific or existential – stress the moral contents of their creeds or anti-creeds and in their organization and 'life-style' often take on, quite unconsciously, the trappings of religion. Perhaps this explains why the notions that man cannot live without religion and that religion and morality are inextricably mixed, which lack credentials in either philosophy or history, die so hard, even among those whose own lives testify to the secular view and who would explain away their non-devotions on the grounds that 'religion is irrelevant'. That it is irrelevant to one's moral state in this life and possible fate in another I would agree. But so precise are its claims and tenacious its hold that the veracity or otherwise of these claims cannot be regarded as an irrelevant issue. So I have given a large, and some will deem disproportionate, amount of space to considering it. Partly this results from the great complexity of rival religious views compared with political and other alternative, or complementary, responses to the world. From a moral standpoint the intrinsic truth or otherwise of these views is of scant importance so long as people believe them, save in so far as a nation's laws and educational system, with their influence on all citizens, mirror the degree to which public credence is accorded. Given the 'inward' interpretation of religion it hardly matters whether Zeus was a phallic symbol or Jesus a fly agaric [8] rather than their customary representations. Humanistic, scientific and existential views of the world can be equally inward. Politics however, in relation to economics, is by its very nature of immediate practical importance. Hence its appeal to modern man. Rarely is it described, outside the extreme Left, in moral terms; though 'freedom', 'social justice' and other vogue expressions have strong moral undertones. My thesis is, however, that the historical association of political and ethical theory is as intimate as that between theology and ethics and that political speculation always flourishes when religion has come to look speculative.

This may be seen in the life of the individual no less than in the life of nations. Such, at any rate, is my observation. For this is essentially a book of observations. Most accounts of ethics read like extended bibliographies of other accounts of ethics. All the big guns, past and present, are wheeled out again, oiled and polished, fired once or twice, then returned to their museum. Coming from some of the greatest minds of civilization, these batteries cannot but impress. But I sometimes wonder what relevance they have to the real battles of morality. To me their shots are far more interesting as a relic from the past than as an arsenal for the future. Their theories represent a reaction against specific injustices of their own place and time, or a response to an individual psychology or physiology. Even the most visionary of them have dreams whose raw material can be identified in a biographical way. In referring to this as a book of observations I hope that it may be practical. True, it considers many ethical theories – even formulating some that have largely been inchoate

– but it does so largely to dismiss their supposed moral application. As such it is chiefly a 'negative' book. This is not fortuitous, for I believe that the 'negative' is ultimately the more 'positive', just as life functions most smoothly when its servo-mechanisms of negative feedback [9] are the most sensitive. But the 'positive' elements in the book – the impulses which the servo-mechanisms refine – will no doubt provoke the claim that this is yet another theoretical venture dictated by the limited constitution and experiences of its promoter.

It is appropriate therefore that I give further autobiographical details so that the reader may sample the soil in which the thoughts which follow germinated. According to the theory of selective observation, yet more fundamental than my 'experiences' is the personality-type which is experiencing them. I do not, however, propose to psychoanalyse myself, being uncertain whether I am basically introvert or extrovert, and psychoanalysts are likely to agree that I am the last person who should make the attempt. Nor do I propose to set out my dreams or my sex life. The autobiographical details that follow will be of the more conventional kind.

One of my first recollections is starting at Sunday school before I began day school. It was an average-sized affair, run by the Plymouth Brethren. Most of the stories were from the Old Testament and, by any reckoning, of dubious morality – as many churchmen will now admit. When the choruses were not entirely vapid ('I'm H-A-P-P-Y') they tended to be doctrinal ('What can wash away my stain? / Nothing but the blood of Jesus'). Few of them were concerned with moral responsibility, and then only in a non-specific way ('Jesus wants me for a sunbeam / To shine for him each day'). Almost every class at this Sunday school contained one member of a numerous problem family. One of the little girls, who was a notorious liar and thief, developed the ingratiating habit of waylaying everyone she met, children and adults alike, and asking them 'Are you saved?' To those unfamiliar with this world I had better explain that this cryptic question meant 'Have you taken the Lord Jesus Christ as your own personal Saviour?' Because of my Sunday school connections my parents, of Anglican and Methodist origins respectively, were persuaded to join a Brethren assembly. No pope ever reigned more augustly over the One Holy Catholic and Apostolic Church than did a handful of elders over this tiny community. Outside the meeting-place one of them had a reputation for sharp practice in business and another for spying on lady guests through holes providentially formed, or drilled, in his outside weather-board toilet. The lives of the general membership were enlivened by their efforts to smear on make-up, visit cinemas, buy lottery tickets, smoke, drink or read Sunday papers without detection. At about the same time my grandmother turned Seventh Day Adventist and tea-drinking became one of her secret and constant sins.

After a time my parents, with me in tow, drifted away from the Brethren via the Baptists and Church of Christ to the Methodists. There were interludes with other evangelical groups and at American hot-gospelling rallies that made anything which has appeared in Britain along these lines seem decent and decorous by comparison. At university I had a lot of Catholic friends, some of whom told equally hair-raising stories of the tyranny and puritanism, in another context, of their own school-days. On the whole I was happy with the Methodists, especially with those who, I see on looking back, wore their religion lightly and regarded chapel and its adjuncts as a social club with an aura of uplift. Religion, I came to believe, did not produce the 'changed lives' beloved of revivalist meetings; for I had the opportunity of seeing the day-by-day conduct of some of those who on such occasions witnessed for Jesus. Good men did not need religion to make them better while bad men through it added humbug and fanaticism to their other vices. Despite the constant associ-ation in literature, law and public opinion of religion and ethics, few people, I considered, turned to and stayed in the churches for moral reasons. Instead they were seeking respectability or belongingness or certainty in an uncertain world or immortality or some other fundamentally selfish benefit. The universal love they spoke of did not stretch across their neighbour's fence or even permeate their family circle. Some people in the churches were assiduous in hospital visiting and other kindly acts, but typical members of this group acted thus before joining a church or after leaving it. And, when I came to move in wider circles, I found similar people who had never had church connections.

As I was one of the small group that stays interested in religion after ceasing to believe it, after a period in the ideological wilderness on leaving the Methodists I entered the infidel movement – or, as it now likes to call itself, the humanist movement. Here, if only because of size and resources, there was less opportunity for fanaticism to be dangerously manifested, while respectability was hardly, in the historical circumstances, a goal of membership. In so far as there were no creeds, dietary and other tabus there was less occasion for humbug. I did, however, find that there were some humanists, particularly in the ethical church tradition, who thought, even when they did not talk, about 'changed lives' as a result of some new humanist insight into living. What precisely this was I was never, despite involvement at the centre of humanist affairs, able to find out. I happened to find a materialist interpretation of the world more plausible and a libertarian attitude to sex and other appetites more congenial than the one I was brought up in (perhaps I was never really 'saved'), but I was unable to see that in everyday matters of tolerance, balanced judgement, truthfulness, trustworthiness and the rest humanists were any better than anyone else.

A fair number of humanists are scientists and most of the rest talk a lot about 'scientific method' even if they seem to have an imperfect knowledge of what it means. This was another field that, at least for a time, I was able to observe at the grass-roots. For I was educated in medicine into the clinical years and modern medicine is a science, however inexact, rather than an art. In the preclinical years I also saw the physical and biological sciences at work. Now, it seemed to me that in science faculties (including medicine and engineering) even more than in the arts the great bulk of people involved, staff as well as students, were chasing a meal-ticket or social status rather than quenching any passionate thirst for knowledge. In so far as they did seek enlightenment it was largely confined (by necessity, some will say) to a very narrow specialism. Within the rigours of their own disciplines, trendiness, deference to authority, purblind commitment to pet theories, however discredited, wilfulness, jealousy and One-up-manship were more noticeable than outsiders imagine. Outside their professional competence, they showed no greater resistance than non-scientists to mythology, ancient or modern (and in spiritualism–psychical research–parapsychology they have often shown themselves more gullible), and no less tendency to 'irrationalism' in everyday life. Even when their professional researches were models of objectivity and humility, these qualities did not necessarily spill over into their private lives and influence their moral judgements.

Outside my own formal education, as an only child who did not go to boarding school or hall of residence and had few close friends, I was in a good position to have existentialist[10] thoughts While they may have encouraged individuality and self-reliance, as these words are commonly understood, I was never tempted to think that the isolated individual gained new insights into human relations. On the contrary, while such a stance may give a clinical approach to other people's failures to 'relate', it also produces a disinclination to form personal relationships oneself and may, at its extreme, echo the cry in Sartre's *Huis-Clos* that 'hell is other people'. Shut off from peer pressures, one can become contemptuous of them. Certainly one arouses peer suspicion and hostility. Now while this may become the stuff of great art and even, with exceptional individuals, of great moral insights, it is hardly the stuff of day-to-day practical morality. That is why I am distrustful of what is called 'individual morality', with its concentration on individuals' 'responsibility to themselves to develop their individual uniqueness'.[11] For the most part this will produce individual unhappiness and – if indulged in by unstable minds 'freaking out' with a 'hippie father' like Charles Manson – tragedy. What I describe as 'persomorality' simply recognizes that every individual necessarily follows his personal computer, which is programmed by a multiplicity of sources in one of an infinity of different combinations. It is not intended to suggest, as 'individual morality' does, that the 'moral instinct' is some strange property arising from or injected into the individual's innermost self as a manifestation of 'the transcendental and the spiritual',[12] which curbs our animal nature and achieves feats of altruism that astonish us. This concept is, I believe, a ghost of the theologian's 'soul' left behind when religion has ostensibly died.

From my school-days politics has fascinated me as a study, though its practice I find distasteful. At one time I was a vice-president of my university's Liberal Society. This meant very little, since it had no formal links with the Liberal Party outside and Australian Liberalism has for a long time been, on most social questions, more reactionary than British Conservatism. Since those days I have found the company of 'socialists' more congenial because of their interest in social reforms, but I doubt whether most of them have really thought about the full implications, let alone the practicability, of economic socialism; while they, with ample justification, suspect the strength of my class-consciousness.

I was brought up in sundry working-class districts, or what would in any other country be so described, and have since visited the best-known proletarian shrines in Europe and America; while for some years I have read much about theories of class origin, description and transformation. All that has struck me from observation is that, in the last analysis, people are pigeon-holed into classes according to what they possess, regardless of how they came by it. In Britain, as distinct from Australia or America, this includes the ability or inability to buy a special type of education with the accent, manners, tastes and other attributes that go with it. This definition of classes readily suggests that the upper classes must be more unscrupulous than the lower or they would not be in possession of so much more. Or at least it readily suggests this to the modern mind. For a long time social classes were assumed to have a divine or quasi-divine origin and the upper classes were looked up to as the chosen vehicle for moral revelation. Whether or not morality still in practice diffuses downwards rather than upwards is a talking point for sociologists, but, outside the mystique of monarchy and the churches of Christian Science, it is no longer fashionable to assume that virtue brings material rewards or possessions confer moral status. Rather, the contrary view prevails. It is found among Marxists of all class origins, but among non-Marxists it is especially the joy of middle-class theoreticians. The working classes, it is now declared, are some strange repository of goodness denied to other, more acquisitive classes. It is a theory which has the practical, if not the philosophical, advantage of being non-invalidatable. A proletarian saint is a demonstration of the goodness of his class; a proletarian crook is a demonstration of the evil of other classes. Class-consciousness is a virtue when practised by the working classes and a vice when practised by other classes.

From my vantage-point within the working classes I have been unable to detect that nidus of virtue whence, we are told, the whole of society can be purified and reconstituted. I have met good people and bad people, as in every other class. Neither have I met what is described as a peculiarly working-class virtue, 'solidarity'. On the contrary, history suggests that ruling classes have, when the crunch comes, been more inclined to overlook personal interests and varnish over sub-class fragmentation. But working-class solidarity, as represented by a 100 per cent strike, signifies, when it does occur, more the sort of self-interest investors display when they look for profits than any stand on high moral principles. Viewing this position the unthinking Tory may say, privately these days, that the masses are too unintelligent to appreciate such subtleties. To me it does not seem unintelligent for the better organized of the workers to let radical 'bourgeois' intellectuals, many in straitened circumstances, agonize over working-class wrongs while they, heedless of the claims of radical minorities or pensioners, relax over beer and bingo. Nor does it seem particularly moral.

A variant of the class interpretation of morality I have found is the people interpretation. This is the facile assumption that national and international corruption would be eliminated if 'ordinary people' were in control; but, alas, they are led by the nose by their rulers. Here again, I was moved to investigate the anatomy of power and responsibility by personal observations. This view may be held by those who, at the same time, believe that evolution depends on social forces and emphasize that those improvements in health and living standards which we have seen have nothing whatever to do with our 'rulers'. Whipping-boys when things go wrong, nonentities when things go well – such is their thankless task and, no doubt, their social function. Being hostile to theories that are both untidy and unjust, I early came to exonerate rulers of both exceptional sagacity and exceptional depravity. Franco, Stalin, Vorster, Hitler, Mussolini and the rest all, in my view, testify to national moods and political systems and are not strange biological sports mysteriously swept to power. For this reason, and because of my interest in social rather than dynastic history, I was more than willing to believe that a lot of the trappings of government, bureaucratic and legalistic, might safely be dispensed with as redundant. Some form of anarcho-syndicalism seemed the way to let nations express themselves directly. But again my observations intervened.

It was soon apparent to me – long before I was able to appreciate political theory – that a generous display of headmasters in schools and policemen in slums was necessary to stop violence from breaking out or remove it when it did. With adults and in more favourable situations, though, things might be different. Yet my experiences have failed to encourage this further hope. However worthy their aims, organizations I have known have depended for their effectiveness on leadership. Even when this is good there is no shortage of critics to denounce the monstrousness of constitutions, officers, annual reports, confidential files and the other consequences of organization. Interestingly, these apostles of extreme libertarianism show marked authoritarian traits in themselves and, when they establish their own non-organizations or communes, as they not infrequently do, they show a noisy dominance that nobody in 'the great grey monoculture'[13] of orthodox society would tolerate for ten minutes. I have had contact with the New Left, Student Power, Women's Lib., the drugs scene, the 'Underground', the 'Free University', communes and other power-houses of the 'protest industry'. They show the same mixture of active and passive types as may be found in the outside world, but lacking a formal structure their non-organizations soon tumble to earth (if they ever get off the ground); while their sincerity seems often to match their efficiency. In my recollection are meetings of indescribable incoherence;[14] spurners of corrupt society who break off harangues only for visits to a bank to cash cheques from rich parents or to a Social Security office; a teeny-bopper reporter who, on the strength of six months' apprenticeship on an Underground paper, expected to command the heights of Fleet Street features journalism; a not-so-young young man who, after writing his autobiography of a dropout, hoped to drop in again in a big way; a good assortment of compilers of sub-Ginsberg *graffiti* and

20

revolutionary slogans who dominate the poetry 'circuit'. Personally they may be charming if not 'beautiful' people, but so, I discovered, was the founder of the reactionary John Birch Society in America and so, by all accounts, was Hitler. Some aspects of their life-style may be attractive: their contempt for physical violence and war,[15] the free love of 'group marriages'. At least I find them attractive. But only as an excrescence on an affluent society, an eccentricity of the young or childless. For how could society as a whole be organized, or disorganized, on this model? How would children – assuming they escape the probably exaggerated hazards of congenital drug addiction or deformation – survive the instability of this *milieu*? One anxious modern *communard* speculates that 'perhaps capitalistic society does give people a sense of freedom – some strange sort of freedom – in that they are not actually tied down to concrete undertakings'.[16] Yet this is precisely the motivation, I would say, of most of the Underground.

It is hardly necessary for me to say that I have met *poseurs*, idlers, eccentrics and young men on the make in the worlds of conventional business and politics, many with less ability and gaining greater rewards than those I have met in the Underground; and it may be wondered why, unless I am an arch-reactionary, I should single out one relatively inoffensive group for special comment. Now I am, I hope, a card-bearing and heart-baring liberal, but that makes me the more anxious to analyse what is put abroad in the name of liberalism. The traditional wide boy or wastrel is frankly self-absorbed and does not offer his life-style as a universal model. Indeed he has no relish for further competition. The Underground, however, makes a virtue of its prejudices and idiosyncrasies and often displays a proselytizing zeal that invites apathetic, astonished or even hostile bystanders, as C.N.D. did in its heyday, to 'join the march'. At the same time a number of 'square' commentators have, rather tendentiously and prematurely, identified this life-style as an important ingredient of modern 'adolescent protest'.[17] Sometimes it is suggested this may be more than a growing-up pain: nothing short of a prodromal symptom of tomorrow's 'new morality'. And, in the 'silent majority' mind, the 'permissive society' is similarly identified with everything 'from drugged students in digs and blue films in Soho, to nudity on stage'[18] and public love-making at pop festivals.

Now, the permissive society, properly understood, is what I regard as essential for future harmony, the expression of a tolerance of, if not of a sympathy for, a wide range of individual tastes and national customs or political systems, without which the earth will explode in riots and world wars. With it, exotic life-styles and forms of government will arise and may spread by emulation. But it is important to examine every brave new discovery which claims to have found the answer to greed and war. Millennia ago Indian *gurus* made similar claims and it is not surprising to find that Indian mysticism features prominently among today's *avant-garde*. Yet Indian history shows not only a failure to abolish greed and war but a notable capacity to spread pestilence and beggary. This, I suggest, could be hippiedom writ large if all its social implications were accepted. So I found myself returning, reluctantly, to traditional forces in society – law and bureaucracy, communications and pragmatic government – hated, with some reason, by good progressives, to see whether they were dispensable and, if not, how they could be humanized and made accountable. In so doing I became convinced of the moral need to preserve social stability in the midst of social reform. Not only must a permissive society permit people to be conventional, but fostered unconventionality seems to lead to either new and narrower conventions[19] or disorder which is morally subversive.

These observations of how people actually behaved in certain circumstances led me to investigate ethical theories. The technical analyses of philosophers[20] are interesting mainly as a reflection of educated opinion in their own slice of space-time and, more recently, for their brave, but not altogether successful, attempts to understand and systematize moral language.[21] Of greater impact in the world at large have been those ethical views, explicit or implicit, enshrined in the great religious, political and other world-views. In studying them and systems erected on them I became convinced that they either had no effect on individual morals at all or that, by forcing 'solutions' to moral problems regardless of circumstances, brought only harm. So I tried to analyse what really influenced morality, for better or worse, and what might benefit it. Rejecting traditional religious answers I was impelled to reduce[22] not only society but man to what I felt were his essentials in the absence of a spirit or soul. For whether or not the whole is greater than its parts its function cannot readily be understood without identifying them. Increasingly I have come to believe that much moral terminology of a non-technical kind – willpower, free will, altruism, autonomy, ego and superego, creativity, introspection, spirituality, transcendence – are survivals of the religious outlook, and that man is only a super-computer. This will, I know, at once bring the charge of nineteenth-century materialism or mechanism or reductionism of the grossest sort. There are historical reasons[23] why it should in a world that has experienced the new technological barbarism. But I do not believe we can any longer delay facing what may be to many an ugly fact. Neither do I believe that such an admission will necessarily degrade man even below the level of a naked ape. On the whole, society looks after its computers better than it looks after its apes. But if man is a computer the manner of his programming becomes of prime importance.

In coming to this view I was not tempted to make do with the language of behaviourism. While much can be explained by conditioned reflexes, or conditioned responses, other factors, hereditary or spontaneous, are as important. To jettison 'consciousness' together with more dubious psychological terms is arbitrary and unconvincing, while 'social engineering'[24] conjures up the worst excesses of psychiatric tyranny and totalitarian planning. So, as has happened before, I was induced, reluctantly, to invent terms of my own. 'Persomorality' has already been distinguished from 'individual morality'. 'Nucleoethics', a more arbitrary term, is explained later. Throughout the book I have tried to use 'ethics' for theory and 'morality' for instructions. Of ultimate importance, however, is how people actually behave. This I call 'moropractice' where it is in keeping with the individual's own moral code, and 'moromalpractice' where it is not and makes him ashamed. The latter is, I suggest, far less common than is usually supposed. Within this terminology the sort of behaviour I should like to see is 'persomoropractice' and to avoid is 'persomoromalpractice'. As such ungainly words are equally to be avoided I have made do with ordinary expressions like 'desirable conduct' (despite the disadvantage that this invites the question 'desired by whom?') and 'antisocial behaviour' respectively. 'Antisocial' is to be taken in the sense of causing demonstrable harm to society and not simply offending against those tabus, customs and manners which happen at any one time to be fashionable. For such behaviour I use the term '*immores*'.

To dodge those confusions which are widespread in the literature of ethics and even more so in the moralistic prose of the devout, I try wherever possible to avoid the unqualified word 'morality' and particularly 'immorality', which may mean,[25] by my nomenclature, persomoromalpractice, moromalpractice or (frequently) *immores*. 'Morality' usually appears in the text with a prefix to denote the moral codes that tend to result from specific ethical views of the world. Here again ordinary adjectives are inadequate. 'Religious morality' might suggest the moropractice of the clergy or morality which is especially binding. 'Religiomorality' is devised for a specific usage, viz. to describe those moral codes deduced from 'religioethics' (religious belief in its ethical context). Similarly 'political morality' might suggest the moropractice of politicians; 'politicomorality' is the morality derived from 'politicoethics'. Naturally an infinity of religious and political views might have been analysed. I have confined myself to those which are most influential or most distinctive. The disproportionate attention I have given to Christianity is not intended to suggest that it is a more plausible or complex interpretation of the world than other religions. On the contrary, if religion is regarded as a purely abstract system seeking to interpret the natural order from the standpoint of human justice, the Hindu–Buddhist notion of *karma* may well seem more reasonable than Christian 'justification by faith'. But Christianity is likely to be more familiar to most readers than other religions and has, apart perhaps from Buddhism, been more successful. It is also the religion whose nuances and sects I understand best. So I have felt justified in referring to it often enough to justify 'Christoethics' and 'Christomorality' as further neologisms. The alternatives of 'religioethics[2]' and 'irreligioethics', with their moral equivalents, are explained fully in the appropriate section. For the sake of uniformity I have used 'endoethics' and 'endomorality' instead of 'situation ethics' and 'individual morality', which are more or less what they connote.

In this way I hope to lay bare the anatomy of authoritarianism and mythology, ancient and modern, to the unsentimental gaze, and present the permissive society, not only naked and unashamed but healthy and responsible, to admiring suitors.

Part One
Is There a Moral Crisis?

1   The Crisis of Authority

It's a mad, mad, mad, mad world:
The only thing you're sure of
Is that nothing is sure.[1]

The cinema of shocks reflects a world of instant experience. What lies behind it? Or before it? What is in the head of electronic man among the image fragments of communication? What umbilicus of ideas binds him to his ancestors? Does he escape drowning in an internal soup only to sink outside in an ocean of alienation?

In his speech at New York to mark the twenty-fifth anniversary of the United Nations, the British Prime Minister, Edward Heath, observed that in the 1970s 'civil war, rather than war between nations, will be the main danger which we face. We are ourselves experiencing this in the United Kingdom.' The main divide in Northern Ireland he saw as that between 'those who believe that constructive change is the only sound basis for peace, prosperity and security' and 'those who reach at the first opportunity for the gun or the bomb'.[2] There is some evidence to support this view.

Every week we see mirrored on television a hundred riots and uprisings, crimes, revolutions and *coups d'état*, colonial and neo-colonial wars and border disputes. In the late 1960s American newspapers listed campus upheavals in ready reference tables, like sporting fixtures. From Japan to Germany, Sydney to the Sorbonne, Rio to Rome, Mexico City to Moscow, the picture has varied only in intensity. In England and Wales, despite compulsory religion in schools and better-equipped police in the streets, the number of known indictable offences almost trebled from 1950 to 1967. In the same period the number of convictions among males between seventeen and twenty-one more than quadrupled. Those who leave the churches do not join humanist organizations. Politics is held in contempt, or not held at all. The world seems to be exploding with napalm and population beyond the wit of international agencies and technological expertise to solve.

Much of the crisis is in our minds. We know that there have always been wars and rumours of war, student riots, delinquency, intellectual doubt and political apathy. Today we collect more disturbing statistics because we collect more statistics. Populations are exploding not because reproduction is accelerating but because the great scourges which acted as governors have been dismantled by antibiotics. As the tempo of history races, special problems are thrown up. The *malaise* in Britain has overtaken every great power that has 'lost an empire and has not yet found a role'.[3]

When the Industrial Revolution undermined ancient religious and political faiths that bestrode nations with their solid chilly masonry, and made space for gaily painted *bijou* ideologies in pluriform suburban precincts, anxiety first developed. In Britain

at this time a cry of discontent is gone forth, the apostles of anarchy take advantage of a temporary and partial distress, and by imposing upon the ignorance of the multitude, flattering their errors and inflaming their passions, are exciting them to sedition and rebellion.[4]

In France an early warning system showed how

one excess succeeded another, each more extravagant than that which went before it; follies were generated by follies, crimes begot crimes, and horrors were produced by the monstrous intermixture of both, such as former times had never seen.[5]

The writer could almost be Malcolm Muggeridge or Arthur Koestler or Stephen Spender. It was, however, Robert Southey in 1816. As the years passed, the Roman Catholic Church met at a council in the Vatican to survey a world disintegrating. The bishops

occupied themselves with Pantheism, Rationalism, Naturalism, Socialism, Communism, indifference in matters of religion, Regalism, the licence of conscience and of the press, civil marriage, spiritism, magnetism, the false theories on inspiration, on the authority of Scripture, and on interpretation.[6]

This was not the Second but the First Vatican Council of 1869–70. After some time young people felt that their parents

lived in an intellectual world which bore no relation to our own; and cut adrift as we were from the intellectual moorings of our up-bringings, recognizing, as we did, that the older men were useless as guides in religion, in science, in philosophy . . . we also felt in-stinctively that we could accept nothing on trust.[7]

Thus Edward Pease described the background of the early Fabians in the late nineteenth century. Our problems are older than we imagine. Jeremiah and Bildad were even older.

Yet there do seem to be ways in which our situation is un-precedented. Not simply in the hardware we can create for affluence or destruction, but in our world-view. Or our lack of it. The 1960s promoted a number of words: dialogue, consensus, participation, power, violence. This represents the approximate time order. Cynics might say it represents an escalation. Different as each concept looks at first glance, they all belong to the same ideological family.

In the old closed societies with little literacy or travel the bulk of the population tended to accept the official creed, or some popular compromise between it and ancestral memories, locally modified by the *ethos* of any tolerated subculture. As the scientific revolution moved men mentally and physically into new thought patterns and new situations, the state monolith fractured. But domestic icons remained intact, increased in number and decoration. Individuals still clung to authority, but it was self-imposed and heterogeneous. Those who complained of the breakdown of authority were the heirs of formerly dominant systems. What they lamented was the breakdown of their own authority. No longer able to oppress, they could still orate in the name of ancient virtues. Gradually their orations failed to convince themselves. They came to regard conformity as an ideal but not as a dynamic.

It would be congenial to protest that modern dialogue and consensus represent a new tolerance, sympathy and under-standing. In the few years of their fashion, however, there are few signs that man's inhumanity to man has been washed away in a flood of universal brotherhood. The flow of 'permissiveness' is not so much a wish to accommodate as an inability to curb. A

31

recent opinion poll on basic British attitudes was reported as 'The great leap Right'.[8] The supporters of liberal reforms show little inclination to submit their proposals to referenda. With authoritarian impotence has grown apathy. As the chairman of the adolescent unit at the Tavistock Clinic observed in 1969, we live in 'what is not a permissive but an uncaring society'.[9] The Roman Catholic Church has had dialogue in turn with other Christian churches, Jews, international humanists and communists. The Christian denomination that has shown most interest in this is the Church of England, which some regard as a whited sepulchre and others as a white elephant. Some dialogues are purely political. Catholics and communists have diplomatic problems in each other's countries. All they seem to share ideologically is a crisis of internal authority.[10] 'Catholic Marxists' could arise only in an age doubtful of both Catholicism and Marx.[11]

In Lent 1969 the Pope distributed an agonized rebuke with his Maundy. Protest, he said, was 'crucifying'[12] the Church and threatening schism. Two months earlier Cardinal Heenan had been more conciliatory with critical Catholics:

It is not their fault if they are disturbed. Remember that the Church is in the world and every institution is passing through a turbulent period.[13]

His auxiliary, Bishop Butler, put it down to cybernetics:

At the very point where authority fails to communicate its message to the conscience, it fails to *be* effective authority.[14]

In the Soviet Union language is even more cautious but the problem is the same:

Soviet young people are just as identified with socialism as their fathers. But that makes it all the more essential to admit that youth problems exist and see that they are dealt with – by the young people themselves in the first place.[15]

If such monoliths are shaking it is not surprising that lesser idols lie in ruins.

Though junior clergy and laity, workers and students often call for participation, it is questionable how many really care about it. Apart from those who are conservative and do not want responsibility, there are the dropouts and the militants. The hippies follow the advice of Timothy Leary's League for Spiritual Discovery: 'Turn on, tune in and drop out.'[16] The Yippies and the drugless activists want action. Often, it seems, any sort of action. They are in search of 'power'. Society they regard as a form of institutionalized violence and 'Violence must be met with violence'.[17] Drug-taking is itself regarded by the police as a way whereby youth turns on violence rather than mystical experience, while social workers regard it as 'one part of a many-sided social revolution' involving 'rebellion against authority and bureaucracy'.[18] Nothing would be new if this were all. The downtrodden and those who feel themselves downtrodden have erupted spontaneously throughout history, after coming to believe, like Chairman Mao, 'that politics is war without bloodshed while war is politics with bloodshed' and 'only with guns can the whole world be transformed'.[19] But they had plans and programmes and a belief that they were furthering the cause of humanity, or at least rose up against an immediate grievance.

It is true that behind the world's turmoils there are genuine grievances. Black Power, Student Power, Pupil Power[20] (and the half-serious fear of Infant Power[21]), Gay Power,[22] Cunt Power:[23] they all represent groups of the underpowered, and, in so far as power brings privilege, underprivileged. American universities have been notoriously paternalistic, banning even the most conventional kind of political organization. They are the archetypal academic factories turning out organization men as a human investment. Protest against this reification was behind the seminal Free Speech Movement at Berkeley in 1964. Those Negroes at Cornell five years later who found rifles the best negotiating machinery also had real grievances and positive demands. In the universities of Tokyo and Rome, at the Sorbonne and the London School of Economics, overcrowding combined with bureaucratic administration and the study of sociology to raise discontent above the threshold of violence. Yet it often seems that those who call for power have no clear idea of why they want it and how they will exercise it.

The French sociologist Alain Touraine sees the student movement, 'in principle at least, of the same importance as the labour movement of the past'.[24] In other words, left-wing and

33

potentially revolutionary. The Western press gives most attention to the anarchists and Trotskyists and fosters this impression. Conversely, in Eastern Europe, notably Poland and Czechoslovakia, students are regarded as 'a traditional elite group, overwhelmingly bourgeois or petit-bourgeois by recruitment and outlook, and therefore ultimately a trivial or reactionary force'.[25] Clearly these assessments suit the respective governments. Yet there are edges of the student movement, as of the whole politics of our time, that cut across traditional boundaries between right and left and further scar the face of authority. Some Western observers do not share the usual Western assumptions. In reply to a suggestion that the students' revolt could be termed 'left-wing fascism', Max Beloff retorted: 'The student movement is not "left-wing fascism", it is "fascism".'[26] Similarly, in America 'managerial technocrats' place militant students in the 'reactionary'[27] tradition of the Luddites.

Traditional left-wing language comes from their leaders. One of the dismissed L.S.E. lecturers declares:

The first concern of a revolutionary student movement will be direct confrontation with authority, whether in the colleges or on the barricades.[28]

In practice the students avoid those with real expertise on barricades. To some extent this derives from universal indignation at the belated and half-hearted support of the French Communist Party for the movement of May 1968. The party was denounced as both 'counter-revolutionary'[29] and 'Stalinist'. But the avoidance of all Western Communist Party establishments may have a deeper significance. The only successful communist movements praised by the students are those of China and Cuba, snubbed by the West and forlornly located in the Third World. To student activists a virtue of Mao is that he does not preach 'dictatorship of the proletariat' as a means to a tranquil communist end, but 'perpetual revolution' as an end in itself. Their leading saints are also martyrs, conspicuously unsuccessful and murdered: Rosa Luxemburg, Léon Trotsky, and above all Che Guevara, figures of action and of tragedy. In America the genial Paul Goodman has been replaced as *guru* by the heterodox Marxist firebrand Herbert Marcuse, with his proclamation that 'true pacification requires the withdrawal of tolerance before the deed, at the stage of communication in word, print and picture'. So that the Free Speech Movement now seems committed to 'extreme suspension of the right of free speech and free assembly'.[30] Marcuse is himself a cloistered academic and his influence is likely to be transient. The new ideal is the anti-hero in the anti-university.[31] Protest must be committed to failure and fission or one authority will give way to another.

At a time when the world's communist parties are increasingly treading the peaceful (British) road to socialism, youth turns towards the beguiling paths of 'non-negotiable demands' and violence. In India Gandhi's non-violent non-co-operation is ailing, and it is said the patient never represented anything more than 'the non-violence of expediency'.[32] The similar movement in Britain under the Committee of 100 banner has been pronounced dead. No recipient has gained its heart. On its grave sits the soul of Régis Debray:

Each one of us has to decide which side he is on – on the side of military violence or guerrilla violence, on the side of violence that represses or violence that liberates.[33]

Or of Che Guevara:

Relentless hatred of the enemy . . . transforms us into an effective, violent, selected and cold killing machine.[34]

At a big debate among the British Left in January 1969, Eric Heffer M.P. received enormous, unwelcome applause when he referred to those who want the 'overthrow of the capitalist system by violence'.[35] After the violence, what? To many the act brings its own existentialist reward.

The cult of violence – or sex 'n' violence – is not confined to the young. Or to the goggle-box. Black comedy and sick verse are highly fashionable in the most impeccable suburbs. Ethics has been replaced by ethology as a topic in polite drawing-rooms. Man, we discover, is after all a naked ape constantly urged to aggression by his territorial imperative.[36] Though a Marxist intellectual places this among the 'metaphysical or super-naturalistic theories',[37] most *literati* have agreed with the liberal (or erstwhile liberal) journalist who contemplates her garden and latchkey in a new way and feels 'a lot better for it'. She believes that 'what zoology and the physical sciences were to the end of the nineteenth century, Freud's discoveries were to the first half of the twentieth, animal ethology will be to the second half'.[38] Aggression is seen as innate and inevitable, part of our animal heritage. War hath her victories no less renowned than peace. They are as real on the home front as on the battlefield. Where reason fails direct action prevails. Strikes have spread from blue to white collar workers and to professions like teaching, nursing and medicine where they had been thought unthinkable. The authority of unions is as powerless as that of employers. In Britain today 95 per cent of strikes are unofficial. The pundits say that all authority is dying. Some believe it is dead. And if authority has died what has happened to morality?

But first we must ask what morality is.

2   What is Morality?

It is all very well to justify such terms as 'religioethics' and 'religiomorality', but this does not help us to resolve the age-old dispute over the nature and scope of 'ethics' and 'morality'. Frequently the two terms are used interchangeably. The first definition of 'ethics' given, however, in the *Oxford English Dictionary* is 'the science of morals; the department of study concerned with the principles of human duty'. Other sources tend to agree. In James Hastings's *Encyclopaedia of Religion and Ethics* ethics is said to be, like logic and aesthetics, 'not only of universal application, but refers to constant elements in human nature':

Its subject-matter is human condition and character, not as natural facts with a history and causal connections with other facts, but as possessing value in view of a standard or ideal.[1]

The monumental *Catholic Encyclopaedia* makes these suggestions:

Ethics may be defined as the science of the moral rectitude of human acts in accordance with the first principles of natural reason . . . Ethics is the scientific and philosophical treatment of morality.[2]

What all these definitions agree on is that ethics is the *study of* morality. But what is morality?

From the *Oxford English Dictionary* can be isolated sixteen separate definitions. In so far as they are not tautological, e.g. 'the quality or fact of being moral', they invoke such words as 'duty', 'rightness' and 'goodness' and, like the definitions above, beg more questions than they answer. This has been a common feature of moral dissertation down the years. The nineteenth century was more enlivened by fundamental debate on ideological issues than the technologically prone twentieth century,

37

and the movement associated with Robert Owen for many years produced a popular weekly, the *New Moral World*, which tried to put the subject of morality on a rational and scientific footing. It came to adopt the sensible slogan 'The Character of man is formed for him, and not by him',[3] but the best it was able to do with definition was:

Morality! what is it? That perception and consciousness of the beautiful and true in nature and its laws, which arises from an early familiarity with goodness and intelligence; that knowledge and correct performance of all the holy characteristics of life which proceeds from an enlarged and just comprehension of self-love and sound affection.[4]

The use of the word 'holy' strengthened orthodox opinion of the day – which still adheres to this view – in asserting that morality is intimately associated with religion, and provoked a dissident Owenite lecturer, George Jacob Holyoake, into observing that he 'had the impression that that mysticism which had crept into their morality pervaded their works'.[5]

This tendency to associate, in some mystical way, 'the good, the beautiful and the true' is at least as old as the Greek philosophers. They spoke as though these things were writ large in the heavens, spaceless, timeless, absolute. All we needed were the means to read them. Just as everyone immediately recognized a good apple or a bad apple, so a good deed or a bad deed ought also to be recognized at once. What was right was what was natural, what should be universal. In English and many other languages the same word indicates the type of conduct that is expected and the hand that most people find natural for delicate operations. Up till very recent years great efforts were made at school to force everyone to be right-handed on the assumption that left-handedness was perverse; and there is still a widespread belief that unusual behaviour, especially sexual, is perverse because 'unnatural'. People were not, of course, before our own generation, so unobservant, untravelled and thoughtless as to imagine that there was universal agreement on either ethics or morality. But they tended to believe that such agreement was, at least in theory, possible. As the eighteenth-century Scottish philosopher David Hume put it,

The Notion of Morals implies some Sentiment, common to all Mankind, which recommends the same Object to general Approbation and makes every Man, or most Men, agree in the same Opinion or Decision concerning it. It also implies some Sentiment, so universal and comprehensive as to extend to all Mankind, and render the Actions and Conduct, even of Persons the most remote, an Object of Censure or Applause, according as they agree or disagree with that Rule of Right, which is established.[6]

Eleven years earlier, however, Hume had sounded a less confident note:

I cannot forbear adding to these reasonings an observation, which may, perhaps, be found of some importance. In every system of morality, which I have hitherto met with, I have always remarked, that the author proceeds for some time in the ordinary way of reasoning, and establishes the being of a God, or makes observations concerning human affairs; when of a sudden I am surpriz'd to find, that instead of the usual copulations of propositions, *is*, and *is not*, I meet with no proposition that is not connected with an *ought*, or an *ought not*. This change is imperceptible; but is, however, of the last consequence. For as this *ought*, or *ought not*, expresses some new relation or affirmation, 'tis necessary that it shou'd be observ'd and explain'd; and at the same time that a reason should be given, for what seems altogether inconceivable, how this new relation can be a deduction from others, which are entirely different from it. But as authors do not commonly use this precaution, I shall presume to recommend it to the readers; and am persuaded, that this small attention wou'd subvert all the vulgar systems of morality, and let us see, that the distinction of vice and virtue is not founded merely on the relations of objects, nor is perceiv'd by reason.[7]

If this insight gave any comfort at all, it was likely to be to those religious irrationalists and moral intuitionists of whom Hume profoundly disapproved. Either that, or there could be no morality at all; so that only the moral nihilist could rejoice.

In the wake of nineteenth-century imperialism came comparative studies in anthropology, sociology and religion. These brought out the full diversity of ethical theory and the range and bizarreness of moral precept and practice. For a time it could be pretended that this was merely the product of 'heathen darkness' among the 'lesser breeds without the law'.[8] By the twentieth century, however, the rise of Afro-Asian nationalism and the decline of Christianity and moral certainty inside the imperialist countries rendered this simple view obsolete. Welcome to many as the new insight was, it gave no joy to ethics. If the customs of 'primitive' peoples were not to be subject to paternalistic change by the imperial powers, was this simply a recognition of political impotence or an acknowledgement that there was really nothing to choose between them and the codes of 'sophisticated' nations? Were differences confined to matters of ceremonial and good manners, such an acknowledgement could be graciously, if belatedly, made; but more fundamental conflicts existed. It was found that the Nyam-Nyam of Central Africa ate their enemies while the Dieri of Central Australia ate their relatives. Among the Queensland aborigines the old were cared for; among the Polynesians the old were killed. The ancient Welsh thought murder was acceptable outside the kin; the ancient Gauls made this the only form of capital murder. Women were highly regarded by the Greeks at the time of Homer and poorly at the time of Hesiod. The Polynesians looked tolerantly upon homosexuality; not so the Persians. In attitudes to marital states – monogamy, polygamy, polyandry, celibacy, incest among siblings – criminology and penology, no agreement could be found. The same was true of the organization of society itself. Democracy worked efficiently in ancient Athens while dictatorship worked efficiently in ancient Sparta. The Zuni, Hopi and Dakota Amerindians advocated non-competition, which the European settlers who supplanted them held in the highest contempt. It seemed as if morality were completely arbitrary, the jest of geography and history, and that the only provision that all people at all times have agreed on is that it is wrong to marry your mother.[9]

At the same time there developed in the West an interest in language, including moral language, of the sort adumbrated by Hume. For among the sparks that flew from the fracturing of cherished beliefs in the twentieth century were the bright young men[10] of logical positivism. They said that the only statements which were meaningful were tautological or empirical: that is, based on definitions or based on verifiable claims. If we say 'The sky is blue' all we mean is that 'blue' is the name we have chosen for those short light waves scattered and made visible in the sky; and when we say 'The sky is full of rain' we mean that water vapour can be detected in the sky visually or by the use of instruments. But if we say 'Jones is a good man' or 'I believe in God' we are not, according to the logical positivists, saying anything which is either tautological or empirical and are therefore talking 'meaningless nonsense'. But ordinary people have persisted in believing that even if these attitudes to Jones and God are nonsense they are abundantly meaningful. They are not discussion stoppers and do lead to further conversation. Under the influence of Ludwig Wittgenstein[11] most English philosophers have now changed their position somewhat. As 'linguistic analysts' they agree that if people find a certain statement meaningful there must be something in it. They devote themselves to finding out what these standard meanings are and do not presume to say whether the statements are right or wrong. 'We must,' says Wittgenstein, 'do away with all explanations and description alone must take its place.'[12]

This has become the dominant theme of moral philosophy today, associated with revived interest in Hume's censure of those who pass glibly from an 'is' to an 'ought'. Such an exercise is called the 'naturalistic fallacy'. The term was coined at the beginning of the century by G. E. Moore,[13] who pointed out that we could not detect moral qualities as a property of nature recognizable by the senses. But anxious that such qualities should not be dismissed as pure illusion, he asserted that they are non-natural qualities recognizable by intuition. As the century drew on, framed by the theory of relativity and blotched with great upheavals of war, revolution and the cult of violence as a political theory, his successors came to doubt whether there was anything objective about moral judgements at all. Practically all moral philosophers up to this period had believed in 'normative ethics', i.e. that they had something to say which might help people to conduct their lives. Now it was considered that: 'normative ethics is more than a science – that it encounters its own difficulties, and has its own characteristic functions. Such a view does not require a faith in some higher type of knowledge, beyond that to which the sciences can attain. It requires only the realization that ethical issues involve personal and social decisions about what is to be approved, and that these decisions, though they vitally depend upon knowledge, do not themselves constitute knowledge.'[14] So there developed among philosophers, in place of normative ethics, 'non-cognitivist meta-ethics';[15] and 'ethics' was defined, not as the study of morality, but as 'the logical study of the language of morals'.[16]

What the meta-ethicians point out is that traditional moralists have always deduced their precepts from the supposed state of the world (the objective approach) or of the divine, individual or collective human mind (the subjective approach). It is said, for example, that there is in existence a divine revelation, written or unwritten, or a legal system, formal or part of an oral tradition. It is said that human conduct gives a sense of satisfaction or dissatisfaction to God, or to other men, or to the person himself. But all of these assertions, say the meta-ethicians, are simply statements of what 'is' – or is said to be – so and not of what 'ought' to be so, or why the individual 'ought' to act accordingly. Why should we follow sacred scriptures or human laws? There may be some point in giving satisfaction to ourselves, but why should we trouble to give satisfaction to other people or to God? Failure to do any of these things may lead to punishment, which is a disincentive to wayward behaviour. But is a prudential reason automatically a moral reason? If so, then, where there is conflict among divine revelations or legal systems, does moral conduct involve obedience to what appears most capable of punishing us? Are we free to do as we like if God does not exist or if we can conceal our conduct from our neighbours? If we think only of the mental state of people directly involved in our actions, are we justified in what we do if our capacity for satisfaction appears greater than theirs for dissatisfaction, or in murdering but not insulting them, on the grounds that they would be unconscious of the one but not of the other? Most of these interesting avenues can more profitably be followed in the suburbs of this book. It is the city-centre of morality we are concerned with here.

Undermining profitless ethical theories is a useful exercise. Emphasizing the difficulty, or the impossibility, of passing logically from an 'is' to an 'ought' should at once prune the exuberant outgrowth of moral codes and draw attention to the fact that, however plausible each one may be in itself, the important question is whether people can be persuaded that they 'ought' to follow it. In a world where traditional authority is breaking down, a simple *diktat* will no longer suffice. A moral code is rather like an architectural blueprint: very attractive to look at, perhaps, especially with background knowledge, but pointless until put into practice. So we have to ask, what is the relationship between morality, the belief in what it is right to do, and moropractice, what is actually done? And what is the extent of moropractice? Most people would accept that sticking a knife through a tomato is not a moral issue but sticking a knife through a person is. Does it cease to be a moral issue if the person belongs to an enemy nation during wartime? What about borderline cases all the time? Was a contemporary moral philosopher right to say that 'a man who is infatuated with an unsuitable girl, marries her, and lives unhappily ever after, makes a moral mistake'?[17] A mistake, no doubt (assuming the girl seems 'unsuitable' to him and not merely to outside observers), but is it a moral mistake? In high theory it is even impossible to be sure that it is a mistake; that is, that the man would have done something different if he could have foreseen the consequences, or that it is better to live happily than unhappily. The meta-ethicians[18] have said that the utilitarian happiness criterion is no yardstick of morality, not only because of the difficulty of finding out what makes people happy but because it measures something other than morality: a psychological state with purely personal or even antisocial attributes.

Yet, on balance, it may be doubted whether the logical positivists and linguistic analysts have helped the moral debate, and in recent years there has been some reaction[19] against them. This is overdue. It is, I think, possible to salvage the statement 'Jones is a good man' from any charge of 'meaningless nonsense' by logical positivists, on the basis that it is really tautological. In other words, there is no difference in kind between this statement and 'The sky is blue'; in both cases the adjectives simply define qualities that by arbitrary rules we have chosen to distinguish from others. Today the verification principle is itself under a philosophical cloud. For it is a 'metaphysical' statement that is neither tautological nor empirical. One can 'verify' what is specific and contemporaneous, not a 'principle', which is universal and futuristic. The presuppositions of linguistic analysis have been similarly questioned, critics pointing out that 'ordinary language' is less consistent than the analysts suppose and 'is shot through with the fading hues of past philosophical theories'.[20] But it is at the practical rather than the theoretical level that most anxiety has been occasioned by what is still the dominant trend in British philosophy. At the time when the institutional and ideological authority of particular moral codes is being undermined, philosophy seems to be undermining the whole foundation of morality. On the assumption that we cannot pass from an 'is' to an 'ought', one or other of the following conclusions would appear to follow. Either we are so constituted that we can appreciate only 'is' statements and so are not bound by any sort of obligation, or we come to 'ought' statements by arbitrary impulses which are not susceptible of rational debate and have no necessary connection with the world around us.

The meta-ethicians are, of course, aware of this dilemma. Probably the most influential of them, R. M. Hare, has attempted a solution by looking more closely into the meaning of 'ought'. 'I ought to do X'[21] he decided might mean one of three things: (1) X is required in order to conform to the standard which people generally accept (statement of sociological fact); (2) I have a feeling that I ought to do X (statement of psychological fact); (3) I ought to do X (value-judgement). From (1) arises the concept of *mores*, the support of which is frequently held – wrongly in my view – to be a moral duty. Hare divides value-judgements into non-moral and moral. As an example of one he cites 'You ought to give a second dose' (to a would-be poisoner), and of the other 'You ought to tell the truth'.[22] Both refer to ways of carrying out principles. From these arguments he concludes that moral statements are prescriptive (a branch of language comprising imperatives and value-judgements), universalizable and follow ordinary logic. Apart from asserting that moral statements follow some mysterious sort of emotive logic or no logic at all, the more extreme of the meta-ethicians might argue that prescriptions are simply lists of what we want other people to do and do not satisfy the moral requirement that we regard them as binding on ourselves; or that, while they may be appropriate in particular circumstances, they cannot be regarded as universalizable. This is a metaphysical conception and one, moreover, which overlooks the fact that the circumstances of one situation can never precisely recur.

Despite many brave attempts the language of morals has never quite escaped from the primordial fog of magic and mysticism, religion and 'revelation'. Moralists and metaphysicians, priests and politicians, lawyers and laymen are alike fearful of the social disintegration or dehumanization which they fear would result if human 'value-judgements' were to be stripped of the mythology that surrounds them. That non-human animal societies do not disintegrate without this inestimable advantage they never pause to notice. That some of them are a good deal more stable and not conspicuously more unjust than a lot of human societies they would refuse to notice. That 'value-judgements' are siblings of censorship and oppression as often as they are related to civilized standards they may have noticed and secretly approve.

Now, as other sections of this book illustrate, I have little sympathy with the hippie-anarchist[23] approach to life which is impatient of all restraints and standards apart from its own non-standards. The harbingers of the 'new world' all too often make spontaneity a cult and non-standards a tyranny. 'Doing one's own thing' is splendid so long as the nexus of social duties on which the world depends does not disintegrate and so long as stuffy, conventional people are allowed to be stuffy and conventional without incurring invective or molestation. But trendiness can become its own convention, even more stifling and arbitrary than the traditions it replaces. And perhaps this tells us something about what is enduring and, it may be, ineradicable in human nature, of which moral language is a significant index.

Whatever ideologies we hold or life-styles we cultivate, all of us expect, consciously or unconsciously, our view of the world, which we equate with God's – actual or phantasmagoric as he may appear to us – to be held by others; and we gravitate towards those who share our convictions and fortify our prejudices. God is the personification of our desire to impose our standards on other people, or, if we are self-critical, to change external conditions so that we can more readily adopt other standards for ourselves. When we find that God is dead we hastily create God-substitutes. Our natural tendency is to tell other people to do what we think is correct for them to do and not limply to say 'You ought to do X'. By the same token, if we think something is correct for us we do it or say 'I will do it' and not 'I ought to do it'. Far from implying a categorical (moral) imperative, the use of 'ought' usually implies a doubt. This has arisen because

45

experience has taught us that other people – some more or less than others – do not share the same views of the world as ourselves. It is only in the realm of the ideal, i.e. of religion or religion-substitutes, that one may postulate, as Hume does, 'some Sentiment, common to all Mankind, which recommends the same Object to general Approbation'. When we say 'You ought to do X' we usually mean that we think it right but we have reason to believe that the person addressed does not. And when we say 'I ought to do X' we usually mean that the person addressed, or respectable society, expects it but that we are ourselves unconvinced and probably have no intention of doing it. So that, for practical purposes, if 'ought' is a 'moral' word its use implies that a moral act is *unlikely* to eventuate. For this and other reasons I have the gravest reservations about the efficacy of sermonizing or moralizing to the individual, regardless of whether, unless we are the parents or teachers of small children, we have any acceptable status from which to do it. For moralizing is likely to confirm the doubt present in the 'ought' and confirm people in their waywardness, if that is what it is. A demonstration of the consequences of actions, if necessary of the sanctions we are able to wield or society wields on our behalf, is more efficacious. This is true of other than 'right-thinking men'. Most psychopaths do not commit murder when a police patrol-car is passing and most kleptomaniacs do not steal when a sales assistant is watching. It is true that advice or suggestions may profitably be made to other people and should take precedence over threats of sanctions – for the practical reason that glad co-operation is likely to be more enduring that reluctant compliance under duress – but 'ought' is seldom the language of diplomatic suggestion.

It may well be that anxiety over how we can pass from an 'is' to an 'ought' is a preoccupation of philosophers rather than of ordinary people and that on this occasion at least the man-in-the-street has happily bypassed it. Yet, it will be asserted, whether or not the man-in-the-street is aware of the naturalistic fallacy it is there all the same and educators, penologists and other specialists must face up to it. So it is appropriate to look further into descriptive and value-judgement language. As soon as individual words are looked at, it becomes clear that there is much ambiguity. Some words like 'good' are notoriously difficult, being applied equally to apples, music and people and in various tones of voice with widely different meanings. It is usually believed that it implies a standard, descriptive or evaluative. Sometimes even this may be doubtful. 'This is good music' may mean simply 'I like this music' or 'This is the sort of music musicologists are in the habit of writing about'. Where standards are implicit the word may be applied to the same person for different reasons, themselves incompatible. This is another way of saying that the same action may be judged good or bad by different observers and every person in his lifetime performs different actions. But the same person may judge the same action, and the person with whom it is indissolubly linked, in different ways at different times. In 1938 the agreement with Hitler at Munich was generally described as 'right' and Neville Chamberlain as a 'good' prime minister. By 1940 it had generally become 'wrong' and he 'bad'. In the meantime the goal had changed from appeasement to confrontation, for the consequences of appeasement had become more apparent. Does this mean simply that the situation was wrongly 'described' in 1938 and correctly by 1940, and that the 'value' of confrontation was right all the time? Not necessarily. An apologist for Chamberlain might argue that appeasement was necessary to play for time in which to find allies or build up armaments. (He could, however, be accused of having used his time badly.)

'Good' is a word customarily regarded as primarily evaluative.[24] Is there greater consistency among words regarded as primarily descriptive? Take 'big'. Applied to people it can mean something like 'magnanimous', which would generally be thought of as evaluative. But in most cases, whether applied to things or to people, it refers to size. Is this as uncontroversial as might at first appear? Does this 'simple description' mean the same to everyone who hears it? Can it be controverted? On seeing our first water-melon we might describe it as a big one. Yet someone who has seen many water-melons might recognize it as being quite small. Even with a lot of experienced observers we are unlikely to secure 'universal' agreement, for there are always people who claim to have seen many much bigger water-melons somewhere else (a statement which can at least be tested) or (an untestable statement) at some time in the past. Hare declares that 'value-terms have a specific function in language, that of commending',[25] which distinguishes them from descriptive terms. Might 'big' not be thought of as usually having the element of commending, except on those occasions – e.g. with vegetables or fish which do not improve in texture or flavour as they get bigger – where the opposite intention is present. If then the accuracy of the word as a descriptive term depends entirely on the experience of the observer, of which an outsider may have little or no knowledge, not to mention his veracity, while at the same time the expression has evaluative overtones, it may be that 'big' is more meaningful as an evaluative than as a descriptive word. Something similar may, I suggest, be said of other descriptive terms.

Now, all this confusion is most unsatisfactory from the meta-ethician's standpoint, for the unique role of 'value-language' is important for his ethical theories. Hare admits that paradigm evaluative words like 'eligible' – as in 'eligible' bachelor – become denuded of meaning and have to be replaced by others; while some descriptive terms like 'tidy' and 'industrious' (usually applied to people) have a secondary evaluative meaning. But he seems unwilling to admit how great this overlap is. This is not surprising in view of his main thesis:

Moral principles or standards are first established; then they get too rigid, and the words used in referring to them become too dominantly descriptive; their evaluative force has to be painfully revived before the standards are out of danger. In the course of revival, the standards get adapted to changed circumstances; moral reference takes place, and its instrument is the evaluative use of value-language. The remedy, in fact, for moral stagnation and decay is to learn to use our value-language for the purpose for which it is designed; and this involves not merely a lesson in talking, but a lesson in doing that which we commend; for unless we are prepared to do this we are doing no more than pay lip-service to a conventional standard.[26]

The final sentiment I can at least concur with. In morality, more perhaps than in anything else, actions do indeed speak louder than words. But I would go on to question whether moral language can be anything more than 'lip-service' to standards, conventional or otherwise. To fulfil the dynamic role cast for it by Hare it would need to be much more precise than it turns out on investigation to be. It seems to me that animals, which do not have our sophisticated value-language, manage a good deal of species co-operation and cannot be said to lack 'morality'. To speak of morality as something uniquely human may well be a theological survival related to concepts of 'soul', 'conscience' and vulgar anthropocentricity. Moral language, often tacked on to ideological world-views, may even be a positive disservice to moropractice. But more of this in the second part.

Moral philosophy tends to operate on the humanities side of the two cultures,[27] where, coupled with, one suspects, a certain distaste for the 'exact sciences', there is a frequent misconception of how 'exact' they are. This, too, fortifies the presumptive dichotomy between 'is' and 'ought'. It is often assumed that science is the world of description and measurement, and that these processes are as simple as taping the length of a table and writing down the result. Even here suppositions are at work: that our percepts are a faithful reflection of objective reality and that any distortions of length caused by cosmic motion and explained by the theory of relativity can safely be set aside. As we advance further in science assumptions multiply.[28] The modern scientific world of cloud chambers, electron microscopes and radio telescopes is more accessible to 'imagination' than to 'observation'. We may go further and admit that in high theory it is impossible to dismiss the most extreme phenomenological or existentialist arguments. Each of us cannot even dismiss solipsism, the belief that there is nothing at all outside one's own consciousness and about which some scholars have written, or imagined themselves to write, enthusiastically. Yet as practical men we make practical assumptions which serve us very well in the business of living. Certain things are accepted by common consent. In a community which is accustomed to water-melons in every fruiterer's and most gardens, there grows up a working agreement over what is or is not a big specimen. And, in stable communities, it is much the same with morals. Seen in historical perspective, politics – save during revolutions – has always been in large measure one of consensus; though this is often taken as an infernal modern invention. Certainly it is true of democracies, but it is true of many dictatorships too. If our age is more conspicuous for confusion and alienation than its predecessors, the explanation is more likely to be the mobility of populations and ideas, with the precipitate admixture of moral conventions represented by each sub-culture.

The meta-ethicians have always admitted that, while moral decisions, in their view, 'do not themselves constitute knowledge', 'they vitally depend upon knowledge'.[29] I would submit that the link is so vital that they may well be indistinguishable. When we say that 'a man ought to behave socially' (which I conceive to be the same as 'a man ought to behave morally', but much less ambiguous), we are in effect saying that 'man is a social animal'.[30] The 'is' of conscious beings living socially implies the 'ought' that ensures that their society will survive; while the 'ought' of conscious beings living socially implies their 'is'. If they were differently constituted and did not recognize mutual obligations, their society would not exist. In less contentious areas language can be similarly handled. To say 'This is a peach tree' is to imply that it 'ought to produce peaches'. In other words, we have a certain expectation about it, which may or may not be realized. It may disappoint us completely, or it may produce what some people would call 'nectarines'. Where the dividing line is drawn is an arbitrary matter reinforced by common consent. If the old classificatory system becomes unworkable, new dividing lines are proposed and may in time be accepted. In the meantime the old ones are accepted, as horticulture and commerce would be impossible without some recognized system. Moral systems are, I suggest, similar in theory if more complicated in practice.

All statements may be regarded as matters of assessment. Our first impulse is to regard them as either true or false. But in our calmer moods we concede that some have a high degree of probability and – though they may eventually turn out to be wrong – can be regarded as statements of fact, while others have a lower degree of probability and can be regarded as statements of opinion or value-judgement. If the probability is extremely low we say the statement is false. I use 'opinion' in a statistical sense. 'I like this music' expresses a personal opinion, though as a statement it has a high degree of probability and may be considered as expressing a psychological fact. The more information that is made available to ordinary people the more statements of opinion will approximate to statements of fact. Because of the constant evolution of knowledge this is a continuing process and potentially limitless. There are, however, many things in the world we need not trouble to make an assessment of, or act upon our assessments if we do. Moral questions are those where assessments must be made and acted upon. Sometimes we feel impelled by circumstances into premature assessments and actions, so these are the issues where emotions and regrets are likely to be more apparent than in others. For the most part, though, we are able to formulate a general plan of action which directs what we 'ought' to do in specific circumstances; that is, it determines what is likely to achieve our 'purposes'. I would submit that these, like the promptings of 'ought', have no mystical overtones and are not the scratched record of the voice of God, but arise as solutions to problems raised by our past experiences. We find ourselves – to a greater or lesser extent depending on our vulnerability and temperament – dependent on the good opinion of others, and by trial and error we have found, usually in childhood when people are more indulgent to us, what will secure this. Moreover, we have an inherent sense of the fitness of things associated with self-respect. Nagging reflection on something we have done or left undone and the belief that a certain act will rectify the position impel us to action. When it is done our tensions are resolved.

If this is so, and if morality is not some extrinsic force perceived by intuition or some intrinsic mystery like 'animal magnetism', then our understanding of 'moral', like our understanding of 'peach', will largely depend on the range and consistency of our education. I do not mean education in any academic sense, for it is an imperialist myth that those who lack 'formal education' are both barbaric and barbarous, but family and social training. Whatever the tenor of this chapter, there is a very real sense in which 'morality' is what people think it is. From this has arisen the notion of 'private immorality':[31] the belief that what one does alone, or with consenting adults in private, is immoral if other people say it is or if the individual himself thinks it is. It probably arose from the primitive conception of the individual as someone never really alone but constantly under surveillance by critical spirits or gods, and was fortified by the philosopher's

51

concept of the absolute and the theologian's vision of the body as 'the temple of the Holy Ghost which is in you, which ye have of God, and ye are not your own'.[32] Now, since 'moral' comes from *mos*, the Latin for a 'custom' (whose plural is *mores*), if the word has been understood in an absolute or theological sense for a long time, this may seem an excellent reason for continuing to do so. Clearly people are entitled to do so, whatever moral reformers may say or however much support they should get. No day-spring from on high has visited me or, to the best of my knowledge, any of my contemporaries. There cannot be any 'new morality'[33] in the sense of any new basis for morality. If it is determined by God it will remain so whether or not we cease to worship him or believe in him. If it is socially determined in the way I suggest, it has always been so determined however wide or narrow the area of human activity allotted to it and whatever sanctions, natural or supernatural, have been cited in its support. But if there is any virtue in the naturalistic view – and if there were not I should have been burnt with many another as a heretic long ago – then our views of morality should change when the theory of relativity undermines the concept of the absolute, when theology is being abandoned or renovated (for practical purposes it may not matter whether a new insight is called a hypothesis or a revelation), and when practical difficulties have become apparent in the old view.

The 'new theologians'[34] declare that 'is' and 'ought' are reconciled in God, who gives them ultimate unity. This allows for them to be eternally fluctuant or evolving. I believe that our assessment of what 'is' proceeds[35] inevitably, unless we are disoriented, psychopathic, autistic or mentally defective, to a calculation of what 'ought' to be done in the business of living. Both views are capable of a relativistic interpretation. Now, if all conduct is relative rather than absolute it must be related to something and there cannot be absolute offences. By common consent the 'something' to which it must be related is other people. What is done alone and has no demonstrable effect on other people cannot, and I believe should not, reasonably be regarded as a moral action at all. 'Amoral' has been used in this context but I should prefer to abandon words derived from 'moral' ('amoral' is frequently used for people blind to morality and, if not culpable, morally defective) and call such behaviour 'aesthetic' or anything else which relegates it to the realm of personal taste. Masturbating, reading pornography, drug-taking and other solitary acts (unless it can be demonstrated that they directly lead to the abandonment of incurred responsibilities) should not, I submit, be thought of as 'private immorality' – or 'private morality', should they at any time be socially esteemed – but as actions that are not moral at all. Certain solitary acts, such as putting a log across railway lines, may of course have harmful social consequences and are clearly 'immoral' or 'antisocial'.

Because of the relativistic nature of morality, what we do to others must largely depend on their expectations rather than on the general expectations of society. If they think it is immoral, and we know what they think, then it is immoral. If not, not. During the summer of 1970 a large pop festival was held on the Isle of Wight. A lot of young people took off their clothes and some copulated to cries of 'Do your thing.' The police, explained the local M.P.,[36] were unable to arrest those guilty of 'indecent exposure' because there were so many offenders. Yet the point was, surely, that if there were so many the exposure was not 'indecent' and to keep one's clothes on might have looked ostentatious or unfriendly. Just what others expect is a complex matter which depends on the individual and the relation between the doer and recipient of the action. What is a love-pat to a relative[37] is an indecent assault to a stranger, unless the contrary is indicated by a remark or, more usually, some non-verbal signal.[38] Consensual fucking may not be, as the former Bishop of Woolwich said in the *Lady Chatterley's Lover* trial, some form of holy communion and may involve immorality to a third party who regards it as the breaking of a marriage vow, but it is not immoral between the immediate partners. However liberal, society usually – and I believe wisely – excludes the consent of children from this concession. The reason given is often 'corruption';[39] it should be 'uncertainty whether the consent is freely and knowledgeably given'. For, even if one is introduced to activities one might otherwise not have indulged in, if these activities are not immoral or demonstrably harmful to oneself the act of introduction cannot be 'corruption'.[40]

The notions of common consent, expectation and signalling have placed morality firmly on a species footing in general and, till recently, on a familiar, community, tribal, national, religious or racial footing in particular. Close association with domestic animals in childhood, and again in old age, has brought them within the moral conspectus of most people, while Desmond Morris and other ethologists[41] have shown that human beings respond favourably or unfavourably to (and thus protect or exterminate) 'wild' animals not only according to the absence or presence of any threat they represent to our own survival but also to the degree to which they look like or unlike us in facial characteristics. Far from breeding contempt, familiarity delimits the range of our postulated 'moral law'.[42] It may be argued that in no other generation has man been so conscious of familial, community, tribal, national, religious or racial differences and of the way in which he is driving harmless and beautiful animal species into accelerating extinction. Yet this is, I suggest, a spasm of contrition and the birth pains of a more universal morality conceived and gestated by better communications. In general terms traditional barriers and suspicions between races, creeds and classes are less dominant among younger than among older generations, not because youth has higher moral insights than age (though it may, in a largely sentimental and self-righteous way, be more 'idealistic') but because young people have travelled more and mixed more and been better educated, on the whole, in internationalism and conservation. In many countries this had led to new alignments, determined by new shared values, with young people from different social backgrounds teaming up in confrontation with, even in intolerant belligerence towards, those older people whose different formative experiences gave them different attitudes to life and made them accept, victor and victim alike, distinctions and discriminations that are no longer tolerable. Particularly are the young hostile to the middle-aged, who represent both the parental generation against which it is most natural to rebel and the fount of power in society; the really old may be less comprehending, but they are impotent.

3   Morality in Everyday Life

'Don't pull Mary's hair, John.'

'Why not, Mummy?'

Whether or not John will pay any attention to the answer is a moot point. Parental has declined with other forms of authority. Increasingly parents are looking to schools to shape discipline that is shapeless at home.[1] In the preamble to the 1944 Education Act is stated the duty of the local education authority in England and Wales 'to contribute towards the spiritual, moral, mental and physical development of the community'.[2] It is generally assumed that the provision of compulsory religious instruction and collective worship was intended to fulfil the first two obligations. It is generally recognized that this has failed. In October 1965 there was set up at Oxford[3] a Farmington Trust Research Unit to study how moral education *per se*[4] could be given. Many humanist organizations have been pursuing the same matter informally for considerably longer. Yet demand for legislative reform has been slow to cross the national protest threshold. It would seem that parental apathy and Christian pressure groups are fortified by a widespread uncertainty over what to put in the place of religion to achieve the 'moral development of the community'. For with the crisis of physical authority – which tends to be cyclical and self-correcting – has come the more profound, probably unprecedented, crisis of ideological authority.

What answer is John's mother to give? There are many possibilities:

'Because I say so.'

'Because I'll smack you.'

'Because the policeman will come and take you away.'

'Because the bogeyman will get you.'

'Because when you die you'll go to hell.'
'Because I shan't love you any more.'
'Because she'll pull yours.'
'Because people will say what a naughty little boy you are.'
'Because you'll make her unhappy.'

Are all or any of these answers satisfactory? Does it depend on the age, or the personality, of the child? Will John regard them as prudential reasons or as moral reasons? Does it matter so long as he stops pulling Mary's hair? Will he start again as soon as his mother's back is turned? This parental problem is age-old. Two things make it new. Mother is now more anxious to give the right reason and less certain what it is. Mother – together with father, grandfather, grandmother, big brother and sister – is even less certain how to tackle the gang, or tribal, or racial, or national, or power bloc, or consortium equivalent of pulling Mary's hair.

Elsewhere it will be studied how moral codes arise, how they are transmitted and how they operate. But little will be gained from a study of the contents of these codes in isolation. That is, without regard to the 'total social fact'.[5] This concept arose from anthropological studies in circumscribed communities. In these small, isolated, cohesive and illiterate societies there were fewer potential exemplars to distract individuals from the prevailing *mores*. But even here there were problems. The anthropologists could not be quite certain, without long acquaintance and a good deal of detective work, whether the prohibitions they encountered arose from the fact that a certain form of behaviour was avoided widely enough to make codification a practical proposition or was indulged in so frequently as to make censure a pressing necessity. For, granted that a moral code is relatively stable in an enclosed community, how does one ensure that all members, particularly the young, will respect and obey it? How, in fact, is a moral imperative effective?

Traditional ethical systems have buttressed themselves with a panoply of sanctions, supernal, temporal and infernal. The individual was led to believe he was under perpetual surveillance by powers seen or unseen. Under their imprint moral codes were drawn up which tried to be as precise as possible so that the least opportunity was allowed for behavioural uncertainty. Within this framework stability, status, obligation and obedience were the prime concerns; though justice, benevolence and cautious development came to be added. Perhaps it is necessary to observe that these qualities – all of them – are not entirely without relevance today and cannot be abandoned without peril.[6] But, taken as a whole, the traditional social construct was unable to specify what to do whenever there were conflicting moral claims, and, above all, it tottered when its ideological base disintegrated. When the portico of the old order collapsed during the French Revolution of 1789, there rose from the dust new moral imperatives: liberty, equality, fraternity, opening out in spontaneity and individuality the doorway to morality which had formerly been darkened by compulsion and conformism. And so people came to regard, as they did during the near-contemporary American Revolution, 'the pursuit of happiness'[7] as the prerogative of rich and poor alike. Not just as a political slogan but as a moral testament.

In the year of the French Revolution Jeremy Bentham put forward the 'principle of utility' – later popularized by John Stuart Mill as 'utilitarianism'[8] – as the overriding moral yardstick:

Nature has placed mankind under the governance of two sovereign masters, *pain* and *pleasure*. It is for them alone to point out what we ought to do, as well as to determine what we shall do. On the one hand the standard of right and wrong, on the other the chain of causes and effects, are fastened to their throne. They govern us in all we do, in all we say, in all we think: every effort we can make to throw off our subjection, will serve but to demonstrate and confirm it. In words a man may pretend to abjure their empire: but in reality he will remain subject to it all the while. The *principle of utility* recognizes this subjection, and assumes it for the foundation of that system, the object of which is to rear the fabric of felicity by the hands of reason and of law. Systems which attempt to question it, deal in sounds instead of senses, in caprices instead of reason, in darkness instead of light.[9]

In 1822 he added a note:

To this denomination has of late been added, or substituted, the *greatest happiness* or *greatest felicity* principle: this for shortness, instead of saying at length *that principle* which states the greatest happiness of all those whose interest is in question, as being the right and proper, and only right and proper and universally desirable, end of human action. The word *utility* does not so clearly point to the idea of *pleasure* and *pain* as the words *happiness* and *felicity* do: nor does it lead us to the consideration of the *number*, of the interests affected; to the *number*, as being the circumstance, in the largest proportion, to the formation of the standard here in question; the *standard of right and wrong*, by which alone the propriety of human conduct, in every situation, can with propriety be tried. This want of a sufficiently manifest connection between the ideas of *happiness* and *pleasure* on the one hand, and the idea of *utility* on the other, I have every now and then found operating, and with but too much efficiency, as a bar to the acceptance, that might otherwise have been given, to this principle.[10]

In the form of 'the greatest happiness of the greatest number',[11] qualified by 'everybody to count for one, nobody for more than one',[12] it has been, at least in the Anglo-Saxon world, probably the most influential moral formulation to this day.

'Greatest happiness' or 'greatest good'[13] had originated, with theistic sanctions, in the seventeenth century, but under the influence of Bentham, Mill and Robert Owen, God's governance waned to vanishing point:

The creed which accepts as the foundation of morals, Utility, or the Greatest Happiness Principle, holds that actions are right in proportion as they tend to promote happiness, wrong as they tend to produce the reverse of happiness. By happiness is intended pleasure, and the absence of pain; by unhappiness, pain, and the privation of pleasure.[14]

More recently utilitarianism has been subdivided into the 'act' and 'rule' varieties:

Act utilitarianism states that the rightness or wrongness of an action is to be judged by the consequences, good and bad, of the action itself. Rule utilitarianism holds that the rightness or wrongness of an action is to be judged by the goodness and badness of the consequences of a rule that everyone should perform the action in like circumstances.[15]

'Rule utilitarianism' has been further divided into 'actual' and 'possible' rule. Representative of the latter is Immanuel Kant's precept:

The chief principle of ethics then is, Act according to a maxim, which may at the same time be valid as a universal law.[16]

To which he added the 'maxim of ends': that 'it is man's duty in itself to make man in general his end' and 'he is entitled to use neither himself nor others as a mean barely' (i.e. only as a means).[17]

Clearly these related principles have fallen before the sword of most of the meta-ethicians.[18] Equally clearly they have political – which are perhaps their most important – implications we will consider later. But how can they help the mother of John and Mary, even if all three accept them? If both Mother and Mary are upset by his action, John must defer to their (majority) verdict. Suppose however that Mother is blissfully unaware and John proclaims that, because of his seniority or intelligence or imagination, his capacity for happiness is greater than his sister's for unhappiness. It was to deal with this sort of problem that Mill, and to an even greater extent G. E. Moore,[19] postulated different grades of happiness and a theory of the total amount of pleasure and pain. So there arose the further division into 'hedonistic' and 'ideal' utilitarianism. Whereas Bentham believed that playing push-pin was as good as reading poetry if it produced pleasure, his successors asserted it could not produce equal pleasure, or at any rate equal happiness. There was, in their estimation, a hierarchy of pleasures, of which intellectual or aesthetic or spiritual happiness was at the top and causing pain was at the bottom (if it could be said to rank at all), however much enjoyment John might have claimed to derive from pulling Mary's hair. Indeed, thought some of the ideal utilitarians, probably actions could be said to have a quality of rightness or wrongness besides their pleasure factor; whereupon the whole theory noticeably sagged. In the end what became clearest of all was that the 'greatest happiness principle' was not as simple as had at first appeared. Perhaps it demonstrates only that what is moral is what has moral overtones, and what is likeable is what we like.

There is a clear psychopathic position where pleasurable actions cause almost universal condemnation, which genial moralists avoid by describing them as 'amoral' and doctors attempt to explain in terms of some neurochemical deficiency or extra chromosome.[20] There is also a clear 'saintly' position where pleasurable actions cause almost universal approbation. That this approbation is never universal comes from two factors. One is the tiny minority of apparently amoral people to whom approbation for 'right' conduct or censure of 'wrong' conduct is meaningless, though they respond explosively to grievances, real or imagined, of their own. The other minority is of perverse moralists who do not regard as moral an action which brings pleasure to the doer. On the contrary, they regard pain as ennobling and happiness as corrupting. An action is, they believe, moral only when we do not gain happiness from doing it, when it is a positive burden and we groan and travail over it. Macaulay had this class of person in mind when he said that 'the Puritan hated bear-baiting, not because it gave pain to the bear, but because it gave pleasure to the spectators'.[21]

The psychology of this attitude must be pursued. There is no evidence that the Puritans themselves, to their credit, had any secret wish to indulge in bear-baiting. What does seem clear is that they derived pleasure from their own censure and happiness from their own hate. This impression from history is, I think, confirmed by observation of their spiritual descendants. There is an old joke about the masochist who said to the sadist, 'Go on, hurt me,' and got the reply, 'No, I won't.' Usually, of course, the sadist is happy to oblige and, in the act of inflicting ecstatic hurt on the masochist, derives pleasure from their joint enjoyment. If he does not, it is an example of psychological masochism where the sadist (or sado-masochist) deprives both the masochist and himself of the pleasure of hurting and gains a new sort of satisfaction by the act of deprivation.

There is a more genial and widespread modification of this puritanical version of morality, which states that truly moral conduct is altruistic, that it is displayed in unselfishness for the happiness of others and not of ourselves.[22] The difficulty is how to be sure a person acts in what Moral Re-Armament hails as 'absolute unselfishness'. Combined with absolute honesty, purity and truth, absolute unselfishness has made M.R.A. into a very wealthy organization and provided a socio-political climate in which its members have mightily thriven. Psychologically we know too much today about the powers of rationalization to hold an idealist view of human motivation. But, it will be pointed out, there are cases of people who die rescuing or trying to rescue others, or who set fire to themselves to promote an ideal. We cannot be certain, however, that those in the first category would have set about their rescue attempt had they known in advance that they would die themselves, or that those in the second did not intend to commit suicide anyhow. Interviews with people who do not die during hazardous rescues, or who set fire to themselves unsuccessfully, suggest the contrary. In the second category, moreover, there have been cases of known mental illness among the successful. As well as rationalization we all know about martyr complexes.

History and martyrology nevertheless tell us that in pre-psychology days there were unquestionably sane religious martyrs who rationally made the supreme sacrifice. A number of quibbles must still be made. In pre-psychology days the standard of 'sanity' was erratic to say the least. Many 'historical' and martyrological tales were the purest invention, as even the Pope now admits,[23] and legend tells us even less about real motivation than superficial anthropology. But even if the tales of religious martyrs were all true there is a further complication. Most of them may be presumed to believe in some system or other of rewards for devotion to the faith, bestowed in an afterlife, in either heaven or another earthly existence; and this calculation of future happiness, as an expected *quid pro quo* for their martyrdom, is likely to exert a profound influence. Such motivation is often acknowledged. The gospel Jesus is reported as saying, 'He that loseth his life for my sake shall find it,'[24] which the early Christians took to be both literal and metaphorical; and certain sects, like Christian Scientists, boast that their faith brings material rewards in this life as well as in the hereafter.

There have, however, been martyrs for non-religious causes who do not believe in an afterlife but are still prepared to pay the supreme price. Some of them do not embrace death as a spacious gesture in theatrical surroundings, but submit to it quietly and anonymously rather than recant or betray friends. Is this pure altruism? Usually 'martyrdom' simply involves spells of imprisonment, where some victims have been honest enough to recognize compensations. Amnesty International's Prisoner of Conscience for 1969 has said:

But let's not be absurdly masochistic. During the years I worked for the organization I had the ideal job: no rat-race; travelling; interviews

61

on television; brochures to write; going to prison every now and again. What could be more varied? There is a danger that one will want war in order to go on working for peace.[25]

Others less fortunate have preferred death to a life which would, by the terms of saving it, be intolerable through loss of community or self-respect. This decision is a form of gratification. It brings figures of tragedy into the same category as those who seek euthanasia, or commit suicide, where it is conventional to say – often, it is true, for the sake of religion or relatives or life assurance policies – that 'the balance of their minds was temporarily disturbed'. Today most people would not hold such conduct vicious. Equally it ceases to be virtuous and is at best amoral. Let us then cut the pious claptrap about altruism and recognize that, whether or not people are aware of their motives, in the last analysis they do what they want to. The problem of moropractice is to ensure that what they want to do is 'right'.

This brings us to another important moral consideration. If people do what they want to, do they also do what they 'will'? Just before his exit a suicide may appear as normal as, or no more neurotic than, the rest of us. If he is not held responsible for his actions should the rest of us be for ours? Now, a belief in freedom of the will is one of the most contentious of all human beliefs, and has had strange peaks and declines in fashion. These changes have not occurred in isolation but have accompanied fashions in religion, politics and penology. The belief does not, on the whole, seem to be strong in 'primitive' cohesive societies, including the modern Mafia. There the emphasis has been on the crime rather than the agent, and expiation is a tribal rather than a personal act.[26] If personal, it involves a representative of the tribe who need not be the criminal at all.

Similarly, young children appear to have little notion of free will. In the first few months of life they show no appreciation of the difference between self and not-self and are in any event completely dependent physically on adults. When they move independently, for a year or two they have no awareness of causal relations and whenever they push something over they incline to the view that it moved itself. Between about three and seven years they pass through what the influential Swiss psychologist Jean Piaget calls the 'egocentric' stage, a time of 'confusion of the ego and the external world' and 'lack of co-operation', where rules are imitated but for most of this period 'are not yet coercive in character'.[27] In other words, the child acts on impulse and does not afterwards think that he could or should have acted differently. He may even project guilt on a personalized *alter ego*. When the child does, at the infant school, become aware of particular rules he becomes too aware of them, regarding them as something dictated entirely from the outside by parents, teachers or God and not susceptible of any change according to circumstances. If he is faced with a situation not covered by the rules he has no idea what to do and is likely to act in an entirely random way.

At about the age of ten he gains a degree of knowledge of rules derived by common agreement, and this is the age in Britain that was fixed in 1963 as that when criminal responsibility begins. It is assumed that below this age a child does not know what is right or wrong and has no *mens rea* or intention. Up till the age of fourteen it must be proved in court that the child knew that what he was doing was wrong. At about the age of twelve he becomes capable of codifying rules independently, or thinking abstractly, and some criminologists think this ought to be the age of criminal responsibility. The American psychologist Lawrence Kohlberg has provided a somewhat different *schema* involving six stages, two of them pre-moral, two of conventional morality, and two of self-accepted moral principles. The process has been described by the biologist C. H. Waddington as 'the function of ethicizing', which 'is founded on the formation of "authority-bearing" systems within the mind'.[28]

'Ethicizing' is not used by Waddington in the way chosen for this book, viz. an academic pursuit in which few people engage. 'Moralizing' would be what I should use for his concept if the word did not have another connotation. Whatever vocabulary officiates there is unlikely to be much dispute today over the general trends of development outlined above. The only wonder is that, even in the absence of experimental psychology, ordinary observation had not brought home to people long ago that a child is not a miniature adult. No doubt it would if observers had not been blinkered by those ethical systems to be described shortly, which had absolutist or purely external views

63

on the nature of 'authority-bearing' and regarded any conflict between the system and human nature as a deficiency in human nature. These systems either insisted that people of all ages had similar capacities for autonomous judgement or that they were equally incapable of independent thought: for example, that they all possessed divine reason or intuition or were all divine puppets. Yet there is perhaps a danger that the new theories will suggest that the development process is a series of steps that fall away as the next one is gained. In adults there are rudiments, of greater or lesser size, of earlier stages. Failure to realize this may suggest that a community of adults should not, and after a generation of sound education will not, need external sanctions like police, government or punishment of any kind. This view is surely Utopian. What is important is that sanctions should be appropriate and personalized and accompanied by respect for the individual.

This discussion of anthropology, child psychology and criminology indicates one thing clearly. At a sufficiently early stage it is quite meaningless to talk about free will. Is it meaningful at any stage? Moral evolutionists can make out a theoretical case for believing that the will develops as civilization and the individual develop. But is this practically demonstrable? We all know that before certain actions – what we call voluntary, as distinct from purely reflex involuntary actions like a heartbeat or dropping a hot plate or putting one leg before another as we walk or even 'talking without thinking' – we are conscious of alternatives; as we perform one alternative we are conscious of doing that and not another; afterwards we can think of reasons, good or bad, for what we did. It seems not unreasonable to say that we were perfectly free to choose to do that particular action and that therefore we have free will. But what may seem reasonable is not always right. The issue is no idle speculation. For centuries it has provoked sharp theological debate. Its social consequences are of profound importance. If the human will is really free, then crime is an individual matter. From our righteous indignation punishment can proceed only as retribution. There can be no deterrent or reformative effect, which is a conditioning process, if each individual will remains 'free'. But if, on the other hand, the human mind is completely determined by its heredity, environment and education so that its 'decisions' are simply the result of these forces and thus matters of impulse, can there be such things as individual responsibility or penology at all?

In practice the whole 'psycho-social phase of evolution'[29] is built on the capacity of people to be influenced by education as well as by obvious physical factors, even in subjects often regarded as intuitive. As the Apostle Paul put it,

How then shall they call on him in whom they have not believed? and how shall they believe in him of whom they have not heard? and how shall they hear without a preacher?[30]

Certainly, this does not go very far along the deterministic road. It limits freedom of choice to known alternatives, here Christianity and paganism, but does not deny perfect freedom to choose one or other alternative. Most unbelievers of the Age of Reason, seventeen centuries later, took up much the same position. They saw themselves as simply making a different choice from the believer's. But as the age was drawing to an end grave doubts about human freedom arose. They were best put by William Godwin, now regarded as a pioneer anarchist, in 1793:

Freedom of the will is absurdly represented as necessary to render the mind susceptible of moral principles; but in reality, so far as we act with liberty, so far as we are independent of motives, our condition is as independent of morality as it is of reason, nor is it possible that we should deserve either praise or blame for a proceeding thus capricious and indisciplinable.[31]

That is, the exercise of reason itself depends on predictable laws of deductive and inductive logic; while moropractice is held to be a consequence of what has gone before.

Formerly a parson, Godwin entered the world of freethought with messianic zeal and helped to establish its predilection for determinism, which has persisted to the present. It is an intellectual predilection derived from the 'modern' attitude to science: no longer the reverent study of God's handiwork; but a cool and practical appraisal of the natural world, where predictability[32] is at a premium. For emotional reasons free will, which suggests the 'uniqueness' and psychological omnipotence of man, has continued to hold sway in religious and even in some freethinking circles. It has also seemed to many the only way to uphold 'responsible' attitudes, for it must be conceded that the ultra-libertarianism which would close down all prisons tomorrow[33] is, paradoxically, a byproduct of determinism. Especially is it associated with the psychology of behaviourism. This was expressed most forthrightly by the school's founder, J. B. Watson, in 1926:

So far in his objective study of man no behaviourist has observed anything that he can call consciousness, sensation, imagery, perception or will.[34]

There is nothing surprising in this announcement, taken at its face value. No behaviourist is looking for these things. Nor could he find them if he did. They lie buried in the vaults of the individual mind. To each person they have their own reality; though we must not lapse into 'misplaced concreteness', giving what is subjective or abstract credit for objective reality.

The implications of behaviourism are however disturbing, not to say questionable. Though behaviourists have tended, at least in Britain, to be ultra-libertarians,[35] their theory is consistent with an extreme degree of conditioning which, while it might take place in a psychological clinic rather than a prison, would be interpreted by most people as punishment of the most repressive sort. It hardly seems consistent with a liberal education or the kind of answer John's mother is likely to want to give him. And it conflicts with what we think we know about our own thought processes. Yet behaviourism cannot be lightly dismissed. In a very real way we, like experimental psychologists and other outsiders, 'observe' our own behaviour and our own 'decisions' but not the thought processes behind them. What psychoanalysts have described as the 'stream of consciousness' may better be thought of as a string of discontinuous waterholes in a desert meander, whose overall direction is apparent only from an aeroplane and which flow together for short periods during seasonal floods. On the other hand, a belief in consciousness, sensation, imagery, perception and will has shown great survival value.

In so far as they have moral relevance these concepts will be considered more fully later.[36] It will suffice here to say that, apart from leading to possible action, sensation, imagery and perception form probably the bulk of our 'consciousness'; and that this has at least as much validity as the world around us. Knowledge of our voluntary actions is also part of our consciousness and the reason why they are called 'voluntary'. To the outsider it seems that we could have 'decided' to do something else in a way that we could not have 'decided' to alter our heartbeat.[37] But all our actions are the product of neural events and it would be remarkable indeed if these events were free of the deterministic laws that are the whole foundation of empiric science and without which the flick of every light-switch would be an act of faith or fortune. I would suggest therefore that, while it may be convenient to speak of actions which are 'voluntary' or 'involuntary' and, by reference to the amount of prior deliberation, 'considered' or 'impulsive', the neurophysiology is essentially the same. Voluntary actions follow nervous events in the cerebral cortex which trigger off the motor neurons. Consciousness of this triggering process we call the 'will'. All our actions derive from neural impulses and are essentially 'impulsive'. We cannot 'will' what our total experience makes it impossible for us to 'want'.

'Responsibility', in these terms, means the incorporation in this neural cycle of regard for the rights of other people. It is an educational process within a framework of determinism which is social or communal rather than individual. It recognizes that, whatever the dangers of indoctrination, the infant cannot be left as a 'noble savage'. In the realm of toddlers we see more of what is savage than of what is noble. No one is more selfish than a baby. Yet its endowments and its physical environment are unique and, unconsciously and consciously, constitute ineradicable influences. What Mother can do for John is, in an atmosphere of loving care, to help him to understand that vicious behaviour cannot and will not be tolerated by others, individually or communally. As he understands this he will acknowledge it and make allowance for it. The process will become natural to him, almost as natural as his self-regarding actions. He will 'want' to be well thought of and 'want' to act to this end. Too often, however, Mother does not provide a blend of loving care, stability and patience. Instead she shows possessiveness, authoritarianism and the lack of nerve it masks, all inherited and bequeathed, borrowed from and lent to society, tragically self-perpetuating. The answers she gives to John's question are not incremental and creative. She tries short-cuts, short-cuts that promise not only parental and societal convenience but mystical powers and magical formulae to annihilate inborn emotional needs and reasoning powers, to change human nature itself. So she turns to myths, citing in her defence authorities who, if they trouble to explain themselves at all, assert that 'individual responsibility' within a deterministic world would itself be another myth. A psychological myth it may be, but it enables forethought to enter the neural cycle, modifying what instinct or incitement from moment to moment prompts. These other myths, however, not only pose assumptions but urge practices which are incitements in their own right and often outlive their credal superiors. These we will now consider.

Part Two
Traditional Answers

4 Religioethics and Religiomorality

Religion advertises more than a foundation for moropractice. It offers prescience, or a description and explanation of the universe before the invention of empirical science. Commonly it postulates a world of spiritual reality beyond the visible universe, a soul or spirit at the heart of the human person, and particular beliefs and rituals which will ensure its posthumous prosperity. Politically it may act as 'the opium of the people'. By this Marx meant more than what it has since been taken to imply, viz. a cynical use of religion to deaden the social consciousness of the people in the interests of priests and politicians, though few could deny that it has often been used in this way. What he actually said was that it gave hope to the hopeless and cheer to the cheerless:

Religion is the sigh of the oppressed creature, the feelings of a heartless world, just as it is the spirit of unspiritual conditions. It is the opium of the people.[1]

But what is common to all religions, theistic and non-theistic, ancient and modern, is their supply of ethical systems and moral codes. As Gladstone put it,

In its ultimate, general, and permanent effects upon morality, largely understood, the test of the value of a religion is to be found.[2]

Gladstone was better known as a politician than as an amateur theologian, and in the world of politics there has been a persistent belief that religion is necessary for social cohesion and stability. As he said a little later on the same occasion:

Those who think lightly of the testimony of the ages, the tradition of their race, which at all events keeps them in communion with it, are often found the slaves of Mr A or Mr B, of their newspaper or of their club.

This view was shared by many agnostics and was the basis of Voltaire's famous quip, 'If God did not exist it would be necessary to invent him.'[3]

An equally persistent view, of a philosophical or theological nature, is that ethics and morality are alike impossible without religion, that religioethics is the only valid ethics and religiomorality the only valid morality. Up till very recently, when the facts became too obvious to deny, it was widely asserted that religion was the only guarantee of moropractice and *mores*. Many still believe that virtuous atheists are living on 'Christian moral capital'. In its most universal form the religious argument states that natural man is thoroughly nasty and will never find goodness without special guidance. This may come from mystical contemplation, spiritual exercises, the instruction of certain holy men, tribal myths and legends, communion with the powers of nature in sacramental feasts and other rituals, invocation of the spirits of ancestors, observing dietary laws, sacrificing to friendly spirits and gods to enlist their help or unfriendly ones to propitiate them and reduce their harmful influence. In what is known as its highest form religion consists in coming to know the will of a supreme sustainer-creator God and follow it, and seeking his supernatural help by more sophisticated versions of the above techniques. This knowledge is to be obtained by serious reflection on the universe and the human situation (natural theology), a special revelation in the person of a divine incarnation or through writings divinely inspired or by an individual vision, and the systematic instruction of a consecrated priesthood (dogmatic theology). As a heavenly father God exacts our obedience. Our moral code is what he tells us to do. Moromalpractice is sin, or disobedience. If he is our father then other men are our brethren and we treat them as brothers because this is God's wish. If we disobey any of his injunctions he knows it at once, for he is omniscient. In this life or in an afterlife or in both he punishes us, for he is just, and omnipotent. But if we obey he will reward us. By ourselves we are weak and frail, but he will forgive us and help us in the future if we acknowledge our faults and our needs, for he is omniamorous. If our duty were only to man and we had only man to help us, we should often be negligent, go undetected and unpunished, and fail to find help. God is the good, and the good is God. 'Seek, and ye shall find.'[4]

On the face of it this is a humane and righteous arrangement. In life we observe many injustices and persecutions, virtue that has gone unrewarded and vice that has escaped punishment. In our passionate desire 'that somehow good will be the final goal of ill'[5] we look beyond the material world for another world where justice reigns and sin has gained no visa. On the face of it, a perfect arrangement. But underneath? The first question that must be asked is, 'Is it true?' The arguments one way or another do not here concern us. What matters is that a large and increasing number of people have doubts or outright unbelief. This involves community and personal problems. It is only in recent years that substantial numbers of people have rejected the spiritual world completely. But even when its empire was all-pervasive it was fragmented. At no period did a majority acknowledge any one ruler. In isolated communities there might be majority agreement, even the pretence of unanimity. But across a sea or a river or a mountain were other communities with different allegiances. These aliens were not simply different and strange in their race or colour or customs. As they ignored or defied the universal jurisdiction of the one true God, each group having a pretender God of its own, they were at best ignorant and foolish heathens who needed conversion for their own good, and at worst blasphemous and wicked infidels who deserved extermination. Even within a community of united allegiance to a common God disagreements arose as to his attributes and the discovery and interpretation of his will. The minority in each dispute must surely be motivated by the devil, or pride, or passion, trapped in a heresy that imperilled their own immortal destiny and invited temporal retribution against the whole group. As communications and scientific knowledge increased, growing numbers apostatized to rival faiths or atheism itself. To defend God's glory and man's security no religious war, *jihad*, crusade, witch-hunt, burning of heretics or persecution could be too severe.

Few religious believers support this policy today. It belonged, they say, to a savage and mistaken age. Yet it is a logical outcome of a particular world-view that stressed God's justice before his love. In recent years the assessment has been reversed; and there has come a collapse in the real strength of theistic belief and believers. Even if he does not fall victim to these major hazards the lapsing individual is still at risk. He may indeed be in moral jeopardy. Not because he lacks the divine guidance of his associates. Others have grown up under the influence of different divine guidance, or none at all, and felt secure. But he is now crossing life's chasm on a bridge whose pylons are crumbling, committed to a system of sanctions that have lost their force and precepts that have lost their Preceptor. The guilt of apparent betrayal clings to him, however irrational it may be, and numbs his moral with his other mental processes. He needs a new code, but what should its superstructure or its foundation be? This is the dilemma of many of today's teenagers as they renounce an imposed childhood religion – for what?

Infidelity is not of itself a proof of credal falsity, though it may be a straw in the wind. The religious theory of ethics raises fundamental objections. The popular view has always been that the invocation of God not only aids moropractice but eliminates the 'naturalistic fallacy', that is, allows us to pass from an 'is' to an 'ought' without difficulty. What God wants, or says 'is' right, is what we 'ought' to do. But this is itself an assumption. Why should we do what gives God a feeling of pleasure or describes his psychological state? Evangelists say that we obey because we love or respect him,[6] but this solves no problems. An atheist could say that his only relations were with other human beings and he behaved in a certain way because he loved or respected them. There is no philosophical, though there may be a prudential, reason why we should do as God says. The conundrum to be resolved is: Does God give certain commands because they are right, or are they right because God gives them? In one case right or goodness are independent of and logically prior to God, and he is limited by ethical and moral rules like everyone else. In the other, his commands are purely arbitrary. But are they really good? How can we know? His postulated attributes of spirituality and transcendent power are no guarantee. The devil has similar powers, and it is a matter of speculation whether he will be finally defeated by God. In the whole course of recorded human history there have been good gods and bad gods and the individual has been expected to distinguish one lot from the other. But if our God is, in the long run, uniquely powerful, so that the prudential reasons[7] for obeying him are overwhelming, are they also moral reasons? Is virtue no more than cowering conformity to the divine will?

If everything depends on keeping God's commandments it is of vital importance to know what they are. This is a matter of real difficulty. If there is one universal God with consistent expectations, it is singular indeed that religiomorality should be so varied in time and place. Changes in marriage customs down the ages or across tribal frontiers may be explained in terms of God's recognition of particular human needs, but what of more fundamental differences? At certain times in most world religions the anchoretic tradition has been strong. But is going off into the desert as a hermit to spend all one's time in lone meditation morally commendable? Was it perhaps initially immoral to walk out on worldly responsibilities, and can a life lived in isolation be moral at all? Are other people not necessary to be moral to? This is an extreme example of what in Christian history has been the running battle between faith and works, the relative importance of duty to God and duty to one's fellows. Added to this are basic dichotomies between righteousness and kindliness; rigidity and sentimentality (hating sin but loving the sinner); introspection and evangelism; neighbourly neglect and neighbourly intrusiveness; social apathy arising from a belief that 'whatever is, is right'[8] because God made it that way, and political fanaticism arising from a belief that the world must immediately be changed in a way God has just revealed.

Now, these are problems that face us all. The naturalist may try to resolve them by plumping for the Aristotelian mean.[9] The supernaturalist is usually limited by the solution which exists in his own circle, according to which religion or sect or theological school happens to be in the ascendant; and as each tends to arise by violent reaction against and in sharp contrast with alternatives, at any one time religioethics and religiomorality lean to one extreme or another. The dominant theory and practice cling to power as long as possible. As they claim to emerge not from changing social circumstances but from unchanging divine dispensations, they are usually inflexible. They arise under the impact of local history and geography. The Christianity taught in British schools, for example, has been described as 'Hebrew history and Syrian geography'.[10] And it proves very difficult to make changes as history evolves and geography expands. That combination of local *mores* and reactive *immores* which constituted the social teaching of the religion when it arose, lingers. Like old soldiers, it never dies but only fades away. In theological terms, behaviour which is based on custom and scientific (prescientific) knowledge at one point in time, modified by the ideas and temperaments of particular religious leaders, is written up as 'natural law' or 'moral law', absolute, timeless, spaceless. This is one, and the commonest, form of 'moralism'. In the following pages this will be taken to mean unwarranted generalization from the particular in the moral field. Like 'scientism' and 'historicism'[11] it is the encapsulation of certain present and past events – perhaps dubiously observed – in a shell of words and formal logic and their projection into the future. For all the elaboration of detail it is a superficial venture that fails to understand and apply underlying principles.

In practice, of course, religiomorality does in time change by force of circumstances. A certain adjustment is then made in religioethics to justify the change. The old will no longer suffice. As a British 'Catholic Socialist' recently put it,

Whole sections of the Church will ignore it; priests of a later, more liberal generation will continue to enter the institutions of the Church; the laity will go on acting by humane values rather than by 'natural law'.[12]

Moropractice has then successfully rebelled. But in the act of rebellion the old stability is overthrown and the old sanctions weakened. There is still divergence between practice and precept, even after authority has been forced in part to yield. This is a period of great soul-searching, guilt and neurosis. It is our situation today. Not only is there tension within each ideology, the individual in a plural society is bombarded with other ideologies, each with its own ethics and morality, each with its own claims on his allegiance, each with the threat of inner conflict or worse to the heedless. Lucky is the man who escapes confusion.

The foregoing generalities need clarification by reference to particular families of faiths. Certain principles and rules are common to all religions, indeed to all humanity, if seen in their functional instead of their organic aspect. In the broadest sense it can be said that all societies have the same functional relationships, as the next part of this book will outline. But the actual diversity of moral codes that is at once apparent grows within very varied world-views. The sign 'religious' marks off a large allotment whose boundary line is indistinct. Within each patch, be it Christianity or Hinduism, many highly individual plants can be seen to grow.

Animism

This is held to be the earliest form of religion or prereligion. Anything which lives or moves or has being – plants, winds, mountains – is tenanted by a spirit. Animals and plants, often associated with ancestors, provide totemic symbols which regulate dietary tabus. They are also 'the basis of an ethic'[13] Morally this suggests a relationship between man and lower forms of life, so that in Australia's Cape York Peninsula the natives call dogs 'brothers' and 'sons', while the Ioway and Winnebago Amerindians respond similarly to both dogs and horses. As the French anthropologist Claude Lévi-Strauss observes, 'Everything takes place as if in our civilization every individual's own personality were his totem.'[14] Society is divided into moieties or castes and clans or totem-groups.[15] One category ensures stability, with division of labour and endogamy (internal marriage). The other promotes variety, evolution and universalization, with exogamy (external marriage) and the spread of genes and ideas. Special powers are claimed through ritual, sympathetic or antipathetic magic – using objects associated with a person in a friendly or hostile way – and the wearing of amulets with protective spirits. By these arrangements great community of feeling and collective responsibility are fostered. The Chinook of the north-west of North America, for example, do not say 'The bad man killed the poor child' but 'The man's badness killed the child's poverty'. It can be said that ritual 'conjoins' or brings about union, while our games are 'disjunctive' or bring about conflict. Left to itself an animistic society is highly stable, while its institutions are, despite Western allegations of 'primitiveness', complex and sophisticated.

Animism, which succeeded so long in relatively isolated communities, soon broke down before rival systems, though not as much as they often imagined:

There is no religion without magic any more than there is magic without at least a trace of religion.[16]

While it integrated life within the known world it fostered considerable suspicion and hostility outside. Foreigners were often regarded as 'dirty, coarse sub-men or even non-men: dangerous beasts or ghosts'.[17] In many cases they turned out to be more powerful than the tribe; for while totemism might encourage classificatory science, magic discouraged technology. Foreign imperialism, equipped with better weapons, destroyed both tribes and tribalism. The survivors attributed these powers of foreigners to superior magic and the colonial authority gave every inducement or threat to promote conversion to the alien faith. As Australian aborigines on the fringes of civilization illustrate, animists too easily lose their own virtues and gain alien vices.[18] With the modern collapse of imperialism and the rise of nationalism there has been some recrudescence, especially in Africa, of 'primitive' religion, but politicoethics or scioethics is more likely to be embraced.

Polytheism

With polytheism religion narrowly so-called can be said to arise. Its raw material is a plurality of gods, some of whom are the spirits of animism given greater powers and universality. But they have other functions. To satisfy speculation about first and final causes they are given responsibility for the creation, or at least the moulding, of the world, human life and death, rewards and punishments. Animism was never able to offer adequate penology. Its sharing of responsibility became unrealistically general; its concentration on the crime instead of the criminal made culpability 'objective'[19] and led to magic to restore the 'damage' through expiation in a material sense. No autonomous[20] feeling of personal responsibility could ever develop. Polytheism studies the relation of the agent to the action and the full complexity of human emotions and impulses. Though in practice social systems under animism are more complex than is usually believed, polytheism recognizes the functional nature of social divisions and relates them to celestial organization, whose polycentricity more accurately reflects the natural world than does the autocracy of monotheism.

Yet this is its moral undoing. At the same time as social responsibility is undermined, personal responsibility is offloaded on to one or other ruling deity. In a polytheistic society actions can all too glibly be attributed to the caprice of a wayward god. One particular god is held to be especially favourable to each community (Pallas Athene for Athens) or to mankind at large (Zeus), another especially unfavourable (Hades); and they respond to sacrifices of gratitude or appeasement respectively. No stable system of international justice can be built on this arrangement. Nationally, by making divine reflect human institutions at one point in time, polytheism tends to fossilize society in its existing class relations. It is by nature reactionary.

Hinduism

In what is described as its pure, though not, it would seem, its original form, Hinduism is a system of mystical pantheism. Pictured by a modern scholar,[21] it believes in an 'omniscient, omnipotent, impersonal and yet personal power' of which we are ourselves a part. 'We all are one, and that oneness is God, who is within and without.' The spiritual and material are 'two sides of a single coin'. Religion is also the 'centre of gravity' or 'balancing wheel' in society, so that Hinduism has strong political implications in the interests of stability. Though modern India is a secular state Hinduism lends itself to theocracy, and the brahmins or priests form the highest caste. It is, however, essentially tolerant and believes that in a real way all religions are one. In its popular form it is polytheistic, giving particular attention to the preserver-god Vishnu and his ten-plus *avatars*,[22] or reincarnations, and the destroyer-god Siva (Shiva). Reincarnation is the crux of popular Hinduism. By the law of *karma* (action or causality) as we sow so shall we reap.[23] Animals and plants and even inanimate things and gods are arranged in an evolutionary scale. After death souls pass up or down according to net merit or demerit and enter a new life. The whole of the natural order thus becomes the vehicle for Hindu religiomorality. A Jain will not kill any living thing. For all Hindus immortal well-being is not decided by divine favours, the right sacrifices or even right conduct in a single life-time. The entire course of history provides an opportunity for the righting of injustice and progressive elevation through good moropractice. Projected into human society this evolutionary scale leads to an extreme class division or caste system. This is not to be regarded as hereditary privilege for the fortunate but the reward of former virtue. High-caste parents do not choose to bestow privilege on their children; the souls of the children themselves have parents chosen for them by the law of *karma* – parents who are in a position to offer the privilege deserved.

Pantheism is a doctrine which, as Spinoza showed,[24] cannot be logically refuted. By the same token it has little descriptive value. Morally, it could lead to an extreme egocentricity, a belief that our every impulse is a hallowed prompting of the divine mind. As a form of polytheism popular Hinduism is subject to the general critique of this idea. But it is the law of *karma* which has made Indian society unique. It is indeed a prime example of the social dangers of speculative ethics. In theory nothing could be juster or wiser than morally-based reincarnation. In practice it has proved a disaster for social consciousness and political advancement. Caste discrepancies are not only justifiable but essential if the theory is true. The privileged get no more than their rights; the unprivileged no less than their deserts. Envy and sympathy are equally out of place. They amount to an impious questioning of *karma* itself. But if the theory is not true? Then it is a very convenient excuse for the indefinite perpetuation of class privilege and deprivation. In the lifetime of a member of the lowest caste (or outcaste) nothing he can do will improve his position. There is merely the hope that if he accepts his station with a good grace he will advance to something better in a new life. Not surprisingly the system is breaking down among middle-caste intellectuals, who are turning in increasing numbers to scientific humanism. Under the influence of Mahatma Gandhi[25] and the administration of Pandit Nehru the position of 'outcaste' was officially abolished, but it stays a reality in the remotest villages. Certain other social customs were long ago censured by reformist movements within Hinduism itself, beginning in 1828 with the Brahma Samaj of Raja Ram Mohan Roy, who helped the British to outlaw suttee. What remains among the modernists may still be called Hinduism, just as any Western mumbo-jumbo may be called Indian mysticism, but it lacks the uniqueness of Hindu religioethics and religiomorality.

Buddhism

Reform overtook Hinduism much further back than the nineteenth century. Under the influence of Gautama Buddha two and a half millennia ago there was the first notable questioning of Hindu social institutions and traditions. The Buddha sought to free morality from these foundations and erect it on 'the universal truths, which are to be revealed in every one's wisdom and attainment'.[26] He retained the notion of reincarnation, but considered the supreme good was to escape the awful, endless wheel of rebirth. The aim is *nirvana*[27] (enlightenment). This has been variously thought of as extinction of the personality or its extension to embrace infinity. The way towards this, the *dharma*,[28] is the Eightfold Path: right views, right thoughts, right speech, right actions, right living, right exertion, right recollection, right meditation.

Not to commit any sin, to do good,
And to purify one's own mind, that is the teaching of the Buddhas.[29]

It makes much of the symbols of the 'middle way' and the 'raft'. One resembles the Aristotelian mean. The other suggests the practicality rather than the spirituality of religion. Like a raft the Buddha's teachings are means to an end, ways of getting to the other side of the stream of life where *nirvana* is waiting. Once safely across we abandon the raft. It is not like the opposite shore, an end itself. Thoughts and actions are thus to replace creeds and rituals.

While Buddhism is essentially atheistic its most popular form – *Mahayana* or the greater vehicle – has effectively deified Gautama and introduced superstitious practices. Though the attainment of *nirvana* is not intended to be selfish and purely philosophical, its pursuit too often is. Social apathy is a common concomitant. Like Gautama himself the initiate often feels it necessary to abandon his family without undertaking other social responsibilities. All one's energy is put into steering the raft away from the known shore. And, apart from escape from day-to-day neurosis, it is not at all sure what is on the other bank. Meantime, in an effort to ensure right thoughts and actions the voyage is spent in obsessively cataloguing possible *immores*.[30]

Confucianism

Though Buddhism and Taoism have been influential in certain aspects of Chinese thought, they have promoted in China a morality which 'is entirely borrowed from the Confucian system'.[31] Confucius himself did not claim to have founded a school or to be concerned with ethics. It was morality which interested him. Virtue he considered to be a golden mean, and man by nature good. So too did his leading disciple Mencius, though some later Chinese philosophers[32] have asserted the opposite. Princes were advised that if they wished to govern their states wisely they should be sure that their families, themselves, their hearts, their thoughts and their knowledge were similarly governed.[33] So throughout the centuries in China mandarins have traditionally been men of learning and culture, and filial piety and benevolence have been prized even above patriotism. This derived its sanctions rather from the emperor and the social hierarchy than from 'heaven', to whose possible inhabitants the Chinese gave as little attention as the Epicureans. While advising his followers to 'love all men',[34] Confucius made a realistic assessment of human nature. He did not advo-

82

cate the do-gooding impertinence of doing unto others what you would have done unto you, but counselled instead 'not to do unto others what you would not wish done to yourself'.[35] Asked if he believed in repaying injury with kindness, he replied:

'With what then will you repay kindness? Repay injury with justice, kindness with kindness.'[36]

This positivist derivation of morality from existing social relations too often produced mere conformity, while filial piety degenerated into ancestor worship. The system might work well under benign rulers, but the imposition of dictatorship was accepted too readily. With morality geared to the precise political unit of the empire or an independent kingdom, it was unable to devise an easy formula to apply to other nations. This is one of the dilemmas of modern Maoism. Ostensibly pure Marxism–Leninism,[37] it demonstrates many aspects of Confucianism without the sage's linguistic caution. Though peasant in origin, Chairman Mao displays traditional qualities of the mandarinate, which was, after all, a form of meritocracy. He is venerated because he is old, wise, cultured, practical, militarily successful and in office. Because he has so succesfully supplanted (reinterpreted) Confucianism, his followers believe he has a message for the world. They have perhaps forgotten that Confucianism never succeeded in spreading beyond China. True, it made no great effort to.

Judaism

With Judaism we encounter the first great monotheistic religion and one of the great seminal faiths of the world. From this stock have sprouted Christianity and Islam. Because of the origins of Karl Marx some have even attributed Marxism to it. 'Quasi-monotheism' would be a more exact term, for not only are there traces of polytheism in Judaism's legends and first word for God, 'Elohim',[38] but there are elements of the dualism of Zoroastrianism.[39] (This evolving Persian faith divided the universe into the forces of light and dark, good and evil, spirit and matter, under the governance of the gods Ahura-Mazda and

Ahriman.) Lucifer-Satan has features of the divine and the infernal. But Judaism postulates that ultimately the universe is governed by Yahweh, one and supreme, who judges our actions, rewarding virtue and punishing vice. His justice is retributive: 'an eye for an eye and a tooth for a tooth'.[40] a logical simplification of the legalistic religion of Babylonia, whose myths and Code of Hammurabi greatly influenced the Jews who were in captivity there in the sixth century B.C. Man is pictured as in original communication with God until in his pride he disobeys and incurs the penalty of death. In his fallen state he sets about reproduction and so passes on 'original sin'[41] to all the generations of men. The only way in which they can regain God's favour and perhaps eternal life (the Sadducees denied the latter was ever possible) is by rigorous attention to God's commandments, which mingle impartially the moral and the theological, dietary laws, ritual purity and good works. This is the way to God's personal favour. His national favour towards the Jews is already guaranteed by patriarchal covenants, for Yahweh is in many respects still a tribal god who looks after his own and confounds their enemies with scant regard for universal equity. Since Jewish history, as distinct from legend, gave little support to this theory, it was postulated that a Messiah – or, rather, two Messiahs, one earthly and the other heavenly – would presently come to deliver the chosen people from suffering and bondage.

The Old Testament prophets reacted to this scenario in two ways. The more moralistic of them declared that the Jews had temporarily lost God's favour through infidelity and religious laxity. Hosea, Amos and the second Isaiah sought a broader vision. Jews were chosen not to receive privilege but to accept responsibility. The oppressed Jewish nation was a 'suffering servant'[42] bearing the sins of the world. As the Greek playwright Aeschylus was also to proclaim, the ways of God to man were justified in: 'Whom the Lord loveth he chasteneth.'[43] Traditionally the Torah (Jewish law), including the Ten Commandments, had been seen as a necessary and self-sufficient revelation. In those parts of the ancient world where no codification, legal or religious, existed, too often political instability and chaotic mythology flourished. The Jews hoped that people would be freed from uncertainty and know exactly what they

84

ought to do if there were tablets inscribed and scriptures inspired by God himself, plain for all to see. But it soon became clear that life was more complicated and words more elusive than this. Interpretation and elaboration were needed. In this way rabbinical teaching in synagogues gained ascendancy over priestly sacrifices in temples.[44] One of the great rabbis was Hillel the Elder. He was concerned to replace formalism with humanity. Man's duty to man was more important in the sight of God than perfunctory ritual. Like Confucius he interpreted morality in a realistic way: 'What is hateful to you, do not to others.'[45] When Akiba systematized Jewish law, reconciling oral tradition with the Torah, this sensible precept was incorporated.

Despite the exertions of liberal prophets and rabbis, Judaism (at least in its Orthodox form) never completely escaped the formalism[46] and self-righteousness that the Gospel Jesus attributed to the scribes and Pharisees. Everything was done because God said so. There were direct duties to both God and man. Those to God were obviously more important and, if time were short, were the only ones that got done. Ritual impurity ranked with more obvious *immores*. Even good works as usually understood were in danger of becoming entirely prudential and loveless, unrelated to the true needs of the recipient and likely to provoke more resentment than gratitude. Nevertheless, especially within the family and towards other Jews, Judaism did succeed in fostering close ties and a sense of communal responsibility, with significantly low delinquency and crime rates. In relations with Gentiles the position was less satisfactory. The tribalistic and nationalistic origin of Judaism proved as hard to escape as its legalistic one. Indeed it is only in very recent years that converts to Judaism have been recognized, for traditionally it has been believed that only the 'seed of Father Abraham'[47] inherited the covenant. As the centuries passed, however, and persecutions continued, the dream of its fulfilment faded. Jews became obsessed with suffering, fatalistic before oppression. Whole columns were marched off to the gas chambers during the Second World War by a single guard, without any show of resistance. The younger Jewish generation has reacted sharply against this passivity and the whole notion of a 'suffering servant'. Understandably they see it as no more than the gospel of the ghetto. The establishment of the state of Israel in 1948 suggested to many – Christians, and perhaps Muslims, as well as Jews – that God is belatedly fulfilling his covenant. As a result the new nation has shown considerable insensitivity to the human situation in Palestine and world opinion concerning the displaced Arab population.[48] In contemplation of a religious dream the mind readily shuts out moral nightmares.

Christianity

Under the Roman occupation two millennia ago the Jews grew increasingly restive. As demand for the long-awaited Messiah rose, so did the supply. Essentially the candidates were great patriots and partisan leaders, but while they may have been regarded as messiahs in their brief moments of glory, their ultimate failure undermined their claims. At last, however, there did arise a Messiah who, though his historicity[49] is in dispute and his recorded life may be mythical, made a profound impact not on Palestine but on the Gentile world. This impact has been adduced by his followers as evidence of the truth of his claims; but it attests more the technical superiority and evangelical fervour of the nations that took him up than any particular merit in his teachings. Significantly, though he may be said to have arisen as a Jewish heretic with certain overtones of the revolutionary leader, and seems to have made his first impact among Jewish colonies scattered round the Roman Empire, he led two deviations from the accepted messianic path. Like that of the Graeco-Roman philosophers his teaching was universalized, and though he promised a kingdom to the faithful it was 'not of this world'.[50]

It is a little difficult to say, assuming his historicity, precisely what his original message was. Christian denominations are themselves in violent disagreement. 'Christianity' is everything from an esoteric mysticism to a doctrine of good works, from a belief that Jesus Christ was God himself, part of the one and indivisible Trinity, to an opinion that he was simply a great ethical teacher. What is usually known as Christianity is an amalgam of Jesuine and Pauline teachings as they were mulled over and transmitted in the first four centuries[51] of the Fathers. Broadly speaking, Jesus generalized and Paul particularized. Jesus spoke to those who had left or might leave all to follow him; Paul spoke to disciples still living 'in the world' beset by sin and temptation, especially from sex. Though dire warnings[52] are given to those who reject it, the simple teaching is one of love instead of law. God expects us to do certain things for our benefit, not for his; we should obey him out of love, not out of fear. On to this ethical stock were grafted moral traditions and sanctions of earlier and contemporary religions. Zoroastrianism was then blossoming in the form of Mithraism, whose dualism strongly influenced Christianity. The Jewish heaven and hell were Babylonian in origin and marginal[53] in impact. Under Christianity however supernaturalism became the dominant sanction. Zoroastrian dualism also appeared in Gnosticism, and a little later in Manicheism, which both prompted Christian asceticism. The embryonic faith also caught up elements of Egyptian ritualism, Mediterranean cultic nature-worship, Graeco-Roman Stoicism and Babylonian numerology. But its underlying principle was Judaic.

The fall of man was taken as axiomatic. What could be done about it? Were human rituals and good works enough to blind God to the defilement of his once-perfect universe, or human death sufficient expiation? Christians decided they were not, and thus returned to those primitive ethical notions Judaism was beginning to live down. Only the death of God himself, in the person of Christ, could redress the balance. By acceptance of this perfect sacrifice and the exercise of sympathetic magic in communion (later formalized as the mass), man could share in this act of expiation and return to harmony and eternal life with God. This conversion should produce a changed earthly life. Christians were asked to follow what was described as 'a new commandment':

'That ye love one another; as I have loved you, that ye also love one another.'[54]

There was nothing really new in this, apart from its rooting in Christ. Religious leaders and secular philosophers had been saying similar things for centuries. What was, it seems, new was an injunction to 'resist not evil'.[55]

Love your enemies, do good to them which hate you, bless them that curse you, and pray for them which despitefully use you. And unto him that smiteth thee on the one cheek offer also the other; and him that taketh away thy cloke forbid not to take thy coat also.[56]

Without at this stage considering to what extent Christians have tried or been able to live up to this ideal, we can see that there were already three major ingredients in Christianity – faith, sacraments and works – where there was scope for disagreement over details and relative importance. Another basic conflict concerned the way the individual came to salvation. One school, fathered by St Augustine, Cornelius Jansen, John Calvin and to some extent St Thomas Aquinas, held that man was pre-destined to salvation or damnation; another, citing Pelagius and Jacobus Arminius, believed in free will. Predestination is not just scientific determinism. It states that whatever a man may think or do his fate is sealed in advance by God. The theory was put forward to rescue divine omnipotence from the implications of genuine free will, draws upon many Pauline texts[57] and has in the past cut across denominational boundaries. It is essentially a continuation of the 'chosen people' idea in a non-racial connection, but in these more democratic times is decidedly on the wane, in relative as well as absolute terms.

The great strength of Christianity has been its versatility, its capacity to be 'all things to all men'.[58] Like other hybrids it has grown sturdily, though it has been largely sterile of new ideas. It has a complex theology, or theologies, but they can be abandoned for a simple article of faith:

For God so loved the world, that he gave his only begotten Son, that whosoever believeth in him should not perish, but have everlasting life.[59]

It has a strong moral content but it is not like Zoroastrianism, which is 'in the fullest sense of the word a religion of morality'.[60] The higher flights of its precepts are purely idealistic and no one has really tried to live up to them. Yet it has such a profound conviction that its beauty, goodness and truth are wedded to practicability, that its adherents have had an unrivalled urge, prompted by Christ himself, to 'go . . . and teach all nations, baptizing them in the name of the Father, and of the Son, and of the Holy Ghost'.[61] Allied with imperialism and capitalism it has provided an incentive for navigation and contacts with other cultures. Cross-fertilization of ideas has inevitably resulted, even though the original intention was to supplant foreign customs and absorb nothing in return. In some areas a *pax Britannica* (*Hispanica*, *Gallica*, etc.), attributed to the Prince of Peace, has descended on warring and bloodthirsty tribes. At certain periods in history the arts, with their socializing role, have found patrons in the church they could not find outside. For the church claimed jurisdiction over all avenues of life and wanted learning, art, sex, daily occupation and thought all to glorify God.

Till recent times the assessment in the last paragraph would have been accepted, with few qualifications, by most people, whatever their views on the essential truth of Christianity. In 1933 the *Church Times* began to detect a change:

In England, the atheist and the agnostic of the nineteenth century generally recognized the precepts and inhibitions of the Christian ethic. Such a man as Charles Bradlaugh, for example, was something of a Puritan. Today it is the Christian ethic that is most virulently assailed.[62]

The Church of England was clearly seeing the dawn of what is now called the 'permissive society',[63] which most commentators still associate with sex. But the 'permissive' attack on Christoethics and Christomorality is much more fundamental than that. To such an extent that a Scottish psychologist, Margaret Knight, a few years ago declared her inclination 'to the view that the conversion of Europe to Christianity was one of the greatest disasters of history'.[64] Though few like-minded critics have cared to speculate what Europe might have been like without this conversion, her basic view is now widely shared. This is largely a moral judgement, though some would concentrate on what they see as intellectual mistakes and superstitions. Today most Christians offer apologies rather than apologetics for much of Christian history, regretting that 'the spirit indeed is willing, but the flesh is weak'.[65] Non-Christians however assert that objectionable moropractice springs largely from Christoethics and Christomorality themselves.

At the heart of Christianity are the doctrines of original sin and atonement. Regardless of whether or not they are true, they have unfortunate moral consequences. Inevitably they present a thoroughly pessimistic and one-sided view of human nature. True, they also suggest a way of redemption and reconciliation. But this is only for loyal Christians. Though views on the character and fate of pagans, and in more recent times of apostates, have mellowed down the years, too often it has been assumed that those beyond the circle of faith are irremediably evil. Irrationally apostates may believe this of themselves, for moral judgements run deeper than intellectual and those who have ceased to believe in the truth of the atonement may be unable to shake off fear of indictment for original sin. Both Christians and non-Christians within their orbit may, therefore, too readily accept views on the inevitability of wars and other destructive or antisocial activities. For most Christians believe that God is active in individual lives rather than in society at large, and many go so far as to put this 'dispensation' under the government of the devil. Predestination is a particularly amoral, if not immoral, theory. Though it is mitigated by the rider that only God actually knows who has been chosen for what, it suggests, perhaps unconsciously, that neither the elect nor the damned have any stake in their actual conduct. One group has nothing to gain, the other nothing to lose. And while the notion is intended to be theological rather than ethical, concerned with Judgement Day and not every day, it can also suggest that one is entirely a puppet of God's caprice with no personal responsibility.

Today many describe Christianity as simply a way of life. Historically, however, it has been a way of faith, and people have been held morally responsible for what they believe. Great attention has been given to creeds – the Apostles', Nicene, Athanasian – and often to catechisms. The Athanasian Creed is most precise about intellectual requirements:

Whosoever will be saved: before all things it is necessary that he hold the Catholic Faith. Which Faith except every one do keep whole and undefiled: without doubt he shall perish everlastingly.[66]

This preamble points the meaning of 'done good' and 'done evil', which are the passports to 'life everlasting' and 'everlasting fire'.[67] Now, intellectual belief is not necessarily related to conduct, or credal belief to fact. Humility before the facts and the scientific method of investigation and experimentation are quite alien to orthodox Christianity. But sins of the mind and intellectual 'errors' are no strangers and are dealt with harshly: so that inquisitions, book-burning, heresy trials and rigorous censorship, especially of an ideological kind, have flourished in those closed societies where Christianity has gained dominance. These practices were not heresies or deviations that arose when it became the established religion of the Roman Empire. Though its founders may not have endorsed specific penalties for unbelief, they were clear about principles. Jesus appears to have approved of the nobleman in the parable of the pounds (talents), who declared, 'But those mine enemies, which would not that I should reign over them, bring hither and slay them before me.'[68] Paul was also sharp against heterodoxy:

But though we, or an angel from heaven, preach any other gospel unto you than that which we have preached unto you, let him be accursed.[69]

In his epistles right opinions were consistently extolled over good moropractice. Though on one occasion he echoed James's view that 'faith without works is dead',[70] his prevailing teaching was that salvation did not come from one's own merit:

For by grace are ye saved through faith; and that not of yourselves: it is the gift of God: Not of works, lest any man should boast.[71]

As the Pharisees were not slow to point out, Jesus associated a lot with publicans and sinners, prostitutes and prodigals, as if the unvirtuous had a peculiar claim on God's love. In his view it was the outcasts of society who especially needed his help; and, outside Jewish communities in the Gentile world, Christianity seems to have made its initial impact among the forgotten slave population of the Roman Empire. This concern for social outcasts (who are not necessarily vicious and may be virtuous) is undoubtedly worthy, but it can easily magnify sin to exalt salvation, as the whining humbugs in Shaw's *Major Barbara* realized.

From the foregoing it is clear that Christoethics has traditionally regarded itself as the only form of ethics. It might almost appear that no Christomorality could exist, if 'morality' be used in the usual sense; and some Christians[72] have in fact believed that they were freed from the moral law. The apostle Paul himself declared that 'all things are lawful unto me', but went on to observe that 'all things are not expedient'.[73] Rather more than Jesus, he elaborated, at one time or another, long catalogues of inexpedient things; so that Christomorality can certainly be said to exist. Because of Christian attitudes to faith, revelation and sacred scriptures, its prescriptions and prohibitions have also inherited an absolute quality and Christomorality is often regarded as the only genuine morality. Its basic ingredient is said to be love. But, as we have seen before, this is not unique; and, as we shall see later, it may become dangerously possessive and obsessive. When law becomes legalistic it may be right for love to replace it. Emotion is a better stimulus to action. Yet it can be an arbitrary, unreasonable and wayward guide. If 'love of God' is the form it takes, then life may be devoted largely or entirely to spiritual exercises, prayers, rituals of thanks-giving (to replace rituals of propitiation or purity) and other unsocial activities. If basic human needs are thereby neglected, these activities can be called antisocial.

Some would say that 'love of one's neighbour' is the primary Christian concern, and it would certainly seem easier, morally, to have a relationship with man than with God. But when New Testament injunctions and Christian practice down the ages are studied closely, love is found constricted by formalistic bonds. This is especially notable in the field of sex. With some justification modern Christian spokesmen may say that in our world of Freudian psychologists, dolly advertisements and X-certificate films sex is unduly promoted. This obsession – if obsession it be – may be regarded as a reaction against Victorian sanctimonious-ness and the general tenor of Christian culture. For within societies under this influence a person has been declared 'im-moral' not so much for cruelty, greed, defamation or aggression as for grounding 'marriage' in love instead of in heaven. Restrictions, or attempted restrictions, on human sexuality are part of a general air of joylessness, inhibition and unreal idealism that has fanned the halo round the head of Christ and sounded disapproval in the throat of Paul. So that followers who seem incapable of liking their friends lyricize on the need to love their enemies.[74] This extraordinary injunction forms part of the much-praised Sermon on the Mount. Here too we find the beatitudes.[75] We may all commend their praise of the merciful and peacemakers. There will be less enthusiasm for the 'pure in heart' and 'they which do hunger and thirst after righteousness'. But there will be widespread anxiety over the blessing of those who are poor, poor in spirit, meek, persecuted and hungry, when it is seen that their reward is supernal and no earthly effort is urged to remove those conditions which have occasioned their suffering. Against tyrants, oppressors, exploiters and scoundrels of all descriptions there is to be no resistance. In the hereafter God will compensate their victims. 'Many that are first shall be last; and the last first.'[76]

Paul reinforced this teaching, urging 'servants' (slaves) to 'be obedient to them that are your masters according to the flesh, with fear and trembling, in singleness of your heart, as unto Christ'.[77] Not only social outcasts, who may themselves have been antisocial, but political outcasts were thus appealed to. After the failure of the Spartacus uprising in 71 B.C., slaves of Rome, like those of America several centuries later, were willing to settle for a faith which promised beatitude some time, somewhere. But while we may sympathize with the motives of both the preacher and the proselyte, it is hard to ignore the retarding effect on social and political reforms such doctrines have had for most of Christian history. Psychological anodynes readily come to promote masochism and reaction. Yet if Christianity fostered personal pacifism (a notion that is at least endearing even when it is inexpedient) it singularly failed to push it nationally. Evangelism was not universally welcomed. When it was resisted it grew aggressive. The facts are historical and the details do not here concern us. In some cases a Christian, or a Protestant, victory in a colonial or religious war may seem in retrospect an avenue towards advance, though historicism can easily bemuse us. In others the suppressed culture – of the Graeco-Roman world, say, or the Buddhist – was in many ways superior to what took its place.

Before we leave Christianity we may glance over five influential forms it has taken to see whether the parts may in fact be

93

greater than the whole. Similar developments have taken place within other world religions, but Christianity is best suited to this survey as it is more familiar to Western readers and has been most subjected to scrutiny.

Catholicism

The Catholic Church ideally is the universal community of believers. Even in the days of Constantine this never attained a genuine organizational form. Bishops, who were originally elected, were autonomous in most respects. Eventually 'Catholic Church' came to mean that body of Christians who accepted the authority, and eventually the infallibility, of the Bishop of Rome. Based on tradition and the Petrine texts:

Thou art Peter, and upon this rock I will build my church; and the gates of hell shall not prevail against it.

And I will give unto thee the keys of the kingdom of heaven: and whatsoever thou shalt bind on earth shall be bound in heaven: and whatsoever thou shalt loose on earth shall be loosed in heaven.[78]

this arrangement was the logical development of a faith which claimed revelation of abiding relevance. The teaching church would explain the gospel, relate it to changing social circumstances, and combine in one system reason and creed, faith and works. God would ensure that its teaching was sound. Christo-ethics and Christomorality would both be guaranteed by dogmatic theology. Believers would be left in no doubt as to what God expected, and if they transgressed, what penance God exacted. They would then be absolved and given confidence to face life anew and sin no more. Organizational and personal moral stability would both be assured.

Practice has proved less satisfactory than theory. Setting aside such questions as whether the Petrine texts are genuine or correctly interpreted, we have the evidence of centuries that stability cannot be so lightly achieved. Rebellion against what was seen as an intolerable or alien discipline inspired countless schisms, heresies, interdicts, breakaways and other rifts, which often led to civil and national wars. Meanwhile, within a large body of Christendom, theological stability was maintained. It was maintained, however, at the expense of personal conscience, assailed both by intellectual doubts and by divided loyalties at such times as papal and civic authority were in conflict. Moral crises inevitably resulted. Even in times of intellectual and political calm Catholic ethics brought disturbing consequences. It encouraged moral heteronomy and discouraged autonomy. Morality became a mere servant of theology. Before Christianity was officially established in the fourth century there were already the Montanist and Novatian heresies, which centred on whether a corrupt priest or prelate held valid jurisdiction and orders. The heretics denied that he did. To safeguard whatever sacraments he might have celebrated – and perhaps to avoid undue depletion of ministerial ranks – the church plumped for validity. Similar heresies broke out and were denounced in Catholicism down the years. Administratively the orthodox ruling may have been necessary. Morally it was disastrous, suggesting that Christianity was a matter of right views and sacraments rather than right conduct. Century by century the catalogue of 'sins' lengthened, largely with doctrinal offences, and it grew increasingly desirable that formal misdemeanours should be offered formal absolution. In the process, however, formalism was enthroned in all spheres of social conduct. To the unstable mind Catholic ethics brought an unhealthy mixture of moral cares and moral carelessness. Emphasis was placed on the unworthiness and depravity of man, required to debase himself before his creator. Outside church the more active spirits redeemed their self-respect by violent assertion.

Throughout the world Catholics have shown a higher than average propensity for crime,[79] especially crimes of violence. Psychologists describe them as 'extrapunitive'.[80] Catholic catechisms suggest to children sins they had never thought of committing. Penance, with its ready-reckoned tables of reparations, and extreme unction bring a perfunctory or cynical element into moral calculations. Too often they appear to bypass the human situation which precipitated the sin and may well recur, and concentrate instead on a ritual formula of expiation. Sometimes the impression is given that a crime against a non-Catholic is less serious than one against a Catholic. In 1819 Shelley made a shrewd observation on Italian Catholicism:

It has no necessary connection with any one virtue. The most atrocious villain may be rigidly devout, and without any shock to

95

established faith, confess himself to be so. Religion pervades intensely the whole frame of society, and is according to the temper of the mind which it inhabits, a passion, a persuasion, an excuse, a refuge; never a check.[81]

In the later middle ages, scoundrels and wide boys used to take minor religious orders. Without interfering with their way of life this gave them 'benefit of clergy', the right to be tried in ecclesiastical courts, whose sentences for serious *immores* were notably lighter than those of the secular judicature.

Protestantism

What is usually called the Reformation was closely connected with economic and political forces. As will be seen later, they were themselves not without moral overtones. Luther, whose famous ninety-five theses against indulgences precipitated the first successful challenge to Rome's authority, moral and political, was relatively conservative in his theology. The great Protestant monarch Henry VIII was less adventurous still, and gained his title Defender of the Faith for controverting Luther's modest radicalism. True, it was not long before profound doctrinal changes were proposed by the Swiss theologians, but the whole 'protest movement' in the church was as much moral as ecclesiastical and had a long history. Briefly, the private lives of the elect, especially of the clergy, were thought unworthy of their calling. One of their characteristics was, or was thought to be, idleness and luxurious living. The Protestants thereupon advanced the dignity of labour and the virtues of hard work, sobriety and simple living. Deciding that the medieval ban on usury, which in the Italian and Germanic city-states was honoured more by mendicant friars than by financiers, was quite unscriptural, they invested the money they saved in trade and then in industry. This pattern of life is now all but universal, though American sociologists still call it the 'Protestant ethic' or 'Puritan ethic'.[82] What aided these developments was a return to the tradition of independent thought that had flourished in parts of the Graeco-Roman world. At first there was an assertion of the individual aesthetic spirit over medieval formalism, a change which had begun with the Catholic Renaissance. Then came a rescue of independent judgement in matters of faith and morals. Combined with respect for the equal independence of other private judgements, this became known, about 1890, as the 'Nonconformist conscience'. A bonus to independence of thought accrued in the form of scientific discovery, when tradition as a vehicle of knowledge about the world was overturned by free inquiry. In this way Protestantism contributed to the more radical investigations of non-Christian freethinkers, and prepared the way for the Industrial Revolution.

Whatever practical benefits may have come in certain situations were overshadowed by ethical and moral disadvantages. Genuine humility before the facts was not achieved, as the authority of the church was replaced by the authority of scripture. As this is by no means self-explanatory there soon followed what Catholics had long foretold: the full hazards and horrors of individual interpretation and the 'enthusiasm' of latter-day prophets allegedly filled with the Holy Ghost. Often this led to beliefs and practices, and particularly to a religiomorality based largely on Paul, more rigid than the system they supplanted. This Puritanism awakened an echo in Catholicism. Under the guidance of the Jesuits there evolved the Counter-Reformation, which tried to come to terms with intellectual and practical objections to Rome by formulating casuistry and accepting usury, and with moral strictures by giving more attention to clerical purity. But Protestantism always kept a lead in this field and, because it tried to suppress harmless everyday pleasures, soon gained the lion's share of sanctimoniousness, neurosis and depression. Unfiltered by exegesis, the bible disturbed the faithful by being, on the one hand, 'a history of lust, sodomies, wholesale slaughtering, and horrible depravity',[83] and, on the other, a set of strictures and sexual tabus that had arisen in a millenarian climate that believed the end of the world was at hand and family responsibilities could, even should, be neglected.

The stress on individualistic religion often led to selfish preoccupation with personal salvation and the eccentricities of instant conversion. It was suggested that however lost in sin one might be, a changed life could be had simply by accepting the Lord Jesus Christ as one's own personal saviour. With some individuals, in the short term, moropractice may be aided in a heady atmosphere of conversion, but without a stable intellectual or moral commitment behavioural gains tend to be lost when the evangelist leaves and the novelty wears off. But moropractice may not be helped at any stage, since an unstable convert can literally accept the advice of Martin Luther: '*Pecca fortiter*'[84] (sin boldly). This tendency may be exaggerated by a belief in predestination which, under the influence of Calvin and John Knox, came to be almost exclusively, though far from universally, Protestant. More particularly Protestantism came to be associated with biblical literalism, sabbatarianism and puritanism, enforced wherever possible by pledges. That of the nineteenth-century Social Purity Alliance is representative:

I promise: (1) By the help of God, to protect, as far as I have opportunity, all women and children from degradation. (2) To discountenance all coarse jests, conversation, and behaviour derogatory to women. (3) To maintain the equal obligation of the law of purity on men and women alike. (4) To endeavour to spread these principles amongst my companions, and to help, by counsel and warning, my younger brothers. (5) To use all possible means to fulfil the injunction of God's Word, 'Keep thyself pure.'[85]

To the pure all things are impure.

New Theology

There is room for doubt as to what extent Paul accepted the historicity of Christ, or the disciples the Christology of Jesus. A British lay theologian recently observed:

There is an enormous amount of evidence that Jesus and the early Christians used the term 'God' to mean something much closer to the kind of thing modern scientific humanism stands for than anything traditional religion has stood for.[86]

Naturally, he is himself a scientist and a modernist. The New Theology began with the 'tortuosities of the Teutonic theologians'[87] in the early nineteenth century, in the second half of which it reached Britain as the Broad Church or Modernism. It was then said that the theology of the Anglo-Catholic Canon Liddon was 'impossible to believe', while that of the Modernist Dean Stanley was 'not worth believing'.[88] There was a flurry of New Theology inside Nonconformism at the beginning of the twentieth century,[89] and more Teutonic activity thirty years later. Soon after a humanist, Julian Huxley, found 'religion without revelation',[90] Christian theologians discovered revelation without religion. Dietrich Bonhoeffer called it 'Christianity without religion';[91] Rudolf Bultmann, 'demythologized Christianity';[92] Paul Tillich, 'the depth of existence' or 'the ground of our being'.[93] This has been variously identified as love or creativity. Love sounds less exacting and received a notable boost with the Bishop of Woolwich's *Honest to God* in 1963. America has responded with the 'Death of God' school of theologians.[94] Whatever the motives of its promoters, the New Theology has moral significance in that it attempts to separate Christomorality from Christoethics and rescue it from the ruins of Christian theology (which is 'morally intolerable' as well as 'intellectually superfluous' and 'emotionally dispensable').[95] Taking love as the centre of Christianity, and perhaps of all religions, it tries to make this shine within conventional language and traditional institutions. If our attitudes are right, illumined by love, we shall see how to behave in the darkest corners of human life.

Love will be considered more fully in the next section. Here it may be apposite to comment on its relevance to Christomorality. If traditional theologians saw the natural man as a ghost in the dark night of the soul, the modernists see him as a cherub, in the blaze of the beatific vision. Psychologists have also been active in prospecting the ground of our being. While some behaviourists have announced happy finds, the psychoanalysts have found only the skeletons of diseased thoughts immolated in the *id*. They were not a pretty sight. Let us, however, suppose that the new theologians are right and we all have a vein of untapped love deep down inside. Is love the ore to smelt into shining moropractice? Has it anything in particular to do with Christianity? If not, is it desirable to pretend that it has? Love is undoubtedly a powerful passion. It can be creative and constructive. It can also be obsessional and destructive. The *crime passionnel* may be its fruits as easily as the act of reconciliation. Alternatively, it can dissolve into a feeling of generalized philanthropy without yielding any particular action at all. Yet most of us would agree it is likely to be more constructive than hate and stands among the sympathetic virtues. But it is not as such specifically Christian. To say that it is either becomes a self-righteous claim that will irritate and antagonize non-Christians or, if it is based on the reciprocal I–thou existentialist formula, suggests that love is like a club badge with its currency limited to Christians. The New Theology has unquestionably involved verbal junketings that to many imply a lack of frankness which alienates traditional believers and outsiders alike. One section already feels itself, as a British parliamentarian puts it, adrift in 'a world starved of moral certainty' and populated by 'publicizing priests and trendy "leading laymen" '.[96] The other can find many philosophies of 'love' that do not involve meaningless (to them) Christian rituals. For the days when holy communion with the elements of harvest festival really suggested a 'love feast' are too far back in the history of our culture for easy recall. The net result is that Modernism has lost familiar moral sanctions without gaining a plausible new dynamic for moropractice.

State Christianity

Apart from its sectarian interpretations and reinterpretations, every successful religion tends to acquire a political expression, whether or not it began with it. To Jesus is attributed the ambiguous formula, 'Render to Caesar the things that are Caesar's, and to God the things that are God's.'[97] The broad outline of his presumptive biography suggests, however, opposition rather than commitment to constituted authority. So that, with a certain plausibility, he is advertised to young people today by progressive parsons as an authentic revolutionary and anti-hero. His real life and intentions are conjectural, and Albert Schweitzer[98] has postulated a dramatic change from rebel to mystic as his fortunes waned. What is important is that institutionalized Christianity, especially in countries where it is officially established, has been anything but a revolutionary force. It has, on the contrary, been the handmaiden of the 'law and order' men. Perhaps because of their professional experiences criminal lawyers have tended to hold melancholy views on human nature. Without the direst sanctions people would, in their view, tear one another to pieces. Fortifying their own sentences, Christian judges have always regarded the other-worldly sanctions of Christianity as indispensable to good conduct; and this view has remained unshaken however many rascals take the oath with every show of piety. In an important Judgement in 1676, when civil strife was in living memory, Lord Chief Justice Sir Matthew Hale observed:

Such kind of wicked blasphemous words were not only an offence to God and religion, but a crime against the laws, state, and government, and therefore punishable in this court. For to say, Religion is a cheat, is to dissolve all those obligations whereby civil societies are preserved, and that Christianity is parcel of the laws of England; and therefore to reproach the Christian religion, is to speak in subversion of the law.[99]

In 1812, when the French Revolution was a living memory, the publisher of Thomas Paine's *Age of Reason* was in the dock. Recalling the Hale Judgement the Attorney-General asked the jury

To what did they look for the performance of the duties of their domestics, but to the obligations of religion? By what tie were these classes bound, if that was removed?[100]

Endorsing this view Lord Chief Justice Lord Ellenborough announced that he would 'leave it to the jury as Christian men sworn on the gospel of Christ, to say whether the present was not an atrocious libel on the Christian religion'; and the jury brought in a verdict of guilty without retiring. Even before the French Revolution similar views were held by middle-class sceptics. Hume was careful not to discuss religion in front of the servants. This attitude has long been abandoned by sceptics, but, despite the repeal of the main statute[101] against blasphemy in 1967, legal circles tend to cling to the statement in Blackstone's eighteenth-century *Commentaries on the Laws of England*:

Doubtless the preservation of Christianity, as a national religion, is, abstracted from its own intrinsic truth, of the utmost consequence to the civil state: which a single instance will sufficiently demonstrate. The belief of a future state of rewards and punishments, the entertaining just ideas of the moral attributes of the supreme being, and a firm persuasion that he superintends and will finally compensate every action in human life . . . these are the grand foundations of all judicial oaths.[102]

Blackstone gave every evidence of sincere belief in the general propositions of Christianity. Not every disciple has. In objecting to the taking of an oath in the House of Commons by an atheist, before affirmations were permitted, a Conservative member declared,

As for the argument that the members already admitted to the House hold various religious beliefs, I would put out that among them there is one common standard of morality and a general belief in some Divinity or other.[103]

It is this perfunctory approach which has categorized national religions throughout history, especially where the established church is, like the Church of England, Erastian, that is, subject to political control by the state. Ecclesiastical establishment may mean little more than national endowment while the church retains autonomy. The Vatican has always tried to secure establishment on the Guelph pattern, where, with or without concordats, it dictates policy to the state on questions of 'faith and morals'. In this way its views on censorship, divorce, family planning, abortion, education and other socio-moral subjects are imposed on the whole community through the laws of the land. Within this territory in Catholic countries some of the fiercest political battles have been fought in recent years.[104]

Even where there is 'no . . . establishment of religion',[105] as in the United States, the state may effectively promote all religions by its tax laws and especially Christianity by the pronouncements of its public figures. A large measure of socio-moral (usually prohibitional) legislation is based on views derived from Christianity, whether or not their origin is recalled. This legislation usually has the almost impossible aim of being 'undenominational'. Where an established church loses the effective support of the majority of the population it too has to accept and be grateful for 'undenominational' Christian legislation. In 1944 British state schools acquired 'undenominational' worship and religious instruction with the approval of the Church of England, though neither the Catholic Church nor many fundamentalist Protestant sects accept the doctrinal possibility of undenominationalism. Whether established or unestablished, implicit or explicit, state religion boldly seeks to provide a ceremonial and a basis for the legal system if not a foundation for personal morality and political theory, that will unify and pacify, give a sense of national purpose and perhaps a conviction of national destiny. Ideally it is to impregnate the country's political and diplomatic decisions with those spiritual qualities appropriate to the religion concerned. Within Christianity they may be assumed to be love, peace, humility, poverty, obedience, chastity.

The stimulus to law-enforcement provided by state Christianity must be tested by statistics. They can, and often do, lie; but are likely to lie in favour of religion. When the established faith of England was Catholicism, or Anglicanism without access to non-sectarian oaths or affirmations, freedom of worship and freedom of conscience, statistics hardly existed and many, perhaps most, crimes were unreported and unrecorded. The nineteenth-century constitutional emasculation of the Church of England eased with the passing of the Oaths Act in 1888.[106] Thereafter, though credal Christianity has greatly declined, state Christianity has not declined at all. Indeed the introduction of religious broadcasting and statutory religion in state schools in the twentieth century may be said to have advanced it. If, therefore, there is a collapse in moral standards and moropractice it cannot be attributed to a collapse of state Christianity. But there have always been good theoretical grounds for believing that state religion has no effect on personal morality except perhaps a bad one. Even without state education or admass the individual grows up with some knowledge of the conduct of public affairs, if only at the local level. In one way or another he is also indoctrinated with the state religion. He is told that personal belief influences personal behaviour, and he must therefore assume that national belief influences national behaviour. As he grows up he looks around and assesses the quality of public life and national politics. In a Christian country he asks himself whether the pursuit of love, peace, humility, poverty, obedience and chastity is conspicuous in the counsels of the nation or the lives of those who lead it. A prominent Methodist, Lord Soper, recently broached just one of these questions:

The plain teaching of Jesus with his injunction to love enemies and refuse to resist them violently has never, of course, been officially repudiated by his followers. All the same, exceptions have been found and consecrated, time and again, to this general prohibition until these exceptions have proved the rule, and the Christian church has taken its place alongside all the other violent institutions which have cursed mankind.[107]

He is himself a pacifist. But there has never been a shortage of clerical captains to bless military colours, Polaris submarines and any and every emblem or weapon of war. With such an example constantly before them ordinary people assume that morality and moropractice need have no relation, or that the morality that is proclaimed is very different from the morality which is actually believed. This impression of national humbug is strengthened where undenominationalism is concerned. To the naturally sceptical this is little more credible than a fully sectarian position, while it is demonstrably a myth in its own right. People may accept an old-time religion or a new-time religion, but a denominational average or a committee compromise is the religion of no one at all. If no one subscribes to the religion need anyone subscribe to the religiomorality? This assumes that there is one. All too often a state religion seems to be quite devoid of moral content and be simply a means of promoting conformism or nationalism. History has indeed furnished many examples where this was consciously done. The most recent was the folk religion elaborated in Nazi Germany by Alfred Rosenberg.

Popular Christianity

Every successful religion acquires a popular expression; or rather, a range of expressions peculiar to various regions. The official religion itself includes elements of former religions, magic and social customs found in its land of origin. Popular religion introduces changes related to other areas and the emotional needs of people generally. If the official religion has been silent about the gods or immortality or some other specific the people of the time demand, they cheerfully incorporate it. The change may be so radical that in effect a new religion is born: but surprising modifications can take place under the old banner. In this way popular religion does for the individual what state religion does for the nation. It announces certain intentions to the world or creates a feeling of virtuous conduct without the inconvenience of moropractice, and offers a cement to the personality under threat of dissolution in times of stress. Popular Christianity is the religion of the *rites de passage*, of the Jesus freaks, *Godspell* and *Jesus Christ Superstar*, of crucifixes without rosary beads, of St Christopher medallions and good luck charms (whose currency is likely to continue though St Christopher has been pronounced non-existent, just as Christianity would persist in the name of the mystical Christ even if it should be established that Jesus of Nazareth never existed). Among Catholics it adds a belief in the efficacy of healing fountains, the magical properties of shrines and relics, Mariolatry and other practices not officially endorsed, though connived at, by the Church. These comfort the individual with little capacity for theology, abstract thought and meditation, who would otherwise feel adrift on a sea lashed by evil spirits.

However understandable these emotions may be, they demonstrate with striking vividness an important dynamic of religion. Too often orthodox religion masks an obsessional self-interest, a neurotic concern for personal salvation or survival which stultifies life and gets in the way of day-to-day living. Granting that at the point of crunch self-interest is the prime motivation of individuals, we may still distinguish between enlightened self-interest which does not forget the legitimate rights of others and accepts unavoidable adversities with a philosophic calm, and obsessional self-interest which is utterly engrossed in the wellbeing of one's immortal soul or the magical solution of life's problems and performs the most trivial kindness less out of spontaneity than from a calculation about reserves of spiritual grace. Popular Christianity tarts up this formalism with a good colouring of humbug and sends it out into both the spiritual and the material world. Spiritually it employs unsuspecting or prevaricating parsons to assure the bereaved that a deceased scoundrel is now safe in the arms of Jesus; or to accept from pagan godparents at infant baptism promises that they will look after the spiritual and moral well-being of the child, promises which everyone knows to be false; or to gather bogus commitments to the indissolubility of marriage from spouses with every intention of breaking up whenever it suits them. These discrepancies between sacraments or oaths and actual conduct may encourage similar discrepancies throughout life between stated and real intentions. Moropractice becomes as thoughtless as staging a 'proper' funeral, having the baby 'done' and giving the bride (blushing for the photographers and not for shame at being, in many cases,[108] already pregnant) a virginal 'white wedding'. Materially, popular Christianity offers the faithful a miraculous solution of problems and protection from hazards without the exercise of effort or prudence. This is, in every sense, superstition.

Islam

As herdsmen and nomads the Arabs led similar lives to the ancient Israelites. Islam was their attempt to return from Christian mystery-cultism to the simplicity of Judaism. Jesus was recognized as a great prophet, but the religion that centred upon him was rejected because of the elements of materialism, polytheism, ritualism and nature-worship that seemed to exist in incarnation, trinitarianism, churches and sacraments. Christianity was the religion of Cain, of an agricultural people in the sybaritic and corrupting Mediterranean basin. Like Judaism, Islam was to be the religion of Abel, of a pastoral and tribal people displaying the stern virtues of the desert. When its founder Muhammad gained influence and affluence in the city of Medina his own life became less rigorous, and there was a similar development in parts of the great empire the Arabs soon succeeded in establishing. This was especially true of areas like Mesopotamia with a long history of settlement and culture. Down the centuries Islam has thus evolved and diversified, producing its ascetics, epicures, mystics, theologians, rationalists and modernists.[109] But its original teachings, based on the Koran and the *Sunna* (sayings of the Prophet), have remained a widespread Islamic ideal; and where it has been necessary to introduce changes the accepted method has been by forging more *Sunna*. The minimal religious requirement is prayer five times a day facing Mecca and reciting the creed 'There is no God but God (Allah) and Muhammad is his prophet.'[110] Frequent cries of 'There is no might or power save by Allah'[111] are thought efficacious morally but not essential theologically.

'Islam' means 'submission' or 'obedience' to the will of God. Its religioethics is thus one of theocracy, authoritarianism and heteronomy. There is no clear division between the sacred and the secular, the theological and the moral. Like Christianity it postulates posthumous rewards and punishments in heaven or hell. These regions have an unmistakably earthly, or even earthy, aspect. Tradition has it that women are bound for hell, so heaven is obligingly peopled with houris (nymphs or, rather, nymphets). Predestination is accepted generally. One sect, the Murji'ites, say that it is possible to transgress the whole law and still remain a believer, that uttering the creed automatically brings forgiveness. But Islam is essentially a formalistic religion with precise instructions on religious duties, dietary laws and social conventions. There are five categories of actions: enjoined absolutely, commended, permitted, reprehended, forbidden absolutely. Though there is some scope for consensus or public opinion, the tendency is to rely on the authority of the Prophet or, in its absence, on that of a sheikh, *imam*, Mulla, Mahdi or secular sultan. High among the virtues are loyalty, obedience, courage, hospitality, endurance and simplicity of life. High among the sins are murder, usury, refusal of *zakat* (arms) and unchastity. Men are allowed to have four wives and as many concubines as they can afford, and look after them jealously. Yet Muslim ceremonies, especially the pilgrimage to Muhammad's birthplace Mecca, which most believers like to make at least once in a lifetime, stress the equality of all believers. Like Christians, the faithful strongly believe in the social and moral, as well as the spiritual, blessings of Islam and are active proselytizers. To fight in a *jihad* (holy war) is a mark of great virtue, and death in one will gain a celestial reward. Yet Islam has often been more tolerant to the religion of subject peoples than has Christianity.

Moropractice based on this rigid religiomorality has two general characteristics. Some provisions, like teetotalism, are unreasonably severe and widely disregarded. Individuals thus tend to be led into moromalpractice with the resulting guilt feelings, or hypocrisy as they privately reject the morality while publicly pretending to uphold it. Where the moral system is observed there is lack of moral autonomy. No internalization and little development is possible. What is true of the individual morally is often true of society politically. Muslim regimes are at best paternalistic and at worst autocratic. It is not coincidental that within the Islamic world are to be found vestiges of slavery. Here too women have probably the lowest social and political position that survives anywhere. Among the men equality may be a religious ideal but it is not a secular reality. The prosperous are encouraged to become more prosperous so as to earn merit by bestowing alms, which have all the features of Christian 'charity' in its Dickensian application. The unprosperous are encouraged to remain beggars denied a welfare state. So the gulf between rich and poor, for all the alms, increases. Though in its heyday the Arab world made many scientific discoveries and advanced trade through navigational inventions, social customs and the ban on usury discouraged commercial and personal enterprise. Islamic countries have for centuries been backward. Meanwhile proselytization has periodically encouraged aggression, chauvinism and imperialism, which are often curbed more by technological inadequacy than by moral restraints. Wherever Arab countries have avoided these consequences it has been by the effective demotion of Islam.

Shinto

Shinto, or 'the Way of the Gods', is usually listed among world religions, though it has not spread beyond Japan and today is largely dead, or dormant, even there. Its origin and antiquity are uncertain. What is known is that down the centuries Japan was dominated by versions of Confucianism and Buddhism, and that for much of its history the emperor, on whose *persona* Shinto is erected, was subservient to shoguns (dictators). When a hundred years ago the shogunate was finally destroyed, Shinto was revived to fortify the imperial power. For this religion is a blend of theology, morality and politics. Ancestor and nature worship are peripheral; worship of the emperor as God incarnate is central. Higher than filial piety is devotion to the emperor. Chauvinism is the main moral requirement and, in a country where *hara-kiri* (suicidal disembowelling) is traditionally honourable, leads to cheerful self-sacrifice in wartime. Bushido, the cult of the samurai or fighting knights, encourages the military virtues of loyalty, bravery, discipline and chivalry in times of peace.[112]

A nationalist religion like Shinto can readily promote aggression and militarism, as the nineteen thirties and forties showed. Then finer feelings sink in a flood of what are seen as national interests and cruelty is exalted as justice. On certain Pacific islands years after the Second World War Japanese soldiers refused to accept the war was over. When it was lost and the emperor lapsed into humanity, Shinto lapsed with him. The most conspicuous thing about religioethics and religiomorality of this sort is that they are utterly dependent on the prevailing political force and when this changes they collapse. In the short term they bring internal stability, breaking down lawlessness and civil wars, but they have dubious survival value. Nor are they capable of developing an international morality.

5   Irreligioethics and Irreligiomorality
(or Religioethics [2] and Religiomorality [2])

Traditionally religion has claimed governance over all aspects of life. Arising from a particular world-view, religious attitudes to science, politics and morality condense at their peculiar level. As knowledge of the universe increases, the old world-view becomes untenable and a process of secularization [1] sets in. There then comes a crisis for the organizations and individuals that have hitherto supported that view. For a time the organizations can assert orthodoxy superficially while their members rebel inwardly. At last the rebellion surfaces and enough walk out, or stay in and fight, for reformation to occur. Reluctantly the organization yields where it is most vulnerable, usually in its demands on the moral or professional life of the individual. The more authoritarian the church, the greater the stresses and greater the split if it should not give in time. But it is less prone to slow erosion than a looser structure. For if discipline is weak, secularization can go a surprising way without real ideological confrontation.

The process is best seen in our attitude to ordinary problems. The full sequential slide is down this slope: (1) I am ill and pray for a cure; if it does not come I meekly assume it is God's will that I suffer. (2) If my prayer is not answered I go to the doctor. (3) I go to the doctor; if he fails to help I pray. (4) If the doctor can do nothing I resign myself or go to a quack. It is unlikely one individual will pass through all these stages in a lifetime, though he may negotiate most of them. It is rather society that makes this journey as a statistical average. Either the individual or society may stick at one stage for a very long time. This progression can be called 'progress',[2] but it is simplistic to see it as a development of rationalism. Rather, each step reflects a different view of what agencies are likely to be helpful in solving our problems.

In the tempo of change since the Industrial Revolution, particular dilemmas have been created for religious organizations and individuals. If the church 'shakes its foundations' and tries to remove a theological pylon or two, the other pylons may topple and the whole moral superstructure may collapse. This is the crisis facing both conservatives and liberals in the Roman Curia today. The church-goer faces a situation no less agonizing. He can vacillate between faith during devotions and doubt at other times; go through the sacramental motions without genuine belief or emotions; leave the church sadly; leave the church angrily. Once outside he may become a sensualist or a reverent agnostic or a 'god-bothering' atheist, depending on his temperament and assessment of the good or harm he believes religion to do to others. Unusual spirits found a new church. Most remain unconnected. Some join an infidel organization. Similar divisions overtake unbelievers who have never believed. As they grow older a proportion are caught by the hound of heaven in disillusioned or senile flight from the world and return to the fold. The initial rejection of belief is an intellectual matter, the product of 'doubt', but this is not the full story. Some have equal doubts but contrive to stay where they are as, say, 'Christian atheists'[3] or 'Christian sceptics'. The doubts may arise over theoretical matters of belief or a moral concern over practical issues: the lack of social commitment of the churches, the bad personal example set by believers, the crimes endorsed by God in the bible. Religious apologists often assess apostasy as an emotive or psychoanalytical thing. 'Rebellion against the father-figure' is a common diagnosis. Active freethinkers have, however, almost invariably made a wide-ranging critique of the documents and articles of faith; though it is probably true that their activity depends on the strength of their convictions about the moral harm done by religion. For many of them would be inclined to say, with an indulgent smile, that if myths brought comfort and did no harm it would be churlish to denounce them.

Outside the familiar churches there is, then, a wide range of organizational and personal life that forms a continuous spectrum from piety to impiety, a spectrum that depends more on emotional and moral attitudes than on the degree of scepticism. As the moral philosopher Alasdair MacIntyre recently put it:

Humanists have their place in the genealogy of religious sects as surely as do Philadelphians or Friends. They are the spiritual descendants of those English Presbyterians who became Unitarians, who in turn became Rationalists and attended Ethical Churches. It is therefore not surprising that they exhibit many of the symptoms of extreme Protestant religiosity; and perhaps it is not even surprising that they so markedly fail to recognize this.[4]

Another academic observer, Basil Mitchell, has identified two extremes of humanists: those who 'accept the ethical teachings of Christianity and reject only the claim that these are in any way bound up with Christian doctrine', and those who 'are in the line of descent from Voltaire with his "*écrasez l'infâme*" and Hume in his attack on "the whole train of monkish virtues" '.[5] Humanists themselves recognize this polarization of attitudes. To some extent it corresponds with William James's 'tender-minded' and 'tough-minded' personalities.[6] Partly it reflects a semantic battle over whether humanism is or is not a religion. The outcome of this is especially doubtful in that, as will be seen later, many of the terms that unbelievers apply to themselves have previously or subsequently been used by religionists to indicate a preference for one or other theological school. Yet even within the ranks of the organized infidels there is, and has always been, disagreement over whether their beliefs are 'religious', unrelated to religion, an 'alternative'[7] or an enemy to religion. Usually the assessment is on moral grounds, depending on the degree to which, while religioethics is rejected, religiomorality is accepted.

For so long has religion claimed to be the origin of authority, civic and moral, in society, that the sceptic is still asked, and asks himself, 'Yes, but if you destroy religion what will you put in its place?' Many have decided there was no alternative and kept their doubts to themselves. Others have tried to find some new absolute. With his characteristic frankness Bertrand Russell admitted:

Up to the age of 38 I gave most of my energies to the first of these tasks. I was troubled by scepticism and unwillingly forced to the conclusion that most of what passes for knowledge is open to reasonable doubt. I wanted certainty in the kind of way in which people want religious faith.[8]

Russell sought his certainty in mathematics. Even that failed him. So he came to terms with uncertainty. Lacking Russell's mathematical talents most freethinkers with a yen for absolutes have turned to 'Truth', carefully undefined and capitalized, the 'principles' of some new 'ism', or the 'creative centre in Man',[9] again carefully undefined and capitalized. In her autobiography the nineteenth-century freethinker Annie Besant quoted a verse from Mrs Hamilton King:

For some must follow Truth from dawn to dark,
As a child follows by his mother's hand,
Knowing no fear, rejoicing all the way.[10]

For her this was a moral issue:

The total loss of all faith in a righteous God only made me more strenuously assertive of the binding nature of duty and the overwhelming importance of conduct . . . no subject was more frequently dealt with in my lectures than that of human ethical growth and the duty of man to man. No thought was more constantly in my mind than that of the importance of morals, and it was voiced at the very outset of my public career.[11]

By many devious paths 'Truth' led her to theosophy and a belief that 'man is a spiritual intelligence, sharing in God's Eternity and unfolding the divine powers of his Father through countless ages of progress'. In this way she hoped that 'human ethical growth' could be speeded up. For, alas, she had not found enough 'pure living and high thinking'[12] among secularists.

There has been little recent discussion by either believers or unbelievers on whether freethought ethics and morality should be regarded as irreligioethics and irreligiomorality, or a latter-day development of religioethics and religiomorality. Usually claim and counter-claim have been related to the good or bad opinion that religious and humanist organizations and individuals have had of each other. On the freethought side the view has gradually hardened that morality is a discipline independent of religion.[13] This raises an interesting question: what is the role, or social use, of a freethought movement? Mostly its supporters assert that, if freethought does not predate religion and magic – there would seem to have been times when supernaturalist thinking was universal, though this must be a matter of speculation – it can be traced back a very long way, often to before the dominant religion of a contemporary culture, for example, Christianity. In the realm of ideas this is undoubtedly true. All the modern humanist positions can be traced back to the empiricism, pragmatism, dialecticism, materialism, humanitarianism, determinism, utilitarianism and universalism of the ancient Greek philosophers. Yet as organized movements they stand out historically as protests against established religions and their natural histories follow the trend of religion. Clerical fascism may artificially submerge them, but in democracies the interest they arouse is more or less proportional (directly, not inversely) to that roused by religion.

Now, some humanists resent this position and try to ignore it. They declare that they are simply living without God and have no views on whether or not he exists. If however he does exist and belief in him aids moropractice, they are foolishly turning their backs on available help. If he does not exist – as most of them in effect think – and religious belief does not help moropractice, is any belief at all efficacious? Bluntly, what is the use of humanist beliefs and organizations if they seek to avoid equally the contention of the anticlericals that religion leads to certain deplorable activities, that is, to misguided *mores*, and of liberal religionists that religion is useful but has been misinterpreted and needs to be reformed? It might be argued that certain educational or psychological techniques could aid moropractice regardless of ideology, but ecumenical humanists are not necessarily professional educationists or psychologists. On inspection it usually turns out that while they do not believe religion aids moropractice they do believe that humanism does. The question then arises: is humanism a belief or a way of life? If a belief – or belief-system – what moral bonus can it yield that other beliefs are held not to yield? If a way of life, how does it arise and what assumptions is it based on? Is this belief, or these assumptions, in the tradition of religion or of scientific materialism or of some vague no-man's-land? These are questions fashionable humanists prefer not to answer, or even to ask.

In the early days of freethought movements it was customary, as will be shown, to speak of them as religions. Not only did this description make them less liable to prosecution under one or other of the many statutes upholding religion, and more respectable to a bourgeois public on which they relied for donations, if not subscriptions, when the going was rough, but it suggested certain characteristics like *rites de passage*, weekly services, and calendars of prophets, saints and martyrs which they shared with the churches. As the decades passed and church-going became unfashionable these elements disappeared from the humanist organizations, and it was then pointed out that they had always been marginal and were introduced by former believers conditioned to such things in childhood. The opinion grew that humanism really had nothing at all to do with religion, though it need not necessarily be antagonistic. You could play one game without 'rejecting' others. Essentially it was 'a secular social movement, discarding any semantic connection or ideological association with the term religion', which 'the "man in the street" . . . will in nearly all cases use . . . with theocratic connotations'.[14] Yet more recently religious assertions have returned. Julian Huxley wrote *Religion Without Revelation* in 1927 and returned to the attack in 1961. Detecting in every religion a theology, a morality and a ritual, he saw in evolutionary humanism the raw material of a new religion. This raw material was 'the stuff of divinity' which came from 'the fundamental mystery of existence, and in particular the existence of mind'.[15] This is akin to the mysticism of Teilhard de Chardin's 'noos-phere',[16] the way in which biologists interpret 'magical, mysterious, awe-inspiring, divinity-suggesting' feelings. Huxley saw this religion as a future development. A couple of years later a humanist philosopher[17] declared that the movement was already beset with metaphysics, which a group organizer sought to avoid by saying: 'The point is that Humanism is something which can be accepted or rejected, but not justified.'[18] This does not seem very different from the Christian's 'leap of faith'. But the important question is whether or not it leaps into better moropractice.

The whole argument boils down to a semantic wrangle, depending on what is the essence of religion. If it is belief in a God who issues moral *fiats* and hands out appropriate rewards and punishments, freethought is in conflict and leads to irreligioethics and irreligiomorality. For morality in its view arises from the human situation, the biological fact of man in community, the educational and other processes of training man in society. The essential aim is to satisfy human needs. These may be assessed by scientific inquiry and democratic plebiscite and implemented with scientific efficiency. But can human needs be detected so easily? And if they can, what is the dynamic which will ensure we satisfy them impartially? What, in effect, is the nature of man, man who has feelings not susceptible of instrumental measurement, man who cannot justify his existence but simply assumes it, man who speaks of an evolutionary future which can be neither justified nor assumed? Freethinkers thus turn out to be people interested in questions of ultimate reality, even if they produce different answers from those of the religionists.

They begin with the inquiring human being asking why he is here, what life is all about, and – in an evolutionary, if not in a personal sense – where he is going. Today most of them do not stay long in these unproductive fields. They turn to social work, current affairs lectures and discussions, political organization and (in bated or bruited breath) criticism of the churches. History records that the most valuable work they have done is as humanitarians, popular educators, law reformers and anti-clericals. But they themselves acknowledge that anyone could take up the first three undertakings from any ideological standpoint, while some of them feel passionately that the last pursuit is 'negative'. They long to be 'positive',[19] and not just in the other three ways. They cherish an abiding belief – it has been described as 'the unquenchable Humanist faith'[20] – that they have evolved a natural system of morality which will advance moropractice. Or, rather, they hold a number of ethical views, with corresponding codes of conduct, just like the churches. Lacking sacraments and confessions, this 'denominationalism'[21] has never been as marked as that of the churches. Sometimes it has not even been organizational. A number of separate strands may run through one body, and the individual may, as in the preceding paragraphs, apply to himself different labels in different circumstances and regard them all as synonymous or at least complementary. Each one may be seen as religious or irreligious according to definition or taste. Some appear more irreligious than others. Though the number of active adherents has always remained small their ideas have caused grave concern to the churches; and, as the authority of ethics based on God breaks, or has broken, down, a morally hungry world looks towards them, through the media, with a mixture of hate and hope. But individuals look and mostly turn aside, and the question must be asked: Regardless of whether the irreligious (neoreligious) world-view is true, can anything which attracts so few to positive commitment have positive moral value?

Freethought

Up till the 1820s 'freethinker' and 'deist' were synonyms, at least in the Anglo-Saxon world. In France the encyclopedists had already passed on to atheism, which Paine was just as anxious to refute as orthodox Christianity in his *Age of Reason*. He is thought to have wanted to set up deistic 'churches' and one or two were independently established.[22] A number of deistic societies were formed. Then one of his publishers, Richard Carlile, while cooling his heels in gaol for his pains, announced that he had turned from deism to atheism;[23] and other British freethinkers, whether or not they admitted to atheism, soon quietly dropped deism. In many respects there was no practical difference between the two ideas. Both rejected theism, the belief that God directly controlled the universe and was accessible to prayer and partial to worship. But from a moral point of view there was an important difference. The deists said that a self-sustaining universe had been set in motion by God, who then retreated from the scene. It was therefore natural to assume that, together with physical laws, he had established a moral law on which world order was based. Indeed, when he rejected rational arguments drawn from the physical world as proof of God's existence, Kant made the same inference from man's moral sense.[24] This appraisal had important consequences. Through deism ethics and morality gained a sort of pre-existent status which tended to make them arbitrary, absolute and inviolate; while man became, in the words of one modern philosopher,

Philip Toynbee, 'a unique creature on this planet, possessed of free will, blessed and cursed with true responsibility, purposive and holy'.[25] Atheism, however, made no such assumptions. There is, of course, in the word 'freethought' itself some suggestion of free will and true responsibility, but adherents usually intend no more than freedom from conventional dogmas, that is, a willingness to explore new ideas. This applies to moral as well as to theological ideas, which must stand or fall on their weight of evidence. It is up to each individual to judge this for himself and not to accept what he is told. Only when a man is thinking freely in this sense can he act responsibly and creatively and help to promote human well-being. Like religion, this is a dynamic for personal commitment rather than the acceptance of any particular social or political programme.[26]

Most freethinkers early recognized the objections to theological free will, but were not sufficiently aware of the degree to which all people, some more than others, depended on the intellectual authority of textbooks and 'experts' and the moral authority of law and custom. Nor did they always follow through the full implications of their theory, especially in the moral sphere. One nineteenth-century freethinker, later to become a byword for 'destructiveness', G. W. Foote, identified 'destructive and constructive Freethought' and declared it 'an unwise and a disastrous policy to go on exposing orthodox errors week after week to people who have for years discarded them'.[27] This preoccupation with theology and cosy concentration on familiar heresies distracted from 'free' inquiry elsewhere. As a 'religious' unbeliever, Moncure Conway, put it to his irreligious colleagues, 'The freethinkers also had their altar. When they gave of their substance to build their hall and support lectures, none of them would propose to devote the money to relieve the physical sufferings around them. They believed, no doubt, that secularism if generally adopted would relieve such distress, but the orthodox also included that kind of happiness in their millennial dream.'[28] In moral matters, moreover, some freethinkers were anxious to curb inquiry altogether. George Jacob Holyoake declared:

It is of the utmost importance that Freethought literature should be kept free from the suspicion of immorality.[29]

By this he meant the advocacy of *immores*. Freethinkers should not be morally unconventional. But if new ideas did not lead to new behaviour they were of purely academic interest. What the freethinkers unconsciously recognized was that there was a limit to which people wanted to be 'free', regardless of their capacity to achieve freedom. In suggesting that they should be forced to be free Plato and Rousseau never gained substantial support, except in the heady days of the French Revolution and the Commune. Yet the basic failure of freethought was its optimistic belief that improved 'thought' would bring improved behaviour whether or not social conditions changed.

Atheism

In 1813 a wealthy industrialist Robert Owen proclaimed 'A New View of Society', in which he popularized Benthamite utilitarianism and declared his belief that those who were educated at all were 'educated upon the most mistaken principles of human nature, such indeed as cannot fail to produce a general conduct throughout society totally unworthy of the character of rational beings'.[30] At a much-publicized meeting four years later he proclaimed:

Then, my friends, I tell you, that hitherto you have been prevented from even knowing what happiness really is, solely in consequence of the errors – gross errors – that have been combined with the fundamental notions of every religion that has hitherto been taught to men.[31]

They had also, he believed, been prevented from knowing what morality really was. In his concern to help them he built up a system which became known as 'Owenism'[32] and had, as we shall see in the next chapter, strong political overtones. But the movement had a basic ideology which gradually came to be seen as ATHEISTICAL, and on this 'the new moral world' was to be built.* In 1838 the country was divided into 'dioceses', each with a 'social missionary', though Owen advised them not to 'hold discussions on religious mysteries or dogmas, . . . which

* For it Owen created his *Catechism of the New Moral World*, 'Sacred to Truth without Mystery, Mixture of Error, or Fear of Man'.[33]

arouse angry, irrational feelings, tending to separate man from man'.[34] For legal and financial reasons the movement became the Universal Community Society of Rational Religionists the following year, and soon the missionaries and station-lecturers were expected to take a Dissenter's oath. This led to a major split in 1841, when *The Oracle of Reason*, edited by different gaoled 'priests' in turn, began as 'the only exclusively atheistical print that has appeared in any age or country'.[35]

On emerging from gaol the second 'priest', Holyoake, offered himself as resident curator of an 'Atheon', which would do for atheists what the Pantheon did for pantheists. Its prospectus announced that atheism 'alarms bigotry, checks persecution, teaches religionists modesty, and establishes freedom of discussion in theology'.[36] This was similar to the views of Shelley, who told a friend that he had written *The Necessity of Atheism* as a weapon 'to stop discussion, a painful devil to frighten the foolish, a threat to intimidate the wise and good ... to express my abhorrence of superstition'.[37] Shelley saw theism as 'fatal to genius and originality'; Holyoake embraced atheism to 'better promote personal improvement, and public fraternity'. Other atheists turned to political activity, beginning with Chartism. While in prison for sedition one of them, Ernest Jones, carried on the sacramental tradition by writing *Sacred Hymns* in his own blood.[38]

It is not perhaps surprising that, as a movement, atheism hardly left the ground. The 'Atheon' was never set up. In their later years Holyoake, Owen and Carlile disappointed their disciples. Holyoake refused to discuss atheism; Owen turned spiritualist; Carlile became a Swedenborgian and began calling himself a Christian, though he was in effect the first 'Christian Atheist'. But it was not any triumph of theism, in either these pioneers or the generations that followed, that eclipsed atheism as a moral force. The heresy had simply begun with too high hopes and a terminology that suggested whistling in the dark. As one Owenite put it,

It was a conviction with them that when truth took possession of the public mind error would die out of itself.[39]

Neither intellectually nor morally, individually nor socially, was this borne out. It proved much easier to chase out the old gods than to debar new ones: spiritualism, theosophy, faith healing, anthroposophy, UFO cults and the whole range of commitment that 'seekers after truth' have found in the sunshine of California. The question became not whether atheism was or was not true, but whether it was satisfying. Some – like the philosophers Friedrich Nietzsche and Arthur Schopenhauer, and the poet James Thomson[40] – found the prospect of a godless world depressing, and retreated into hero-worship or enervating pessimism. Neither attitude was likely to promote morality or moropractice, as both deduction and observation showed. One of the arbiters of a legal dispute between Holyoake and his successor as leader of the British atheists, Charles Bradlaugh, made the acid comment:

Of course I grudge the time: however the case is a moral one and it is interesting to watch what great lengths the two long-range guns of Modern Atheism go in ascribing base motives and conduct to each other. I am pulling choice sample fruit grown in this *New* Moral World and presented by its most advanced minds. It appears as true now as of old, that 'a corrupt tree bringeth forth evil fruit'.[41]

Atheism might be useful as an ethical beginning. It was not a moral end.

Positivism

Marooned in a new moral world, churchless and godless, and finding atheism too frail a raft, the nineteenth-century unbelievers set about constructing more seaworthy vessels to reach an ethical port. At last they decided to call on marine architects with more 'positive' plans. The first positive blueprint that turned up was, not surprisingly, Positivism. This was the brain-child of Auguste Comte and had all the marks of French intellectualism. Its basic ideas were drawn from one of Comte's friends, the socialist pioneer Claude de Saint-Simon, who detected in history three stages of society: theological, metaphysical, scientific or positive. According to Comte, the last stage began with the French Revolution of 1789. Its first phase was 'negative', destroying the old misconceptions; its second, beginning in 1854, was truly 'positive' and established the Religion of Humanity.

Whereas the English atheists used ecclesiastical terms with a certain irony, Comte, who was a great admirer of the stability and cultural unity of medieval Catholicism, created his Temple of Humanity, served by priests, a catechism, a calendar of thirteen major saints (including Moses and St Paul) and many minor ones, images and liturgies, embracing nine sacraments,[42] in all seriousness. Instead of the Decalogue there was the Positivist Sacred Formula (In the Name of Humanity):

Love for Principle
and Order for Basis;
Progress for End.
Live for Others. Live Openly.[43]

In this way he hoped to reconcile the demand for political and social reforms represented by the revolutions of 1830 and 1848, with the sort of stability associated with authoritarian religion. Though peculiarly adapted to French conditions his 'religion of humanity' passed round the world and a friend of George Eliot, Richard Congreve, gave it a home in the London 'Church of Humanity',[44] with appropriate trimmings.

As the originator of the word 'sociology' Comte gave much attention to social science, which he saw in a prescriptive rather than the descriptive role given to it today. For his interests were essentially ethical and moral. The 'ultimate object of all Philosophy' was, he declared, 'the formation of a definite system of universal Morality'.[45] He believed that 'the principal social differences are today essentially not political but moral ones',[46] so that changes should take place in 'opinions and morals' rather than institutions. This was summed up in the Positivist Golden Rule:

Live for others: Family, Country, Humanity.

The Pauline commitment to 'faith, hope, charity (love), these three'[47] was endorsed and given the same absolute but imprecise standing. Comte believed in 'systematically separating political from moral government'; for one employed 'direct compulsion', the other 'the forces of conviction and persuasion'.[48] From a study of man in society human needs could be recognized and, with the right moral attitudes induced by the religion of humanity, a just political order established. He himself preferred republicanism, which he considered to include the moral 'meaning' of communism 'without the same danger'.[49] There was no point, he said, in discussing atheism, which, like theology, concerned 'insoluble mysteries'.[50]

As a self-contained system Positivism was a remarkable creation. Yet it remained an arid thing that attracted few supporters outside France and has little influence even there today. Thomas Huxley's description of it as 'Catholicism *minus* Christianity'[51] was almost literally correct. Catholicism was also a remarkable system in a purely abstract sense, but the important questions were, Was it true and did it work? Though claiming to have transcended metaphysics, to the outsider Comtism seemed to have a lot of the metaphysical in it. A study of nineteenth-century French society hardly suggested that faith, hope and love were the dominating forces, so that the religioethics of Positivism involved mere assumptions and was imposed in a purely authoritarian way. But if it were true, there was no need to change society by political means, for whatever injustices might arise were passing moral aberrations. Positivism was for a century in conflict with Hegelian idealism, whose concentration on the state with its historical destiny was widely assumed to be the precursor of modern fascism and Nazism. There seems however to be some truth in Marcuse's claim that Hitler's Germany was built on the views of Friedrich Schelling, Friedrich Stahl and Carl Schmitt, who, however they began, finished up as positivists; and that Comtism 'arrives at an ideological definition of middle-class society and, moreover, it bears the seeds of a philosophical justification of authoritarianism'.[52] The difficulty was that the creed was committed to 'Progress', while social science is capable of studying only the present and the past. So that intellectual overlords set themselves up to point out to the faithful those aspects of society that were in the path of progress and those that were not, and religiomorality was arbitrarily devoted to the pursuit of the one and the avoidance of the other. Even if the *dicta* were correct, what force gave them the quality of *fiats* and how could they aid moropractice in day-to-day living?

When Owenism collapsed and atheism sickened in the 1840s Holyoake desired a new system. Whatever marginal influence Positivism was to enjoy in England had not yet arrived. With what he claimed to be the encouragement of George Henry Lewes,[53] the common-law husband of George Eliot, he established 'Secularism' in 1851. Not only 'atheism', but curious alternatives like 'netheism' and 'limitationism' were rejected as 'negative', while 'cosmism', 'realism' and 'naturalism' were finally thought ambiguous. The definition he gave of the new system was:

Secularism is the study of promoting human welfare by material means; measuring human welfare by the utilitarian rule, and making the service of others a duty to life.[54]

Though he lost influence in the secularist movement in his own lifetime, this definition has in broad outline persisted till today. But there have been many disputes over how it is to be interpreted. Holyoake maintained that 'the secular is sacred, as that which affords self-guidance and self-trust alone is. But the secular, bounded by the uses and issues of this life, is clearly marked off from atheism or theism.'[55] A British Secular Institute was set up as a 'Free-Centre of Personal Communication'[56] to promote Free-Search, Free-Utterance, Free-Criticism, Free-Action of Opinion, Freethought and Free-Truth. As a Secular Guild it later became somewhat more specific by seeking the 'solution of political, social and educational questions on Secular and unsectarian grounds'.[57] This was in 1870, the time of the first English statute establishing state education and the unsuccessful battle to make it 'secular'. Holyoake conceded that secular education, a by-product of 'secularity' or the separation of church and state, was very different from Secularism, 'a policy of life to those who do not accept Theology'.[58] But he insisted that this was also very different from rejecting theology. In an acrimonious debate with Bradlaugh on *Secularism, Scepticism, and Atheism*, he maintained that an atheistic policy for Secularism would not only prejudice the adoption of secular education (through popular confusion) but would be ethically unacceptable:

If Secularism must be based on Atheism – what better helpers of humanity are we than the priests? They have to wait until they have convinced an inquirer of Theism before they can give him a foundation for moral duty; and the Atheistic Secularist has to wait, in like manner, until he has furnished to the human mind a satisfactory map of the untraceable path to nothing.[59]

This was the row which had split the Owenites and continued unabated after their collapse. Owen's favourite disciple, Robert Cooper, argued with the 'father of Secularism' that 'broadly, emphatically, irreconcilably, is Secularism at issue with theology'.[60] Bradlaugh said that the churches claimed jurisdiction over all aspects of life.

You cannot ignore them or their claim; you must do battle with the priesthood until their power is destroyed.[61]

He had managed to write into the Principles of the National Secular Society a declaration that 'the theological teachings of the world have been, and are, most powerfully obstructive of human improvement and happiness'.[62] Everyone agreed with Holyoake on the necessity of good moropractice in the movement, and Bradlaugh boasted that he had purged the platform of 'men of drunken and immoral character' with a rigour that even Holyoake thought 'a harsh step to take'.[63] One of the founder's objections to atheism was that, as Francis Newman reminded him, among the ancient Greeks the word connotated immorality,[64] just as to many people 'freethinker' suggested 'loose thinker' and 'infidel' a liar. There was general agreement with the Holyoake pronouncement:

Secularism is a development of freethinking, including its *positive* as well as its *negative* side . . . expressing a certain positive and ethical element.[65]

But Holyoake came to believe that his new word signified 'a new form of Freethought, in which we would deal with the agreements at which Freethinkers had arrived'.[66] In, that is, the realm of ethics and morality.

The history of Secularism has been a saga of rows and splits that are of no concern to this book. Holyoake went more or less his own way, except when his name was used to float some new organization. He wrote extensively on the theoretical aspects of Secularism, assuring generations of encyclopedia readers that 'Secularism is not an argument against Christianity; it is one independent of it'.[67] Referring to his writings historians called it 'a system of ethics'.[68] Inevitably it became known as another 'religion of humanity'.[69] To some extent this was because Holyoake's brother Austin, Annie Besant and one or two others gave attention to secular ceremonies, 'hymns', calendars of free-thinking saints and martyrs, ritual anniversaries and holy abstractions like Truth, Duty, Wisdom, Peace and Mother Nature.[70] Despite all this, under the leadership of Bradlaugh and a succession of Bradlaughites the National Secular Society generally pursued the role of an educational and propagandist body, giving particular attention to freethought, civil liberties and humane law reform. On one occasion Bradlaugh said that 'Secularism is, in fact, humanitarianism'.[71] It also advertised 'rational ethics'. By this, however, it ceased to mean any esoteric knowledge or expertise in moral philosophy; simply irreligioethics based on human rather than divine sanctions and nurture.

It soon became clear that, apart from this foundation in atheism (or something very like it), there was no neat political, sociological or other 'positive' basis for irreligioethics among the 'agreements at which Freethinkers had arrived'. Nor was there necessarily better agreement over irreligiomorality. Most of the secularists then – and some of them now – interpreted the pursuit of morality based on 'this world' as simply a puritanical commitment to Victorian *mores* (or assumed *mores*). Where a new issue like birth control arose, though the bulk of the member-ship followed the 'episcopal' guidance of radical leaders like Bradlaugh, freethinkers were as divided as anyone else.* After all, 'this world' contained a bewildering variety of value-judgements. But even if a distinctive and satisfactory irreligio-morality could be arrived at, what means other than an advocacy of sound education and parental concern had the secularists for seeing it would be observed? The non-virtuous could be

* To some of them family-planning literature was of 'immense influence over the happiness of the human race'.[72] To others it was 'full of follies, inde-cencies, immoralities, and crimes'.[73]

expelled from the movement but not from society at large. Was not Secularism in danger of becoming as sectarian in outlook, if not in creed, as the churches? And, as the years went by, Bradlaugh found he had to allow, even on the platform, people whose intellectual brilliance far outshone their moropractice. Nor was it just a matter of enlightened *immores*. By their own professed standards it was clear moromalpractice. Secularism found it easier to take the moral blinkers off the religious than to give moral spectacles to the irreligious. So in recent years secular humanists have been distinguished from ethical humanists by remaining outside the Social Morality Council and the Campaign for Moral Education, declaring that 'the environmental life of the individual ... is much more important than any moral precepts'.[74]

Ethical Culture

From the beginning there were those who doubted whether Holyoake had really found, or even imagined himself to have found, a new system of ethics. A theist republican W. J. Linton said that he had simply 'shuffled out of Atheism when his respectable patrons preferred a less obnoxious title'.[75] But a quarter of a century later in America a more specific claim was made. This was Felix Adler's Ethical Culture. He began with Kantianism, but sought a way of interpreting the term 'social' spiritually, as Kant had undertaken to interpret the term 'individual' spiritually. Darwinism and other evolutionary interpretations of society were rejected because 'they all leave out the concept of inviolable personality, the indefeasible factor in my ethical thinking'.[76] Some of the secularists reproduced the *esprit de corps* of church services in similarly timed meetings garnished with hymns, ceremonies, readings and inspirational addresses. The Ethical Culturists sought also to capture the mysticism and ritual of traditional religion, particularly of the Roman order. This was a fascination they shared with the Comtists. Indeed one president of the London Ethical Society considered that the Vatican was the first Ethical Society.[77] Adler wished to revive the medieval custom of sitting 'different vocational groups' (guilds) in different places in the assembly. And he evolved a prayer-substitute:

The appeal of the God in our neighbour is the substitute for the appeal in prayer to the God in heaven, the call of the stifled spiritual nature in the man and woman at our side, is to draw out of us our utmost latent force, the strengths underneath the strength.[78]

The aim was to create 'fellowships . . . that will hold not religion as a duty but Duty as a Religion'.[79] Or, as a leader of the Chicago Ethical Society put it,

The perfect order of things which Omnipotence was to produce for us in another world we are ourselves to create here.[80]

Stanton Coit, a disciple of Adler's, brought ethicism to Britain. At first he took over Conway's Religious Society in Finsbury and made it an Ethical Society, but his image, images and imagery did not suit the members and so he launched out for himself. Presently he established an Ethical Union whose motto became 'To advocate the supreme importance of the knowledge, love, and practice of the Right', and an Ethical Church in an old Bayswater Methodist chapel, which he furnished like a Comtian chapel.[81] At its services there was a Universal Litany:

That we have been delivered from untold evils:
  By the self-sacrifice, courage and wisdom of countless men and women,
  We gratefully acknowledge.

and Ten (*sic*) Words of the Moral Life:

  Each one of us hears the voice of Duty saying within him:
  I am the Supreme Judge of Men and of Gods; thou shalt exalt nothing above me.
  May no one lead us into temptation; but all men help us to keep this law.[82]

In time Coit discovered that not only was justice equal to love equal to goodness, but that 'Goodness is God'.[83] He proposed a Church of England Comprehension League to universalize the liturgy and 'ethicize' the teachings of Anglicanism, which he wished to remain established.[84] When the First World War broke out he announced that God was 'indwelling in the British People', the Empire was 'the Church of all British Subjects' and all who sought 'a Democracy of Social Righteousness in every nation' were 'co-workers with Jesus Christ'.[85]

By this time the Ethical Church was, in fact, what many had long ago suspected it of being in spirit, just another Nonconformist church, but one with disturbing overtones of the British Israel World Federation or even of the sort of folk religion later to be associated with Nazi Germany. This was an extreme and idiosyncratic version of Ethical Culture, but the whole conception was rather odd. In taking and refashioning the 'stuff of divinity' it only managed to turn out a Christianity without Christ, a deification of the superego. Though claiming to believe in man's Original Goodness, its obsession with the 'perfect' could only draw attention to his Original Sin. A sin, moreover, which, for all the sermonizing and litanizing, was left stranded without a Redeemer. Coit believed that 'atheism' was 'a term of reproach, and ostracizes anyone upon whom it is fastened'.[86] But irreligioethics was at least consistent – an important ingredient of both organization and morality. People knew where they were. He sought a religioethics without the magic of transcendence which genuine supernaturalism is able to give. Sanguinely the ethicists imagined that Duty was as stable and absolute as God, that once we scraped off the veneer of theism we would see it shining in the 'depth' of our being, credible, lovable, free from superstition. But duty to what? Ultimately to the whole human race. An interesting abstraction and more relevant today, perhaps, than before, with our knowledge of world dangers like the population explosion, nuclear testing and pollution. But in day-to-day matters duty can easily become, as it did to the Coitists, an uncritical chauvinism, a moralizing puritanism or a pretentious do-goodism. Like orthodox religion Ethical Culture sought to change society by changing the individual. Though its supporters might, and did, engage in charitable works, it was not basically interested in social conditions as a determinant of character. At the same time it gave the agonizing moral soul nothing to look to for guidance but his own inner resources and a bewildering array of great ones who had gone before. Not surprisingly it 'never attracted any but rare or abnormal spirits'.[87] In 1908 it was thought that 'the surroundings and the selected population ought to justify the attempt'[88] to form an ethical society in Hampstead Garden Suburb. Probably only there, where today a pub-crawl is a feast of 'drink and think', could people be found to understand what Adler and Coit even meant. Whether it was or was not intellectually convincing hardly occurred to the faithful to ask.

But if ethicism were ethically sound was it morally satisfying? Let us suppose 'the autonomy of ethics'[89] and declare Duty to be the mediating instrument, what precisely is it to mediate? There are, after all, in the experience of us all conflicting duties: to oneself, parents, spouses, children, work, community, country, United Nations. Coit's supporters emerged from Thomas Davidson's Fellowship of the New Life. It sounds splendid, but what does the 'new life' consist in? One of the inscriptions at the Ethical Church came from the writer Sir Leslie Stephen, its sometime president:

We believe that morality depends upon something deeper and more permanent than any of the dogmas that have hitherto been current in the churches; it is a product of human nature.[90]

All agnostics of the time agreed. What insight, however, did Ethical Culture have which was at all unique – and operational? From 'human nature' flowed *mores* and *immores*, moropractice and moromalpractice, virtue and vice. Adler's old mentor Kant had even suggested that ethics, as a descriptive academic discipline, had nothing more to do with the production of moral rules, which are prescriptive and practical, than logic had to do with the production of arguments. For all their theorizing the ethicists did not seem to worry too much about this problem. They certainly entered the moral field with gusto. Only a year after the foundation of the Union of Ethical Societies they established the Moral Instruction League;[91] and it is their heirs in the recent Campaign for Moral Education who seem the most anxious to devise formal moral syllabuses. In other words, they have absorbed from the churches a tendency to preach and sermonize. Yet they lack the credentials (real or imagined) of a divinely inspired teaching church. From the autonomy of ethics all one can deduce is the secularist position that the churches' political power and moral influence are wrong, though the ethicists have always been coy about saying so. Duty, their great imperative, we have already seen to be an ambiguous guide or an authoritarian master. What was left to cling to in Ethical Culture?

Now, like many Christians, by making a special study of this problem the ethicists came up with some useful general principles, though nothing more interesting than Kant's precept to use people not as means but as ends. Even this was a problem to those who wished to be practical. It lent itself to a teleological interpretation (that is, declaring that there is a purpose in all 'created' things). The churches had long said that the best way to regard man as an 'end' was to give him an immortal destiny. What the ethicists meant was a need to avoid 'reification' or the treatment of people as if they were things, mere ciphers of sociology. But there were many rival political, social and moral theories of the best way in which this could be done. Then there was another problem to which the ethicists gave scant attention: the passage from morality to moropractice. They tended to assume that all one had to do to induce virtue was to point out 'the good' and sketch plans of 'the good life'.[92] This project alone was as difficult as it was vague. One of the three essential Principles of the Ethical Church was:

In practice the good life is to be realized by performing such duties as are commonly recognized, and are morally acceptable, and, further, by fulfilling obligations not yet enjoined by the general social conscience.[93]

But even if these duties and obligations could be agreed on by the ethicists, how could one guarantee they would be carried out among the faithful, much less in the world at large? Presumably the 'obligations' would not generally be carried out as they were 'not yet enjoined by the general social conscience'. Ethical Culture would therefore glow 'like a little candle burning in the night'.[94] Would the glow even be constant? J. M. Robertson, a secularist who had ample opportunities of seeing Ethical Culture in action, made the point:

While many persons, both in and out of the Ethical Movement, were zealously enthusiastic in revering goodness in the abstract, they did not take sufficient pains to find out how best to put it in practice. The important thing was to *be* good.[95]

The 'consecrating influence'[96] to which Adler referred as the trademark of his creed sanctioned dubious tactics when his successors sought to undercut rival stalls in the non-theistic market-place. Apart from obvious human failings there were genuine disagreements on practical issues. During the Boer War, for example, there was 'a serious difference of opinion . . . as to the proper course for ethically-minded men to take'.[97] Where they were united they were vague. Ethicists declared that moral instruction had a 'two-fold nature':

the formation of right ideas and the formation of right habits. Right ideas are necessary to guide the will, but right habits are the product of the will itself.[98]

Even if these notions were philosophically and psychologically sound, ethicists had still to find a way to reach the 'will'. By 1950 Coit's successor admitted the quest was quixotic. 'The causal approach to moral evils (e.g. exploitation) has proved quicker and more effective than moral appeal and is more congenial to the modern mind.'[99] By that time the movement had almost faded away. People who wanted a 'consecrating influence' wanted God around to direct it. In 1967, to almost universal relief, the Ethical Union changed its name to the British Humanist Association. In most other countries ethicism had long ago died out. Conway's old chapel and the American Ethical Union retain their ethical label but with little of the old content. What survives has, like much of modern Christianity, sounded a more introspective note. 'Ethical meditation' was recently advertised in Britain as a way to 'rid yourself of anxiety, doubt and worry'.[100] The self-confidence no longer involves changing the world.

Rationalism

As a philosophy Rationalism is usually dated from the seventeenth century and René Descartes's famous formula *cogito ergo sum*[101] (I think, therefore I am), which has gained a new significance as one criterion for 'life' in potential heart donors. Originally the concept had no necessary connection with religious scepticism, though the orthodoxy of all its leading exponents is problematical. It simply asserted that revelation and intuition are not always to be trusted, and are not necessary, in the search for God. Pure reason is enough to find him. In this sense some of the ancient Greeks, like the Stoics, and the scholastic theologians of the middle ages were rationalists. But they did not rule out the role of faith and mysticism. Gradually the line hardened into the view put by Georg Hegel:

That faculty which man can call his own, elevated above death and decay, . . . is able to make decisions of itself. It announces itself as reason. Its law-making depends on nothing else, nor can it take its standards from any other authority on earth or in heaven.[102]

At the French Revolution of 1789 the Goddess of Reason was symbolically installed in Notre-Dame. Maximilien Robespierre replaced it with the *Être Suprême* (Supreme Being), which some took to be personified reason and others the conventional God of deism or theism. In England Carlile and Holyoake followed the radical French tradition by calling their bookshops 'temples of reason', while more orthodox minds formed little groups of 'rational religionists' and projected 'Rational Sunday Schools'. Charles Southwell independently established a Rational School in Westminster. Then came the reorganization of the Owenites already considered. In the second half of the nineteenth century Rationalism definitely turned irreligious and stayed that way. Kant's demonstration of the inability of 'pure reason' to discover God was now widely established throughout the Protestant world, which sought increasing comfort in 'faith' and 'divine unreason'. Rome still accepted the Thomist 'proofs' of the existence of God but found it expedient to refer less to the 'rational mind of man'. Those who adopted 'Rationalism' did it to assert their belief that reason had dismembered God.

Though the label 'rationalist' suggests today a heartless academic or a person obsessed with debunking theology, it began as a system of irreligioethics. The first principle of the Ethical Church was:

The good life has supreme claim upon us; and this claim rests on no external authority, and on no system of supernatural rewards or punishments, but has its origin in the nature of man as a social and rational being.[103]

Thus ethicists were, in an unaggressive way, rationalists. When a breakaway of secularists joined some ethicists under the chairmanship of Holyoake to form the Rationalist Press Association in 1899, they took as their definition:

Rationalism is the mental attitude which unreservedly accepts the supremacy of reason and aims at establishing a system of philosophy and ethics verifiable by experience and independent of all arbitrary assumptions or authority.[104]

In accepting the autonomy of reason rationalists were as anxious as religionists to look after morality. This was in the tradition of Robert Owen's *Manifesto* of his Rational Religion:

A system of human existence in all respects opposed to the past and present life of man; a system which will create a new *will* and a new *spirit* in all of humankind, and thus induce each, by an irresistible necessity, to become consistent, rational, and sane in mind and conduct.[105]

Apart from intellectual errors the fault of the old religions was, in the estimation of the rationalists, that they had encouraged an arbitrary and unpredictable interpretation of the universe, subject to the caprice of supernatural powers, which was reflected in arbitrary and unpredictable behaviour by the faithful. If man's actions were to become rational they would also become reasonable. Reason was the most obvious human attribute to take and laud – even, for those who liked symbolism, to deify – for was it not the thing that supremely differentiated him from other animals? Or, if one took a mechanistic view of the world and saw man as a machine, was it not as a *res cogitans* (a thing that thinks) that man had a unique position? Because his brain was the glory of nature he alone had elaborated ethical systems. By deductive logic this same apparatus then elaborated appropriate morality. Because it was elaborated by man for man in a world which, if free of God, was also free of the devil, individuals would naturally obey it. Briefly, ethics would give morality would give moropractice in a continuous, harmonious flow.

The first issue to challenge this optimistic world-view was that of war and peace. As clouds gathered on the Edwardian horizon the rationalists (with the secularists and ethicists) expected all men of good will to sink their several ideologies in a united peace movement.[106] They soon found, however, that it provided a stamping-ground for anyone with a creed to promote. Particularly was this true of the Christians, who proclaimed that the best way to get world peace was to bring the world under the rule of him who was the Prince of Peace. At last in exasperation the freethinkers issued a prospectus of a Rationalist Peace Society which would 'recognize that War and Peace are questions to be dealt with by a consideration of social facts and psychology'.[107] In 1913 the new body issued a volume of *Essays Towards Peace*. One of its contributors, the economist Norman Angell, saw 'War as the Failure of Reason':

It has too often been assumed that what is needed in order to clear up the differences of international relationship is a better moral tone – greater kindliness, and so forth – oblivious of the fact that the emotion of humanity repelling from war may be more than counteracted by the equally strong moral emotions we connect with patriotism . . . The difference between the pacifist and the militarist is not, at bottom, a moral one at all (assuming that we take the best statement of each case), but an intellectual one.[108]

By this he hoped to undermine the simplistic argument that a virtuous person is a pacifist and a vicious one a militarist. But this statement could also lead to one or other of the following conclusions: (1) war is not a moral issue; (2) there are no moral issues, only intellectual ones; (3) by intellectual means we can arrive at contrary moral conclusions. There was no time for the society to consider these disturbing implications (even if they were appreciated) before there broke out what the rationalist H. G. Wells called *The War That Will End War*.[109] Rationalism might have achieved 'a system of philosophy and ethics verifiable by experience', but when it came to inescapable issues like war and peace supporters of the Rationalist Peace Society were as divided as their irrational fellows. One pacifist member was saddened 'to find among the Freethought party some of the most hysterical of the Jingoes'; and, when the Defence of the Realm Act was brought in, was shocked to find its president, Robertson, now a Privy Councillor, 'silent in the face of the grossest outrages against free speech'.[110] Meanwhile the society's committee, while announcing that most of them were 'pacifists of long standing' who believed in 'the pacific settlement of international disputes . . . the progress of civilization, and the growth of those ethical perceptions and humaner ideas which are not the least essential part of a rational civilization', declared that they 'cannot see that we in this country had any alternative but to take part in'[111] the war. In 1917, after being for some time without a secretary, the committee 'reluctantly decided to formally suspend the activities of the Society until a more favourable moment'.[112] This never came. In 1921 the society was wound up and its funds given to the International Arbitration League. There was now a League of Nations and an International Court of Justice. Wells looked forward to a world state. After initially supporting the League he opposed it as a barrier to achieving his real goal. By the time there was another world war, bigger than the one before and climaxed by the atomic bomb he had himself foretold, it was not surprising that Wells found his *Mind at the End of its Tether*.[113]

But 'faith' in rationalism died hard. There arose the Campaign for Nuclear Disarmament and the Committee of 100. Humane and rational arguments tumbled with those that were humane and irrational, inhumane and rational, and neither humane nor rational. Some of these will be considered in the next section. The movement mushroomed up in a dawn of idealism and shrivelled up in an afternoon of cynicism. Here it will be useful simply to note the comments of the late president of the Rationalist Press Association, Bertrand Russell:

I tried first the method of reason: I compared the danger of nuclear weapons with the danger of the Black Death. Everybody said, 'How true,' and did nothing. I tried alerting a particular group, but though this had a limited success, it had little effect on the general public or Governments. I next tried the popular appeal of marches of large numbers. Everybody said, 'These marchers are a nuisance.' Then I tried methods of civil disobedience, but they, too, failed.[114]

This observation raises interesting issues for the rationalist version of irreligioethics and irreligiomorality. The first is whether people really believed Russell when they politely said, 'How true.' The 'science' of psephology, and 'opinion' polls generally, works on the dubious assumption that interviewees tell strangers what they really believe and not what they think is expected of them, what seems to be 'respectable'. Recent polls in England on the attitude to religion, in Northern Ireland to

Ian Paisley, and in Rhodesia to Ian Smith do not accord with actual figures for church-going and voting; or with what most observers would agree, from private conversations, to be the average individual's real attitudes.

But suppose on the nuclear weapons issue people were sincere when they said 'How true' to Russell. Why did they do nothing? Probably rationalists underestimated the difficulty of translating personal views into national action, had idealistic notions about the 'democratic process', and paid scant attention to the 'power game' in public life. This too will be dealt with more fully later. It is a technical matter not really related to ideology. Of power politics, C.N.D. supporters would be inclined to say that its operation favours the forces of reaction, of the Right. Actually it cuts both ways. With skilful enough generalship, reformist legislation (e.g. the abolition of capital punishment) can also be pushed through against the probable sentiments of most ordinary people. The more interesting ideological point is that, in common with most other categories of irreligionists, rationalists have often had idealistic notions about human nature.

They assume that the 'supremacy of reason' in ethics automatically leads to good moropractice. Does it? There are unhappily a number of waterjumps in the course, into any one of which an entrant may tumble. If 'ethics' be defined in the technical sense used in this book, that is, as an intellectual discipline, it can be assumed that reason has a fair chance of being 'supreme' in its elaboration. Only a fair chance. As we have seen, science depends rather more on hypothesis and less on pure 'observation' than is usually thought. This is especially true of the social sciences, where the observer is part of the scene observed. Such is the abiding problem of anthropologists. Through the capacity we all have for 'rationalization', or making the mental best of a bad physical job, it is easy to devise theories congenial to our personal feelings, find suitable evidence to endorse them, ignore contrary evidence, and be quite happy that the whole operation is 'rationalism'. Further, logical systems can be intellectually perfect without having much relation to reality. Mathematicians, for example, happily talk about 'irrational' numbers and phenomena like $\sqrt{-1}$ and dimensions beyond four that have nothing to do with the world of space-time we all know. That is, you can describe ethical systems for angels or brains without bodies or 'perfect man' or any other abstraction, as a purely intellectual exercise like crossword puzzles and having no connection with the practical job of devising moral systems. At 'moral systems' we hesitate again.

A rationalist is all too likely to say that a rational study of the nature and needs of man should lead to *one* moral system, universally valid. Why then do we have so many, not only from culture to culture, but from subculture to subculture and even from individual to individual? It is common to deny the possibility of the last, to say that everyone belongs to a group of some sort which has a group morality, and any deviant who claims an individual morality is either rationalizing his moromalpractice or is 'amoral'. But it is hardly possible for anyone today to deny the existence of several stable moral systems depending on the culture or subculture in which they grow up. The fact would seem to be that moral codes simply recognize what those who support them 'take' to be the vital needs of their social group in one point of time and place. A rationalist may not be the most observant or sensitive person in the community to detect these needs.

Even if he does little to decide what ought to be done, is he the best person to decide how it should be done? There can be little doubt that in judging between possible alternatives reason helps. How much help is it? That is, how powerful is the rational faculty? Is *homo sapiens* as *sapiens* as he thinks he is? The actual way in which moral codes are devised and change as circumstances change is a complex operation about which little is really known. Does some democratic process occur in which all equally participate, or are these codes elaborated by 'leaders of the community'? And if so, do they act in the interests of the community or of themselves? This is a problem for the next chapter, on politicomorality. But suppose that leaders of the community are, if not academic rationalists, specially gifted with reason or that they call in such people to help them frame moral codes for use in schools and other public institutions, and suppose such people are utterly impartial. Then we have rational morality. Do we have rational moropractice? Does a reasonable code of conduct lead to reasonable action, or any action at all? A moral code is to some extent like the Highway Code. It may tell you to sound your horn in a narrow road as you approach a blind corner. You must decide what is a narrow road or a blind corner. Does a rationalist do this better than anybody else? In the last fifty-odd years there has been an enormous advance in behavioural psychology on the one hand and psychoanalysis on the other. Both of them have undermined – some say have blasted out of existence – autonomous reason. The behaviourists declare that we are all subject to elaborate conditioning from outside, which controls our behaviour whether or not it controls our 'thought'. The analysts say we are all controlled by unconscious or 'irrational' impulses and repressed or suppressed 'memories' in the *id* and by the introjected dictates of the superego. While not necessarily accepting one psychological label or the other, rationalists today hesitate to talk about the 'autonomy of reason'. Yet the 'moral autonomy'[115] of today's moral educationists, which may mean little more than that each person is his own computer, often has the old rationalist overtones.

According to the director of the Farmington Trust Research Unit, John Wilson, a man must not only do the 'right thing' but must be 'acting from the right sort of *motives*, or on the right *principles*, for the right reasons, or with the right *ideals* or *sentiments*. For all these words are essentially connected with freedom and intention.'[116] Good moropractice is 'much more than adherence to particular *mores*':

It includes the notion of relating to other people as to equals, and knowing what their interests are, as well as acting in accordance with those interests. It also includes the notion of managing one's own desires and feelings in the right way, even if the interest of others is not obviously involved: this would apply to such cases as choosing whom to marry, what job to do, whether to take drugs or whether to engage in 'perverse' sexual behaviour.[117]

A man's 'moral opinions . . . must be autonomous (freely held) . . . rational . . . impartial as between persons . . . prescriptive . . . overriding'.[118] We must develop in 'perception, awareness of feelings, imagination, and human understanding'. All these compose 'rationality in morals'.[119] It is by 'failures in rationality' that we 'identify cases of moral inadequacy . . . as opposed to identifying them by overt behaviour'.[120] Now, this analysis provokes certain paramount questions. Does rationality give this power of 'managing one's own desires and feelings', and if so are they always managed 'in the right way'?

My thesis is that it certainly does not, and it would not necessarily be a good thing if it did. The high I.Q. organization Mensa,[121] for example, has been marked by internal emotionalism and failure to offer advertised solutions to external moral problems. It may perhaps be argued that 'reason' cannot be measured by 'intelligence'. If not, how can it be measured? More importantly for our purposes, what has either to do with morality? Reason seems to operate powerfully in the mind of the successful master criminal; probably more strongly than in that of the average social worker. We may well wish that scoundrels found some feelings (of honesty and sympathy for the victim) quite unmanageable, as they would be if powerful enough; and agree with Pascal that 'the heart has its reasons that reason knows nothing of'.[122] The Farmington Trust's criteria place impossible intellectual demands on us. If they were ever to become educational orthodoxy, teachers of ungifted children would soon despair of reaching acceptable 'moral' standards. Could even the most brilliant pass the entrance exam? For its requirement of 'motive' rather than action is not very different from the impossible (save for male homosexuals) demand of Jesus:

Thou shalt not commit adultery: But I say unto you, That whosoever looketh on a woman to lust after her hath committed adultery with her already in his heart.[123]

Here we can only say to the moral rationalist, 'Guilty, Lord,' and go sadly away.

Humanism

Most irreligionists (or unorthodox religionists) today call themselves humanists. Under this label they often cling to one or more of the freethinking attitudes previously described. Recently they have been joined by adherents of certain traditional religions, especially Christianity, certain political theories, especially Communism. and certain philosophies, especially Existentialism.

Politics and philosophy will appear under 'politicoethics' and 'endoethics'. Whether or not Christianity can be regarded as a variant of humanism – some adherents call it the supreme humanism – is hotly debated in both Christian and non-Christian circles. Today this debate centres not so much on the nineteenth-century theological argument over the divinity or humanity of Christ (Trinitarianism *versus* Unitarianism) as on whether religion should concern itself with social and moral issues rather than with the niceties of eschatology, or problems of life and death. In the more cautious version of the Archbishop of Canterbury, the Cardinal Archbishop of Westminster and other leading ecclesiastics who from time to time speak of it, 'Christian humanism' may be assumed to be a religious approach which begins from the human situation instead of the theology textbooks. After surveying man's psychological needs and moral inadequacy, however, it finds that only a textbook Christology can satisfy them. Thus one form of Christian humanism may be called a form of scepticism, the other a form of public relations.

The fact that so many people of widely differing world-views can lay claim to humanism reflects a complex history and an inherent vagueness. In its simplest form it means being 'for human beings'. But who is, or admits to being, *against* human beings? Most secular humanists would date themselves from the Sophist Protagoras and his famous slogan:

Man is the measure of all things, of things that are that they are, and of things that are not that they are not.[124]

Throughout their literature the word lights up the page, from time to time, with a spectrum of finely shaded meaning, from prudent atheism to 'the study and dissemination of ethical principles based on humanism and the cultivation of a rational religious sentiment free from all theological dogma'.[125] In 1854, when the positivist 'new age' dawned, a London Humanistic Association was set up, apparently without any formal link with Comte, but for the rest of the century the general public associated 'Humanism' with the Comtian 'Religion of Humanity'. Apart from its Unitarian connotation, Christians more or less confined the word to those linguistic and artistic neoclassical pursuits of the Renaissance and the Enlightenment. The modern usage, with its strongly naturalistic undertones, began in America in the nineteen twenties. For a variety of reasons the United States, though evolving an American Association for the Advancement of Atheism and organizations using all the free-thinking words coined in Britain, has generally preferred softer sounds like 'Liberal',[126] 'Free Religious'[127] or 'Unitarian'. 'Humanism' had the same murmurous softness. In 1946 the American Humanist Association wrote to the World Union of Freethinkers suggesting it change its name to World Union of Humanists, so as to be 'strategic, forward looking, positive at this hour'.[128] The 'hour' was, of course, the war-torn, creed-torn, postwar world. Suspecting that the change proposed was more than one of title, the union declined. Six years later American humanists and ethicists joined with kindred spirits in Britain, Belgium, the Netherlands and India to form the International Humanist and Ethical Union. Since that time the media have popularized 'Humanism' as the 'anti-creed which is itself a creed'[129] for unbelievers, and most of them have accepted the title gladly. It implies, after all, that religionists are not humanists.

New terms within old movements usually accompany either a public relations exercise to sound more 'positive' and, in the advertiser's sense, 'new', or a slight shift of emphasis. Both tendencies may be found among the humanists. The former does not concern us here except as another tribute to 'admass'.[130] In the latter sense Humanism implies a departure from the essentially personal emphasis of Ethical Culture or Rationalism (based on the individual moral sense or reason) towards the social concerns of Secularism. But, among those who do not qualify it with an adjective, it sounds new overtones, or perhaps old Renaissance ones. There is even a suspicion that to some it has the qualities of the cabbala; that the word itself, understood in its innerness and 'plenitude',[131] provides the alphabet of 'Learning to Live'[132] for those of us who 'lay waste our powers and neglect our opportunities';[133] that 'a new emphasis on the "humanness" of man arising from the rise of social and bio-logical sciences and the social and human welfare professions'[134] is mystically destined to turn up more than just orthodox sociology and biology, and is going to achieve a moral breakthrough by discovering that man transcends a mere social animal and is, after all, triumphantly a human being; that 'Humanists believe in the fundamental importance of the welfare and progress of the human race',[135] as if no one else had ever had this belief and recognition was enough in itself to make clear how these splendid things were to be achieved; that 'we should keep Humanism as a positive affirmation of man'[136] to man. The first director of the British Humanist Association, Harold Blackham, declares that 'Humanism proceeds from an assumption *that* man is on his own and this life is all and an assumption *of* responsibility for one's own life and for the life of mankind'.[137] Some humanists have written 'man', 'life' and 'mankind' with capitals, hoping thereby to suggest that the 'whole man' is more than just his physical, mental, emotional and moral components, though most of them would repudiate the notion of a soul or spirit. Humanists, we are told, 'do not dissent from the consensus of mankind down the ages on basic practical moral questions', whatever that may be. Being 'on the side of the angels', they agree with the Golden Rule and the 'ultimate moral relationship of equality as human beings'.[138] What is 'practical' about this is not explained. In practical terms, however, a study of humanist literature and conference resolutions shows a firm commitment to 'liberal' programmes to be considered in the next chapter.

Even if not exactly practical, certain specific goals are marked out for humanists: 'the open mind and the open society . . . the open heart and the open hand'.[139] The 'open' is to be distinguished from the 'pluriform' society, which merely seeks 'peaceful co-existence of different social systems'.[140]

In an open society there is no 'game' for its own sake constituted by its rules. All the rules are ultimately for the sake of enabling people to get what they want and do what they want, whether one for himself or in association one with another.[141]

But Humanism's 'claim to universality'[142] is really to be found in its attitude to man (Man) himself. Universalist Humanists are in the tradition of the seventeenth-century *virtuosi*, who sought God through science, rather than of their atheist contemporaries. Science, however, discovered not God but Man. It also discovered the theory of evolution, genetic inheritance, A.I.D.

(artificial insemination donor), behavioural psychology and educational techniques, thus putting 'man in the saddle'[143] directing the course of both organic and psycho-social evolution. The proper exercise of this great responsibility needs the careful cultivation of individual potentialities. Man must 'make of his own life, and therewith of himself, a work of art', avoiding 'spiritual squalor'.[144] The humanist 'happy man'[145] is dedicated to the philosophic 'dialogue'[146] but is not just an arid intellectual. Humanism must have moral qualities or it is nothing. A good Humanist is 'ready to counsel and to be counselled'. He is 'permissive and tolerant . . . not puritanical, but inclined to be gentle and tender and affectionate, to the point of indulgence . . . active and effective within his scope . . . aspiring to be his own rather than to own and to share rather than to rule . . . giving and outgoing . . . long-suffering . . . understanding and compassionate . . . He does not worship and he does not hate.'[147]

Perhaps the first comment that will greet this statement of Humanism – that is, the philosophy of those humanists who would exclude any limiting adjective like 'scientific' or 'secular' or 'agnostic' – is that it sounds rather claustrophobic and not a little priggish. A confident belief in one's 'universality' does not necessarily make one universal. Most people do not have universalist, but far more modest aspirations. Perhaps it is not surprising that one attender at a humanist meeting heard the comment, 'Of course, it is so difficult, I find others so ignorant,' and went away feeling himself 'too ignorant to join the new master race'.[148] But let us analyse this version of irreligioethics and irreligiomorality to see whether first impressions are justified.

At once it occurs to the analyst that 'religioethics' and 'religiomorality' may be more appropriate terms, and perhaps more congenial to the protagonists. Humanism of this type has certain affinities to Comtism, which the anarchist Pierre Joseph Proudhon had in mind when he railed:

God, according to the humanists, is nothing but humanity itself, the collective me to which the individual me is subjected as to an invisible master . . . Certainly, if there is a prejudice, a mysticism, which now seems to me deceptive in a high degree, it is no longer Catholicism, which is disappearing, but rather this humanitary philosophy, making man a holy and sacred being on the strength of a speculation too learned not to have something of the arbitrary in its composition; proclaiming him God – that is, essentially good and orderly in all his powers, in spite of the disheartening evidence which he continually gives of his doubtful morality.[149]

Catholicism has not disappeared as fast as Proudhon imagined, and many will find his assertion that Humanism is more 'deceptive' than the teachings of the Vatican perverse to a degree. But few will deny some truth in his criticisms. In the Netherlands humanist 'counsellors' have the same status for the unchurched as ministers of religion have for confessional groups, and there would seem to be more than political significance in this. For a priestly mantle appears to settle on their shoulders with easy familiarity. 'Counselling' implies more than the function of a Citizens' Advice Bureau, which tells one where to go for professional services, or the skill in psychological interpretation of a good psychoanalyst, or the narration of personal experiences from which the listener may draw inspiration or *caveats*, or the provision of a shoulder to cry on. It suggests esoteric approaches to the wisdom of man down the ages by a 'priesthood of believers', who gain power to transmit that wisdom to others. It suggests that those who really know the ' "humanness" of man' will find it a mine of information, a tower of strength and a power-house of good. It is all a question of the right 'attitudes' to digging the mine, climbing the tower and switching on the generators. But is there enough ore in the mine, strength in the tower and steam in the generators, and can moral attitudes really be fostered in this intellectualist way?

In the 1860s there was some thought of using 'Humanism' in Britain as extensively as it is today. It was rejected then as too vague. One sceptic thought it suggested 'frailty and crime as well as virtue and rectitude; they all are alike human': so he 're-adopted the Christian name'[150] for its transcendent moral associations. Those who have an idealistic hankering after 'the plenitude of human development and the fulfilment of all' are likely to become depressed with obvious limitations and strain to look beyond them. In professing to find superhuman resources, orthodox religion attracts its millions while Humanism attracts its thousands. Sadly aware of this, universalist humanists try to escape day-to-day limitations by looking to grand human designs. It is perhaps characteristic that they should set up a study group on World Order before establishing order in their own organization. In this there is not only an element of escapism but a survival of the religious idea that if man is made in the image of God ideally one might expect global uniformity of behaviour. To a humanist man is made in the image of man with a 'common humanity'. Now while this is a fruitful concept in private international law and arbitration, it can too easily develop into a belief that attitudes are, or should be, universal and that there really is, or ought to be, agreement on what constitutes 'human well-being' for today and what is man's 'evolutionary destiny' for tomorrow. It is one thing to describe how evolution operated in the past; it is quite another to prescribe how we should manipulate it in the future. To do justice to the common-sense (or inertia) of humanists, though they may talk a lot about 'man in the saddle' of evolution they do not devote much attention to distant horizons. But they do concern themselves with the way the horse's head is facing.

If the source of humanist (ir)religioethics is the universalist man, then a universalist (ir)religiomorality might be expected to result. For though the thoughts of man may differ, his moral attitudes may be expected to show uniformity, discoverable by 'dialogue'. And there are indications that many humanists do, as individuals, have these expectations. A prominent vice-president of the Ethical Union–British Humanist Association was dropped because she failed to support one clause of the Abortion Bill.[151] A Humanist Adlerian psychologist would treat homosexuals by pointing out that they had got 'wrong ideas about sex life and parenthood' and that 'such hidden or out-spoken errors' encouraged 'all sorts of aberrations and perversions'.[152] A former chairman of the British Humanist Association declared that those who supported British involvement in Nigeria against 'Biafra' had a responsibility 'similar or perhaps even greater than the responsibility of ordinary Germans for Nazi atrocities'.[153]

Unless they are mere rhetoric like President Johnson's 'White House study group to define United States goals in health, education and "happiness" ',[154] some humanist slogans have disquieting implications. It is hard to know what to say about the much-vaunted 'open society' and its effects on morality and moropractice. In so far as it is different from the pluriform or secular, the 'open society' is an impossible dream. Constitutional law, established institutions, the taxation structure, what is taught in schools – all imply certain views of the world, whether they be those of multi-party or one-party states, co-operators or bureaucrats, socialists or communists, religionists or scientists. Vigilant pluriform lobbying is necessary to prevent domination by one ideology or one power bloc, producing a fully closed society. Besides stressing, abstractly, the rights of minorities or 'silent majorities', lobbying may show that the privileged creed is false/harmful or the privileged group inefficient/corrupt. An 'uncommitted' society can be achieved only by apathy, universally accepted committee compromises and the compulsory integration of subcultures; or national subsidies for an infinity of social divisions. Is either approach possible or desirable? To a cynic the most 'open' thing imaginable is an infinity of expanding gas.

Humanists appear to have an altogether too optimistic view of the co-operative, universalist tendencies of the natural man. Certainly he wishes to be well thought of, but this is rather in terms of the people he actually knows, who may be fellow-criminals, than of any abstraction called humanity. Nor will it comfort those in distress to be told that humanity cares for them if no particular men and women do. If there is any difference between man and the other animals, studies in ethology suggest that he ritualizes conflict rather less and fights to the death rather more. Folklore, escapist fiction and nationalistic history glamorize figures like Ned Kelly, Robin Hood, Francis Drake, Gil Blas, James Bond, Bonnie and Clyde, that other cultures would call criminals. People seek identification with the family, the neighbourhood gang, the business corporation, the race, the colour, the creed, the nation rather than with the world community. Ostensibly social pursuits like gambling merely express selfishness and idleness. Part of the fascination of pornography, illicit sex and exceeding the speed limit is that they are against the law. The first at any rate has declined in Denmark since it has been legal.

In announcing her departure from the Humanist movement after over thirty years a recent critic declared:

It is the modern myth-substitutes that most Humanists seem to me to worship blindly and uncritically. They are science and technology; democracy and socialism; and the assumption of complete equality of potentiality (in a species that is unique for its *inequality* and for what it owes to the few); and, finally, automatic progress and the unquestioned rightness of all self-styled 'progressive' movements.[155]

In repudiating an advertised connection with the British Humanist Association, Yehudi Menuhin regretted its deficiency of 'the metaphysical' and prevalence of 'the political trend' and 'public relations'.[156] Even in the absence of God and the presence of man, views can be divergent. Many disagree with Menuhin and regard humanist tendencies as ideal, even if idealist. But does idealist morality lead to ideal moropractice? Let me end on a personal note. I move a lot among humanists. The blue-print of the good Humanist outlined above is not the person I meet. He is no worse, but certainly no better than anyone from rival ideologies and similar social circumstances. Indeed, it is admitted that the picture is 'too flattering', like St Paul's account of the 'fruit of the Spirit'.[157] But if humanist moropractice does not exist, we need not trouble too much about humanist morality and ethics.

6 Politicoethics and Politicomorality

For most of history ethical photographers have believed that only a religious or quasi-religious view of man showed him up in a moral light. These several views may or may not have had political and social consequences, but the main appeal was directed to the individual. A 'changed society', if such were desired, was dated to after, not before, 'changed lives'. As the old religious beliefs tumbled, people sought direct appeal to man's reason or moral sense without the intervention of God. But increasingly this did not seem the right order of priorities. To a large extent man is the product of his environment, not just in the materialistic sense of *Der Mensch ist, was er isst*[1] (Man is what he eats) but according to the way his life is moulded by education and regulated by law and social customs. Philosophers have disputed to what extent politics makes him better or worse than he would 'naturally' be. Under the influence of Thomas Hobbes[2] the English have been inclined to believe that the business of politics is to provide 'good government' rather than 'good men', that is, a climate of stability within which special institutions like the family, the church or the school take care of morality. David Ricardo[3] argued that political economy was simply a science of calculus, while William Blake declared that 'general good is the plea of the scoundrel, hypocrite and flatterer . . . He who would do good to another must do it in minute particulars.'[4] This view had been shared by Spinoza, who thought that the state should 'regard nothing as good or evil except what according to its own judgement is good or evil for itself'.[5] Conversely, Léonard de Sismondi, the Swiss historian, argued that politics was 'a moral science'.[6] Finally, Claude Adrien Helvétius[7] thought all government an unmitigated evil except for get-rich-quick politicians, a view that seems to be increasingly shared by electors.

But all political systems have had certain views on essential human interests, which they declare, and probably believe, themselves to be special custodians of, which could be called moral issues or have moral consequences: stability, justice, freedom, opportunity. Indeed, many of these issues are set out in the 1948 Universal Declaration of Human Rights as the responsibility of governments, of whatever political complexion. A close inspection[8] of its thirty articles shows that some of them are contradictory and hopes of realizing all of them illusory; but they do show that while politics may be acknowledged as the 'science of the possible'[9] many confidently expect it to be the messiah of the ideal. Even the English have expected their public men to be virtuous (witness the fate of those who gain notoriety for vice) and are convinced that British parliamentary institutions and legal system are infinitely exportable to the benefit of importers.[10] As the *Encyclopaedia of Religion and Ethics* put it in 1912:

The political genius of the Teutonic races was born out of the conflict between this sense of responsibility – the recognition that man does not live to himself alone – and the intense independence and powerful will of the individual.[11]

Two years later this political genius plunged the world into war. Even after a second, largely Teutonic, world war Wells was astonished to find in the East that Lord Sankey's British version of the proposed declaration of human rights was regarded as 'Western' rather than 'universal'. Consciously or unconsciously European political and religious imperialism had become a moral imperialism too.

The French pioneered in relating political systems to political and moral ends and to religious persuasions. Jean D'Alembert categorized three primary systems: republican, monarchical, despotic, stressing equality, honour and fear respectively. Though 'not a divine but a political writer', Charles de Montesquieu related them to Protestantism, Catholicism and Islam.[12] It is certainly true that where a state allows, or is forced to recognize, religion as the primary vehicle of morality, it chooses, or is modified by, that one which is congenial to national moral assumptions. Today all political systems of any note pay lip-service to 'democracy' as something which is 'right', which is a moral imperative, though the means whereby this is to be realized vary widely. The word itself almost takes on a magical quality and the idea is perhaps something of a folk myth. Democratic politicoethics is based on the notion that the pooled moral insights of the community will bring collective wisdom and check the passions or prejudices of an oligarchy or autocracy. From this will come a democratic politicomorality representing the highest common factor of group *mores*. This will provide the basis of a legal system that will ensure justice for all and education that fosters equal opportunity and social awareness.

Genuinely universal democracy has proved harder to realize than expected. All communities in the past have depended on the exploitation of some group or other: slaves, serfs, a colonial or neocolonial empire, the proletariat, children, women. In our modern technological societies we have departed a long way from the folk-moot that gave everyone a direct voice in matters that concerned him vitally. With the growth of big government, important decisions are taken by the executive and experts with little or no consultation with the mass of the people. But even where there is consultation we may achieve not the highest common factor of group *mores* but the lowest common denominator of the mob or Ibsen's 'compact liberal majority'.[13] Apart from the obvious excesses of demagogy or McCarthyite conformity, there are the more subtle dangers of expediency and convenience. Local areas may be given a large measure of fiscal autonomy less for their self-fulfilment than to ensure that depressed areas continue to have low incomes and all that this entails in inferior housing, education, welfare, police and the arts. We do not need to consider natural inequalities or posit manipulation by 'hidden persuaders'[14] to recognize that 'equality of opportunity' is as nugatory as 'equality'. When this is recognized, deprived communities see national or United Nations politicomorality as something arising from the interests of others and not therefore binding on themselves. The fields of Montesquieu and D'Alembert have seeded recent research showing how there are separate moralities for the different social classes in their internal relations.[15] Since the accepted morality on which law and education are based tends to be upper- or middle-class in origin, there are likely to be clashes with the more aggressive members of the lower classes. Little will be done to pacify them so long as short-term thinking prevails: from which it emerges that, for example, it is cheaper to increase riot control in the ghettos than expand the poverty programme or improve the status of Negroes. Similar considerations have hitherto won on the world scene, notably in the general attitude to China, though now politically recognized.

The following political categories do not follow either orthodox or Marxist analyses, but are related to their overriding ethico-moral concerns.

Slave–Feudal

In some form or other, slave or feudal societies have been widespread. Especially did they flourish in classical antiquity. Anthropologists have identified feudal, but not slave, systems among the most 'primitive' peoples, whose political forms have always been more complicated than Europeans wanted to recognize. In its best form a slave or feudal state is based on a politicoethics of duty, either to serve or to protect, with loyalty the prime requirement of vassals and *noblesse oblige* (privilege brings responsibility) the motto of lords. The politicomorality that results is clear and precise. Stability is achieved. As there is little material or political development there are few problems of adjustment to change. Everything is stratified; people know their place, with its well-defined floor to adversity and ceiling to ambition; the struggle for power is limited and conflict is ritualized like the pecking order in poultry yards. Since there is little possibility of satisfying it, greed too is limited; and Karl Marx and Friedrich Engels were able to look back on the feudal age as 'idyllic'.[16]

Idyllic, perhaps, but far from ideal. 'Duty' became a façade behind which inefficient or corrupt privilege sheltered from the slings and arrows of outrage and fortune. The politicomorality was stable only so long as people failed to think about human dignity and legitimate aspirations. There is little reliable data about moropractice, and if it were 'satisfactory' it lacked freedom and spontaneity and was merely conformist. Nor was the system ever as stable as Marx, Engels and the Utopian socialists pictured it, for it was frequently rent by slave uprisings, civil and baronial wars and brigandage caused by its inability to douse those ardent few who burnt through their bonds, laughed at their duties and defied the accepted rituals.

Capitalism

If feudalism is the economico-political creation of the aristocracy, capitalism is that of the bourgeoisie. While classical economists and orthodox political scientists will protest that a wide range of political philosophies have accommodated themselves to capitalism, from our point of view they can first be considered together since the *ethos* that joins them – belief in the benefits of competition and 'free enterprise' – is morally (and politically when the chips are down) more significant than anything which keeps them apart. Sociologists relate capitalism to the rise of Protestantism. Through its association with fluidity, not only of money but of men and ideas, individual responsibility and scientific research, it is, as we have seen, in many ways more congenial to the Protestant than to the Catholic mind. But this is a simplification, and capitalism was well established inside the Catholic world in those city-states where the guilds were able to gain substantial independence of the bishop. Catholicism has accommodated itself to the system so well that today the Vatican is probably the world's biggest capitalist. From their observations during a particularly nasty stage of bourgeois development, Marx and Engels strongly believed that capitalism was completely immoral, or at any rate amoral, and 'left remaining no other nexus between man and man than naked self-interest, than callous "cash payment"';[17] and capitalists are wont to talk in practical rather than moral terms. But, regardless of any connection with the 'Protestant ethic', the system regards itself as having, in the last analysis, moral justification.

Perhaps it is significant that the 'bible'[18] of capitalism, Adam Smith's *Wealth of Nations*, was written by a professor of moral philosophy. In writing of *Moral Sentiments* he had declared:

One individual must never prefer himself so much even to any other individual as to hurt or injure that other in order to benefit himself, though the benefit of the one should be much greater than the hurt or injury to the other.[19]

Capitalism he saw as the means of producing national as well as personal riches, which would provide the right conditions for good moropractice.

Savage nations of hunters and fishers . . . are so miserably poor, that, from mere want, they are frequently reduced, or, at least, think themselves reduced, to the necessity sometimes of directly destroying, and sometimes of abandoning their infants, their old people, and those afflicted with lingering diseases, to perish with hunger, or to be devoured by wild beasts. Among civilized and thriving nations, on the contrary, though a great number of people do not labour at all, many of whom consume the produce of ten times, frequently of a hundred times more labour than the greater part of those who work; yet the produce of the whole labour of the society is so great, that all are often abundantly supplied, and a workman, even of the lowest and poorest order, if he is frugal and industrious, may enjoy a greater share of the necessaries and conveniences of life than is possible for any savage to acquire.[20]

Not only is behaviour improved but moral fibre is strengthened:

Nobody but a beggar chooses to depend chiefly upon the benevolence of his fellow-citizens.[21]

A hundred years later a doctor lectured so successfully to a 'mutual improvement class' in the north of England that he turned the lectures into a Victorian bestseller, *Self-Help; with illustrations of Character and Conduct*. In this Samuel Smiles set out to show that young people's 'happiness and well-being as individuals in later life, must necessarily depend mainly upon themselves – upon their own diligent self-culture, self-discovery, and self-control – and, above all, on that honourable and upright performance of individual duty, which is the glory of manly character'.[22] He was able to open with quotes from the free-thinking Liberal John Stuart Mill ('The worth of a State, in the long run, is the worth of the individuals composing it')[23] and pious Tory Benjamin Disraeli ('We put too much faith in systems, and look too little to men').[24] Then he proceeded:

'Heaven helps those who help themselves' is a well-worn maxim, embodying in a small compass the results of vast human experience. The spirit of self-help is the root of all genuine growth in the individual; and, exhibited in the lives of many, it constitutes the true source of national vigour and strength.[25]

This heyday of *laissez-faire* capitalism also exhibited, in the lives of many, 'naked, shameless, direct, brutal exploitation'.[26] Adam Smith was able to show by simple mathematics that the mechanical production of pins increased output; but the mathematics of games theory could have shown that under conditions of complete economic freedom the rich get richer and the poor get poorer. Smiles congratulated himself that a former student later approached him as a grateful 'employer of labour and a thriving man'[27] without inquiring into the conditions of the labour employed. Engels had already done this,[28] while Henry Mayhew was in the middle of his depressing study of *London Labour and the London Poor*.[29] In overcrowded industrial cities, uprooted from village communities with the family surveillance, stability and natural recreations they afforded, the proletariat had every access to vice and little to virtue. If society were to be modelled on the pattern of 'all against each and each against all',[30] then any *immores* to the taste of the individual was justified. He could not be accused of moromalpractice, as his conduct was in perfect accord with *laissez-faire* politicomorality.

Broadly speaking, when capitalists have felt confident of their future they have supported Liberalism; when not, Conservatism: creeds whose contents vary somewhat in place and time and are not necessarily associated with political parties of those names. But though they may have a basic politicoeconomic convenience for the bourgeoisie, they also have ethical and moral overtones which have attracted supporters who are in no sense capitalists.

Conservatism

The best definition of Conservatism is a belief that, in the words of the second Viscount Falkland, 'when it is not necessary to change, it is necessary not to change'.[31] The English Tories came into being in the seventeenth century through their support of monarchical legitimacy and opposition to the Exclusion Bill designed to keep the Catholic Duke of York off the throne. But when he became king as James II and his Catholicism proved too Roman and his policies too unpopular, some leading Tories supported the Whigs in removing him.[32] Thomas Osborne justified this action by the formula:

Right may and ought to be defended, and resistance (for the Public Good) of illegal Commissioned Forces, is not resisting the King's Person, but his Forces; not his Power, but his Force without Power.[33]

Not only was this 'no Rebellion',[34] it was an active virtue. 'The Doctrine of Non-resistance gives them Means for a Temptation, and is indeed but a fair Bait to draw them into a Snare.'[35] Though in the eighteenth century 'atheism – "raucous" or "amiable" – was the special privilege of the "upper" classes'[36] (such famous, if very far from perfervid, freethinkers as Henry Viscount Bolingbroke, Edward Gibbon and David Hume were Tories), the Church of England has, during much of its history, enjoyed the title of 'the Tory Party at prayer'.[37] With the formation of the Primrose League in 1883 Conservatism was rededicated to the 'maintenance of Religion, of the Estates of the Realm, and of the Imperial ascendancy of the British Empire'.[38]

Conservative politicoethics is still firmly wedded to 'the eternal verities' which, though not usually regarded as needing (or offering) rational demonstration, are held to be mystical guarantees of stability, continuity and 'law and order'. Those institutions held favourable to stability – monogamous family, church, monarchy, nation, empire, tough police force, stern law courts devoted to retribution and deterrence rather than reformation – are promoted, whatever their credibility or performance. Conservative politicomorality consists in obeying *mores* in minute particulars, even where they are mere social conventions. It may be noted that most of the famous Tory freethinkers went to church. Though William Pitt expressed interest in Adam Smith's writings on manufacture and 'trade', and when Britain's overseas markets were cheerfully expanding all parties came to recognize 'business' and accept free trade,[39] Conservatives have always leaned towards the moral value of 'property'. In the words of Edmund Burke,

The perpetuation of property in our families is the most valuable and most interesting circumstance attending it, that which demonstrates most of a benevolent disposition in its owners, and that which tends most to the perpetuation of society itself.[40]

This feudal ownership principle has since been extended to a Tory 'property-owning democracy'. It is held, with considerable justification, that when enough people have something to lose in a revolution, revolutions will be most unlikely. Since the worst crimes occur under cover of rebellion, stability is a moral force.

However attractive it may sound to some, it is quite unrealistic to build a system of ethics on unprovable ideas and unsatisfactory institutions, especially when their obvious benefits are reserved for the few. If the foundation is weak or crumbling, a moral superstructure for the whole community is imperilled. Loyalty to convention may be nothing but conformism or humbug, and particularly meaningless to future generations who have forgotten how the conventions arose and who have new needs. Interest in property can easily become an obsessive greed, bringing contempt for the property-less. Even if ownership is widespread enough to avoid civil war, it can lead to external military adventures and jeopardize international moropractice.

Liberalism

Liberalism is, as its name suggests, a belief in 'liberty'; but as there are many kinds of freedom,[41] some mutually exclusive (e.g. freedom of the press and freedom from libel or invasions of privacy), there have often been contradictions in Liberalism or non-party liberalism. The ancestors of the English Liberals were the Whigs, who wanted to free the people, or Parliament, or more usually the big landowners, from royal caprice. By the 'people' they meant those in possession of land over a certain value. Largely because they were strong Erastians, wishing to secure the Church of England from foreign control, they favoured a Protestant interpretation of Anglicanism and were more sympathetic to Nonconformists than to Roman Catholics. Like their founder, the first Earl of Shaftesbury, they linked 'Popery and Slavery'.[42] In the eighteenth century Radicalism was born during the 'Wilkes and Liberty'[43] episode. One hundred years later the two streams of Whiggery and Radicalism merged into Liberalism,[44] fed by the expanding middle classes and Nonconformist churches. A favourite author at this time was the American liberal Ralph Waldo Emerson, who in his essay on 'Self-reliance' declared: 'Whoso would be a man must be a nonconformist.'[45] Strongly believing in private enterprise they became associated with such causes and organizations as 'Individualism',[46] the Personal Rights and Self-Help Association,[47] Individualist Club, London Liberty Club and anti-vaccination. While many leading Liberals were temperance advocates, 'Free Trade in Drink' was sometimes announced as the 'only cure for national drunkenness'.[48]

On the whole, nineteenth-century Liberals were against 'big government' and wanted 'retrenchment', that is, reduction of government spending by reducing both social services and military budgets. On what they called moral grounds they were against the Welfare State and the fixing of hours for adults in industry. Bradlaugh said this 'would be giving legal sanction to any fanaticism or prohibition',[49] and people should 'rely more on themselves and look less for salvation to paper statutes'.[50] Like Montesquieu they had no faith in 'the universal decider' and the 'overzealous'.[51] With his usual confidence Smiles asserted:

Help from without is often enfeebling in its effects, but help from within invariably invigorates. Whatever is done *for* men or classes, to a certain extent takes away the stimulus and necessity of doing for themselves; and where men are subjected to over-guidance and over-government, the inevitable tendency is to render them comparatively helpless.[52]

Mill was equally convinced that 'with the personal tastes and self-regarding concerns of individuals the public has no business to interfere'.[53]

The politicoethics of Liberalism is now clear. Without necessary reliance on religious sanctions, it regarded the moral impulse as rising within the individual, having its primary responsibility for the individual, and promoted by self-respect. The context was not a selfish but a democratic one. The self-respect of everyone else was recognized, and to be respected. What minimal rules were entrusted to the government for safe-keeping were rules of the road, an agreement to follow certain procedures in social life to avoid collisions. The principle was 'Utilitarianism' or the 'Greatest Happiness Principle'. To satisfy it one had to be vigilant in detecting and active in overthrowing oligarchies or acquisitive legislation and institutions which looked after the privileges and happiness of a minority at the expense of those of the majority. In the heyday of Liberalism, monopoly in land received great attention and many ingenious devices (short of nationalization, a 'socialistic' measure) were suggested to overcome it. At the same time restrictive legislation which reduced the happiness of an atypical minority while doing nothing to promote the happiness of the majority was also to be avoided.

But what about that deprivation of happiness caused by the onslaught of big business against the individual when trade was not regulated by the government? And what of the unhappiness brought about by personal misfortune – illness, accident, unemployment, widowhood and the like – in the absence of a Welfare State? The answer was personal responsibility and foresight. Workers, peasants, consumers and others who were weak as units became mighty in organization. By the formation of trades unions, agricultural and consumer co-operatives they gained bargaining status with big business, could even emerge as big business themselves.[54] Some Liberals imagined that those with banking or co-op accounts became 'capitalists' or 'property-owners'[55] in their own right. Producers' co-operatives in industry were also possible but not encouraged, partly because joint-stock companies were held to pre-empt them, partly because Utopian socialist experiments in this direction were not promising. To provide security for themselves and families, working people were encouraged to form building, mutual aid, provident, benevolent, insurance and assurance societies. In the opinion of many Liberals their benefits operated not 'so much financially, as a moral means to a great extent'.[56] Was this optimism justified?

To detect and promote the greatest happiness of the greatest number require the fullest democratic processes. Especially in communications. The free-for-all in economic affairs gushes from the flux of ideas. May the best man and the best brainwave win. As we cannot achieve happiness and the 'good life' without knowing what they are, so the search for truth becomes a moral duty. Consider views on the suffrage. A hundred years ago Liberals generally believed in 'democratic' government, and some of them in female emancipation. Even they did not necessarily accept one man–one vote (one woman–one vote). Some thought it perfectly reasonable to restrict voting to the 'virtuous' or the 'wise' (i.e. the middle classes), or at least give them bonus votes in any system of universal suffrage. Often they seemed to want something like Plato's philosopher-kings or today's 'meritocracy',[57] who would guide people in understanding what was really best for them. Once people knew what would bring about their happiness, reasoned the Liberals, they would automatically pursue it, and since, in the aggregate, this amounted to the good, good moropractice and *mores* would follow automatically. In other words, education and the media, self-help and mutual aid, would play the role of government in achieving desirable politicomorality.

Hegel was among those to point out that Liberalism 'sticks to the abstract' and is 'defeated by the concrete'.[58] Such noble aspirations as 'liberty' and 'happiness' are, in practice, even harder to determine than the Conservative abstractions of 'duty' and 'loyalty'. Not only is there no agreement on how best they can be achieved, there is no agreement on what they mean. Though their pursuit may help the individual they really provide no basis for government at all. One man's meat is another man's poison, and what psychological or moral analyst can measure the relative amounts? In its usual expression the utilitarian formula does not eliminate the pursuit of entirely selfish motives or the victimization of passive minorities. Even, indeed, of a passive majority under a economic system that at one period 'brought terrifying distress for most classes of the population'.[59]

Yet more difficult of definition – especially when set beside Conservatism's 'stability' – is the optimistic Liberal dream of 'progress'. In a euphoric atmosphere 'tending (often unintentionally) to prevent the search for the locus of political power and to render more secure its actual holders',[60] there can even be retrogression. Under unscrupulous adventurers, especially in post-revolutionary situations, 'faith in education becomes an instrument for the seizure of political power'.[61] Political as well as economic instability results. With the regulatory theory of John Maynard Keynes the latter hazard appeared for many years to be dispelled, but more recently Keynes has been called to account.[62] The Liberal position may be idealistic and utopian; as such in a world of manipulators and 'hidden persuaders', it is unable to provide a solid basis for politicoethics. For where inherited wealth or personal disabilities exist there is neither equality nor equality of opportunity. By pretending that there is, Liberalism merely increases personal frustration and bitterness and, in the aggressive, innocently promotes organized crime. Its politicomorality becomes 'what you can get away with' and induces a *mores* of the 'rat-race' and exploitation of the weak. Many would not regard this as the right climate for good moropractice. Merely promoting the ideals of 'liberty' and 'general happiness' does not help to recognize or achieve them. Nor does it appear that everyone wants freedom. Some prefer security and certainty in moral and other matters.

Closely related to Liberalism, as might be expected, is 'liberalism' with a small 'l', though today its supporters tend to be in social democratic parties. Its most notable feature is a hot conviction that all its proposals are 'progressive' and all its opponents are 'reactionaries'. Its politicoethics is based on the pursuit of the one and the neutralization of the other. From this comes its politicomorality, which is more concerned with good intentions than with creditable tactics or actual achievement. Historically, 'liberalism' can be said to precede 'Liberalism'. In its Spanish form *Liberales*, 'Liberals'[63] was originally used, by Robert Southey, to connote holders of 'liberal attitudes' rather than the specific economico-political alliance of Whig-Radicalism or the later Liberal Party. According to Southey, the *Liberales* had, as it were, decided that through abolition of such outmoded institutions as the feudal system and the Holy Roman Empire, the 1789 French Revolution and Napoleon were on the side of 'progress' and so became 'good things' whose excesses and crimes should be pardoned, and indeed not referred to. In this sense modern liberalism has taken over a quality implicit in the Liberal belief in 'progress' (which readily becomes just another version of the old formula that the end justifies the means) rather than its commitment to 'free enquiry and debate'.

Opinions may differ as to what are 'liberal' views, just as they may on what beliefs are 'Christian' or 'socialist', but the following are probably among them: that criminals need reformation rather than deterrence, and understanding rather than punishment; that all men are equal and all races, classes and subcultures should be integrated, by compulsion if need be; that science has provided the answer to the world's problems if only we would take notice; that we all really share the same beliefs about the world but individual terminology gets in our way; that men are by nature rational and good and when they see the 'truth' will follow it; that those who put forward conservative views are blinded by class-interest or are simply insincere.

To what extent these views are true need not here concern us. I would suggest that they are by no means 'self-evident',[64] as the American Declaration of Independence said of one of them, and require rather more justification than liberals usually accord them. But what effect do they have on conduct? Granted that a belief in progress is rather more creative than a belief in stagnation or regress, does it really offer moral guidance? In an extreme form liberal politicoethics can justify any and every politicomorality and resultant moropractice, so long as it is in the interests of 'progress'. Everything depends on a subjective interpretation of what progress is. In practice there may develop an opportunist clannishness every bit as exclusive as the conservative clannishness it replaces, limiting and corrupting to those it enfolds. Outside this group the moral effects are no less disturbing. Sentimental views about minorities, especially anti-social minorities, confirm them in a belief that they can 'fool' society, while the majority, angry that less sympathy is shown for the prejudices – if prejudices they be – of law-keepers than of law-breakers, reacts with a dangerous 'back-lash'.[65] This has often been the aftermath of liberal 'revolutions', whether of thought or of action. The attempt to suppress 'reactionary' views because of the curb they might have on the 'freedom' of minorities suggests that the liberal cry of 'free speech' is so much cant and that conservative governments are quite justified in quietening liberals if they get the chance. For if conservative views are to be regarded as insincere, then no respect need attach to the views of any opponent and the only meaningful politics is power politics.

Socialism

Before Robert Owen's New Moral World evolved its Rational Religion it produced Socialism. Its morals were regarded as more important than its economic consequences, and it was defined as 'the science which treats of the history and formation of the human character, and which science is founded on facts discovered by the experience of past ages'.[66] In contrast with the political systems already looked at, there has never been any doubt that it is concerned with politicoethics and politicomorality, that it has ideals even if it is not ideal. The word 'Socialist' seems to have been used first to describe followers of the 'Social Father' by the *Co-operative Magazine* in 1826.[67] For the co-operative and the early trade union movement also sprang from Owen. Though the Co-operative Congress declared in 1832 that 'Co-operators *as such* are not identified with any religious, irreligious, or political tenets whatever',[68] in a couple of years it had changed its name to Socialist. Its leading figures accepted irreligioethics. Under similar influence was the National Union of the Working Classes, whose motto 'Each for all, and all for each'[69] is perhaps the best definition of the basis on which Socialist politicoethics is erected. On the Continent 'Socialism' emerged a little later to describe the views of Saint-Simon, and continued with strong freethought links till recent years. In Britain the disciples of Owen retained their irreligion but mostly turned to political Liberalism. But because of their support for co-operation, trade unionism and land law reform, some of them used a 'Socialist' or even a 'Communist'[70] label from time to time.

In the middle of the century a moderate Christian Socialism[71] entered the co-operative movement, and a revolutionary theistic Socialism came from Continental *émigrés* in the Central European Democratic Committee:

We believe . . . in a social State having GOD AND HIS LAW at the summit, the People, the universality of the citizens free and equal at its base, progress for rule, association as means, devotion for baptism, genius and virtue for lights upon the way.[72]

Both these versions of Socialism were anxious about ultimate sanctions. God's law was recognizable when 'the "Voice of God" and the Voice of the People are in unison'.[73] In the agnostic world Socialism staged a comeback in 1884 with the addition of 'Social' to the Democratic Federation, and the formation of the Fabian Society. Like the Ethical Union this grew out of Davidson's Fellowship of the New Life. It tried to escape his approach, which was 'ethical and individual rather than economic and political',[74] but remained reformist rather than revolutionary.

Up till this time Liberalism had been able to claim the allegiance of most radicals because it was able to deliver the goods. Though Mill was having moral, and to some extent economic doubts, in his later years, most working-class leaders accepted a system where only 'comparatively the few' were 'starving'.[75] But in the 1880s the position changed. For economic reasons that do not concern us, serious depression coincided with a belated English discovery of Marxism. Though few actually called themselves Marxists, many progressives got the message. After years of supporting Bradlaugh's Individualism, Annie Besant found that 'Socialism in its splendid ideal appealed to my heart, while the economic soundness of its basis convinced my head'. To her it was 'intellectually complete and ethically beautiful'.[76] A fellow freethinker, W. P. Ball, asked her pointedly:

Is it wise, is it honourable, is it honest, is it kind, to lead poor ignorant men into undertaking the vast and dangerous enterprise of seizing the whole wealth of a country as the only remedy for their sufferings?[77]

At this time H. M. Hyndman's Social Democratic Federation and a breakaway Socialist League were demanding, with Marx, a world where 'the expropriators are expropriated'.[78] When Besant came to agree with Ball she passed wistfully into Theosophy. Other Socialists turned to Spiritualism. Some returned to the churches.

By the turn of the century the movement itself had largely changed. Its leading figures mellowed – John Burns, the 'man with the red flag', became a Liberal Cabinet Minister – and many moderates moved into it, including religious groups (Jews,

'Celtic Fringe' Nonconformists and Irish-born Roman Catholics) outside the Anglican Establishment, religious and political. The Labour Party retains its 'Clause Four', calling for the 'common ownership of the means of production, distribution, and exchange',[79] but no one imagines it will ever be implemented. In June 1968, however, a section of the party launched a *Socialist Charter* with the preamble:

At the last two General Elections the British people voted for a new Britain. Many have been deeply disappointed and disillusioned by what has happened since. Our country needs a revived faith in the power of the people; a fresh confidence that great changes *can* be secured by political action.[80]

Throughout the world this mood is echoed by those who sadly observe the socialist achievements of the social democratic parties and the moral achievements of the socialist countries.

Some socialist opponents of trends in Eastern Europe and Asia protest that these are not socialist at all. So do rival governments within the bloc. The Chinese, for example, denounce the occupants of the Kremlin as 'a bourgeois revisionist clique', 'fascist dictators' or 'Soviet imperialists'.[81] From the Russians comes publication of protest by a defector from the Communist Party of China:

Mao Tse-tung used the screen of 'cultural revolution' to launch an anti-communist, anti-popular counter-revolutionary military coup and establish a personal reactionary military dictatorship.[82]

Following the lead of James Connolly, who said that 'Nationalization without workers' control is State Capitalism', revolutionary critics of the Kremlin say this or 'Red-fascism' is what it has achieved.[83] Western socialists have never been able to agree whether they are for full central direction, full syndicalist decentralization, or some compromise like Guild Socialism; for the Welfare State or against it on the grounds that it 'reduces the use-value of freedom; there is no reason to insist on self-determination if the administered life is the comfortable and even the "good" life';[84] for advanced technology or, especially in Utopian movements and the writings of John Ruskin in the nineteenth century, a return to rural life and 'values'; for Parliament or for associations of workers, students, consumers and the rest to supplant it; for reform, called 'reformism' and 'a substitute for ... the socialist purpose'[85] by the enemies of gradualism, or revolution – echoing the earlier appeals of 'moral force' and 'physical force' Chartists; for international socialism or the nationalist aim of 'a *British* road to socialism'[86] in Britain; for subjectivism or 'socialist realism' in the arts. Often these conflicts voice temperamental differences or practical suggestions in different circumstances. Equally often they can be reduced to varying emphases on 'each for all' and 'all for each'; that is, the prime duty is for the individual to guard the state or for the state to guard the individual. The only places where a socialist state has actually been achieved have put the first duty first. They are also places where the barricades have been manned on the implicit assumption that the end justifies the means.

It seems to me perverse to say that nothing can be learnt about modern Socialism by looking at the socialist countries and the writings of Marx, Engels and Lenin, on large portions, if not all, of which it is based; just as religions must be studied through the organizations and scriptures that enshrine them and not by some conviction of mystical inner truth which is too elusive to commit to paper or practice. Especially is this true of China, whose doctrine of 'perpetual revolution'[87] fits in better with dialectical politicomorality than any more stable, complacent and thus bureaucratic arrangement. Disputes between the numerous national and sectarian brands of Socialism need not detain us, for they have less effect on Socialist politicoethics and politico-morality than might be expected. On the whole socialists believe that morality arises from the social conditions of man, and that these are largely determined by economic arrangements. Contributions to society will be of different kinds and excellence and will merit different rewards; the formula is 'From each according to his ability; to each according to the work done'.[88] But it must be done for the benefit of the whole community and not for one's personal advantage. So too with behaviour. If society demands more people (to fill empty spaces in Siberia, say, or confront neighbouring unfriendly countries, in the West or China) it is one's duty to be fruitful and multiply. Wherever possible this will be encouraged by financial incentives from the state, operating through nurtured monogamous marriage and disapproval of celibacy, divorce, abortion, contraception and homosexuality. Like other 'unnatural' acts the last is thought to be a particularly blatant form of *immores* and it is often pretended that in a Socialist state it is virtually non-existent. Where puritanism is the social policy, sexual 'permissiveness' is regarded as a bourgeois device, like pornography, to blind people to the lack of permissiveness and decency in economic relations under capitalism, and thus counter-revolutionary. On other occasions monogamous marriage may be regarded as a bourgeois institution to regulate property relations and induce nepotism in public life, and the 'socialization' of sex is then encouraged.[89]

In other ways it is held difficult to divorce the individual's private from his public life. For his biological and intellectual capacities are not for his personal gratification but for service to society. Creative artists have a duty to be both intelligible to, and mindful of the needs of, the general public which, through state publishing houses and other agencies, is their paymaster. If they will not accept this responsibility to produce 'improving' work, then they must turn to some other vocation. They can always indulge their artistic fancies in their spare time, so long as they do not try to discredit their country abroad. Since non-Socialist nations will forever try to undermine Socialist communities and men may be seduced by greed, especially if they were born in the old bourgeois days, it is imperative that the media allow no criticism of the system. Bureaucratic blunders may be exposed, but fundamental policy in the name of the people is sacrosanct. If ordinary men and women are encouraged to think for themselves they will soon think only of themselves. Liberalism cannot be tolerated because, in the words of Mao Tse-tung,

It is a corrosive which eats away unity, undermines cohesion, causes apathy and creates dissension. It robs the revolutionary ranks of compact organization and strict discipline, prevents policies from being carried through and alienates the Party organizations from the masses which the Party leads.[90]

Spying out liberals thus becomes not just a political necessity but a moral duty. This orthodox politicomorality knows no frontiers wherever the people are supreme and following 'real' Socialism, so that within the Socialist Commonwealth there is, or should be, found a harmony of interests, with the disappearance of nationalism and 'limited sovereignty'[91] for each supposedly self-governing unit. In the capitalist world capitalist politicoethics and politicomorality prevail: that is, what promotes the best interests of the ruling classes. Socialists are not bound by these codes and if they obey them it is purely a matter of prudence.

Now, many socialists in democratic countries might dispute some or all of the foregoing assumptions, which are increasingly challenged, out of 'revisionist' conviction or public relations expediency, by Communist Parties in the West. Yet it is hard to see how anything less than this is anything more than a sentimental anarcho-syndicalism, collectivist anarchism or 'democracy' itself. For where, as in Yugoslavia, liberalization has occurred it has been accompanied by elements of a free market, competition and other features of capitalism. George Orwell is typical of liberal socialists in saying that 'in my opinion, nothing has contributed so much to the corruption of the original idea of Socialism as the belief that Russia is a Socialist country and that every act of its rulers must be excused, if not imitated'.[92] Many of the acts of Stalin were not generally known till after his death, for historians and journalists were expected not only to curb opinion but to falsify facts. A Soviet writer has recently admitted – privately to an Australian communist – that 'in our Communist Party are some of our best people and all of our worst';[93] and a Hungarian philosopher, that 'European intellectuals lost their faith in the bona fides of communists'.[94] There is no particular reason why such megalomaniac crimes as accompanied Stalin's 'cult of personality'[95] should occur even in a closed Socialist society, though the inability of the 'people' to curb them must cast considerable doubt on the truth of its politicoethics. To some degree this arose from Communist politicoethics or, rather, the Marxist view that both Communism and Socialism must be preceded by the 'sway'[96] or 'dictatorship'[97] of the proletariat. This need not, perhaps, lead to autocracy; though effective dictatorships, whatever their political ideology, are usually autocracies.

Most socialist countries have passed through a Stalinist phase. Friends of China say it has not; but if it has not, it has also been unusual in that its Constitution declares that the state 'makes use of the positive aspects of capitalist industry and commerce' and 'encourages and guides their transformation into various forms of state–capitalist economy, gradually replacing capitalist ownership with ownership by the whole people'.[98] This is not orthodox Marxism–Leninism. There was, however, in China the 'violent revolution' which Lenin deemed 'inevitable',[99] even if it was an old-style peasants' revolt. Since capitalist and 'mixed' economies are so dependent on the international money market and 'there is no working-class or Left-Wing equivalent of the World Bank, nor of the International Monetary Fund, nor the Gnomes of Zurich',[100] it is hard to see how a genuinely Socialist administration, even if democratically elected, can consolidate itself against counter-revolution during its early difficulties without dictatorship, illiberalism and suspension of elections until stability is maintained. Even the tiny Utopian Socialist communities proved disastrously unstable without paternalistic funding and control by wealthy philanthropists.[101] Owen admitted that, in the absence of his father-in-law David Dale, the Lanark community became 'a very wretched society' and 'vice and immorality prevailed to a lamentable extent'.[102] This was more than just Owen's puritanical response to orderly permissiveness. All the colonies he later sponsored himself collapsed when his support was withdrawn. Since those 'Utopian' days 'socialistic' measures with government support have spread throughout the world, but it remains to be seen whether Socialism and individual freedom in the fullness of both are compatible.

In 1898 the Ukrainian poet Ivan Franko described Marxism as 'a formal religion based on the dogmas of hate and the class struggle',[103] and it is now fashionable in the West to regard it as a quasi-religion. Bertrand Russell[104] has equated its ideology and politicoethics with those of Christianity; its supporters have often reacted like devotees; its politicomorality has many features of Puritan religiomorality. At least among the older generation. It has, however, been recently asserted that 'the old Bolshevik morality has passed into history and nothing has replaced it', that the younger *apparatchiki* 'believe in nothing – except their own power and privilege'.[105] Whether or not this is so, Marxism–Leninism derives from ethical assumptions for which there is no solid evidence. While it is true that certain laws in every country are based on economic relations and there could be no offence of 'stealing' without the notion of 'property', it is highly doubtful whether virtue and vice neatly fall on one side or other of an ownership boundary, be it based on personal property (which is not ruled out by Socialism) or possession of the means of production. No special moral insights are denied the individual because he is bourgeois or accorded him because he is proletarian. There is therefore no less reason to fear the arbitrary powers of a dictatorship of the proletariat than that of any other class or any military junta.

One Marxist writer, Milovan Djilas, has insisted that in the socialist countries this dictatorship has not led to a classless society but to the emergence of a 'New Class'[106] of party bureaucrats who have as effective a control of capital as any ordinary capitalist and display the *mores* of any privilegentsia. Good ultimate intentions are no adequate justification. What ruling group does not, by the processes of rationalization perhaps, come to justify its power as in the national interest? Even the most ruthless of the Nazis believed they would stabilize a wobbling Germany, and in their early days they did. Marxists have been altogether too prone to claim a monopoly of virtue, to vindicate the politicomorality of their party, trade union or sectional interest without reference to the views of others, to whitewash moromalpractice in their leaders so as not to discredit the system. Because of contempt for what they call the vulgar materialistic 'values' of the West, Marxists reject any judgements of socialist or capitalist societies which consider their ability to produce the 'good things' of life. They often reject the Welfare State in the West as a device to bemuse the workers and defer the revolution. Impatiently they dismiss the assertion of nineteenth-century Liberals that crimes that are inevitable with revolutions, even 'just' ones, must be justified – if they can be justified – by the amount of hardship removed from, or the amount of benefit conferred on, ordinary people by the change. As the twentieth-century Socialist Aneurin Bevan said,

Social institutions are what they do, not necessarily what we say they do. It is the verb that matters, not the noun.[107]

In so far as Marxist parties appeal to the material aspirations of the poor, it is only right that the poor should judge by results. Except perhaps for the very lowest stratum Eastern Europe is no showpiece, though in the most backward countries of the Third World it can hardly be doubted that Marxism has brought or will bring improved living standards. Yet it is true, as friends and opponents both say in different circumstances, that 'good things' have no necessary connection with good people. Does Marxism produce a morality that is more tolerant, just, kindly than those of other creeds? And if it does, do those who pay lip-service to it display these qualities in their moropractice to an advanced degree? Even in the most favourable circumstances we look in vain for evidence.

A feature of many socialists, both moderate and extreme, in the West today is the degree to which they are suspicious of the local Communist Party and the oldest socialist country, the Soviet Union. They may therefore say much of the above analysis does not apply to them. But socialists of all complexions share certain assumptions, which resemble social myths. Even if they do not believe that especial virtue attaches to manual labour or blue-collar workers – and many of them do, at least unconsciously – they regard the 'people' or 'society' or the 'General Will' as having mystical moral force over and above the combined insights of individuals. This is especially true of theistic Socialism in its quaint attempt to reconcile the 'Voice of God' and the 'Voice of the People', and Christian Socialism, which most outsiders have found neither Christian nor Socialist. Labelled or unlabelled, seekers of a 'folk morality' are more likely to find old wives' tales. For folk moralists have little love of individual and interpersonal needs but heap their affection on conformity to a statistical average (if such can be worked out). As this will probably be nationalistic, chauvinism prospers. On a world scale moral imperialism that ignores local differences is fostered. Too often majority morality is puritanical, hypocritical, illiberal, anti-intellectual, unsympathetic to moral change in the light of new knowledge. In explaining why the British Labour Party was 'conservative' Hugh Gaitskell declared that 'workers have learned to fear change'.[108] Outside Russia there is a tendency to attribute those aspects of Soviet life a Western individualist does not like to the machinations of a 'police state', whereas a resident has recently observed:

The great majority of workers and peasants are not unhappy to see the too-smart-by-half liberals put in their place.[109]

Only those who have never met a worker or peasant, or have seen one only through rose-coloured opera glasses, need be surprised by this. If reformist legislation had to wait till the majority of the people demanded it, it would be a long time coming. This is especially true in the social and moral fields.[110] It always begins with minority agitation and may not end with vocal majority support. Such agitation need not arise from any particular section of the population, political party or recognizable organ of Socialism. As people become used to it, if it is enlightened, its value is slowly seen. If it should turn out disastrously they will, in a democracy, pretty soon take steps to reverse it. From the start a reformer has to lift or climb over the inertia of a mass population, whose dead weight is not removed by declaring the state Socialist and a vehicle of 'each for all, and all for each'. Nor is there, as the Russians imagine, a neat population division so that young people who want changes need only wait till the older generation that created the *status quo* has died. Preparedness to innovate in moral, as in other matters, is not necessarily related to age. In many ways Nikita Khrushchev was much more adventurous than some of the younger leaders who have replaced him.

If Socialism looks simplistically at politicoethics, it all too often is even less realistic about how this is translated to politicomorality. When Socialists are out of power their views endure in political parties, Freemasonry[111] (on the Continent) and other groups that have not always shone with internal democracy or the probity of their leaders. When in power they, like non-Socialists, rely on the machinery of government – laws, controls, censorship or incentives – to transmit their politicomorality. Even if this is, in every sense, democratic, it may represent the majority and be intolerable for a minority. By party manipulation it may not even represent the majority. As however it is said to operate in the name of the 'people' it acquires a bogus moral sanction. Socialists are thus particularly prone to overlook the role, benign or malignant, of leadership in the conduct of affairs.

During the third week of an unofficial strike a British industrialist, Lord Stokes, declared that 'nothing will happen if
management doesn't manage and leadership doesn't give a
lead'.[112] For better or for worse the same is often true in political
and moral matters. But the power that society is likely to accord,
willingly, depends on the credentials of its managers and leaders.
In this respect socialists do not warrant any more trust than other
politicians, and in so far as they claim a special altruism may need
to be watched rather more closely.

Communism

In common with its other features, the politicoethics and
politicomorality of Communism are largely speculative since,
with fleeting exceptions, there does not seem to have been any
serious attempt to establish it. The early Christians were said to
have 'had all things common'.[113] Under the iron rule of an abbot,
monasteries remain, at least in theory, economically communist,
and there are less autocratic *Brüderhof* and other religious
communities scattered around today.[114] While they have often
dabbled in politics they are not political in the ordinary sense and
their politicoethics is really religioethics. But the Reformation
gave scope to a number of sects, beginning with the Anabaptists,
which, under a cloak of Christian forms and language – accompanied by, it would seem, genuine religious belief – introduced
social experiments owing little to Christianity. In England there
were the Diggers. Theological descendants of the Baptists and
Seekers, they declared their lives devoted to the Golden Rule and
that 'community in God's way'[115] described in Acts. Politically
they were a communist offshoot of the Levellers, a movement
whose name was more radical than its intentions, and believed
that common land was, as the title implied, 'a common
treasury'.[116] So in 1649 they proceeded to dig St George's Hill,
Surrey, and sow carrots, parsnips and beans. But Parliament
would not tolerate spontaneous horticulture.

During the French Revolution there was another outbreak of
Christian Communism, preached by a bishop, Claude Fauchet.
But from that time communist movements, beginning with

François Babeuf's Society of Equals, tended to be non-religious or irreligious, inspired by Owen, Charles Fourier, Wilhelm Weitling, Saint-Simon or Étienne Cabet.[117] With the exception of the short-lived Paris Commune of 1871, they were Utopian in that they sought rather to opt out of the mainstream of politics than to change it. Practicality came with Mikhail Bakunin's 'Free Communism' and Marxism–Leninism. Khrushchev announced that the Soviet Union would pass from its socialist to its communist phase in his lifetime. Then Louis Blanc's formula, 'To each according to his needs, from each according to his abilities',[118] would be realized. At the same time the state would begin to 'wither away',[119] since, according to Marxism–Leninism, it is necessary only when there are vestiges of classes. Instead, Khrushchev's power soon withered away and his successors have declined to give a date to the millennium. Since there are no signs of dismantling of the Kremlin, the elimination of wages, or even of the reduction of differentials in the Soviet Union and its neighbours, it remains to be seen whether Marxian Communism is any less Utopian than its rivals.

Even more than Socialism, Communism springs from strong ethical fountains. During the nineteenth century the two words were often used interchangeably, though the middle classes were more likely to use 'Socialism' and the working classes 'Communism'. Babeuf believed that property was 'the cause of all the evils upon earth'[120] and communists of all schools have believed, with ample justification, that greed triggers off man's inhumanity to man. Apart from their intention of locking the trigger permanently, the politicoethics and politicomorality of Communism and Socialism are similar, though the former may be thought to induce even more uniformity of *mores* than the latter, and to be held with a devotion proportional to its difficulty of implementation. Marx declared that it is 'the solution of the riddle of history and knows itself to be the solution'.[121] Hegel had regarded the state as 'the reality of the ethical idea'.[122] To Marx, Engels and Lenin, who spent most of their lives fighting hostile states, it was no such thing. Life could be rich only in its absence. For it 'is a product of society at a certain stage of development',[123] which, under capitalism, 'calls for seas of blood through which mankind has to wade in slavery, serfdom and wage labour'.[124]

Characteristically, the Communist League was formed in 1847 out of the League of the Just, and it was a sense of justice that prompted the communists to look beyond the dictatorship of the proletariat and socialism to 'equal rights and duties, the abolition of all class rule'.

It may be conceded that equal and classless politicoethics would automatically lead to equal and classless politicomorality. But this presupposes that equality in 'rights and duties'[125] is anything more than worthy sloganeering, and that the only moral problems are those which arise from class and private property. Even in small Communist societies the members manage to keep some things to themselves while their moropractice is more unequal than their politicomorality. Describing our instinctive desire to protect our family or individual lair, ethologists say it is silly to expect otherwise. And are there not moral questions like cruelty for 'kicks' which have nothing whatever to do with greed or possessions? To many critics, however, Communism suggests drabness and uniformity which are uncongenial. Above all, will it work? Will the hate and envy of class struggle suddenly dissolve into classless love and magnanimity? Will people work without incentives, or shall we ever reach a stage of automation where work is superfluous? Will not layabouts always find some way of imposing on their more active or generous neighbours? In the absence of a state can we be sure of fundamental protection of life and limb? If the state is an 'organization for the systematic use of *violence* by one class against the other',[126] will its disappearance remove personal violence? Might not the reverse occur? Lenin believed that 'excesses on the part of *individual persons*' would be curbed by 'the armed people'.[127] The replacement of a standing army by a people's militia was the dream of nineteenth-century European republicanism, derived from the American Constitution. Is America a gentle nation? Have *vigilantes* anywhere removed violence?

7   Scioethics and Sciomorality

Knowledge itself is power.[1]

To the ancients goodness, beauty and truth were all related. If man could only know the ultimate truth about the world he would find it both beautiful and good. Perhaps it should be called God. Not only would it be good in itself, it would serve to make man good. As the Gospel Jesus said to his followers in the philosophical book of John:

Ye shall know the truth, and the truth shall make you free.[2]

At first 'natural science' (from the Latin *scio*; I know) owed little to the modern disciplines of field research, classification and experimentation, and was rather what we should now call 'philosophy'. Even today there are those who believe that 'all we know of science or of religion comes from philosophy. It lies behind and above all other knowledge we have or use.'[3] Ancient philosophy proved too individualistic, too fragmented to stand against religious orthodoxy, but the faithful did not throughout the middle ages regard themselves as the enemies of either philosophy or science. On the contrary, those of them who were scholarly saw Christian philosophy as the pinnacle of philosophy and theology as the 'queen of the sciences'. When the empirical sciences began to flourish in the seventeenth century the church grew hostile to what it presciently recognized as a dangerous rival, though some unorthodox Christians saw the path of science as an avenue to God. Gradually the *Warfare of Science with Theology in Christendom*[4] became endemic and diplomatic relations were broken off. Individual scientists remained Christians but textbooks abandoned pious nods towards religion and came to stress the autonomy of their own disciplines.

As theology ceased to be the queen of the sciences, science came, in the estimation of many scientists, to be the queen of theology. They expected it to be a new, improved road to absolute truth, if indeed it was not absolute truth itself. Naturally the trend began with the stars in their courses and soon spread throughout the physical sciences. By the mid-nineteenth century men were looking for 'a Social Science' which would be 'a body of ascertained laws relating to human society, which, like those that constitute the sciences of mathematics, astronomy, physics, chemistry or physiology, should be definitely accepted and regarded by all men as beyond dispute. Until there be such a body of truths, universally acknowledged and respected, society must remain in a state of profound disorder.'[5] At about the same time a National Association for the Promotion of Social Science was formed. Soon it was promoted so well that many came to believe it had actually achieved the results hoped for. When the old religions vacated heaven, science was elevated in their place. As Annie Besant put it:

Persons may, and frequently are, lifted out of the narrowness of a selfish religion in varying degree by the diviner truths and beauties with which the arts and sciences permeate the minds of their votaries.[6]

And again:

So Science taught him . . . and so he wrought, and learned, and laboured, until Earth took the hues of the fancied paradise, and the fairest dreams of a heavenly life became the realities of a life which was lived on this side the grave.[7]

By the middle of the twentieth century a number of scientific and historical developments had occurred which could have affected, and for many people did affect, this touching faith. But there were others who, if they abandoned Mrs Besant's florid style, held fast to her florid beliefs. This is especially true of the Marxist world, whose founders were convinced of the irrefutable scientific basis of their theories. In broader terms Engels 'believed that the technical and social processes of post-Industrial Revolution society would in fact bring about a new secular set of beliefs in terms of which men would be able to understand themselves and their society and to control their own future',[8] and this is the abiding hope of the socialist countries.

Even among apostates the vision lingers, even in the disillusioned mind of Arthur Koestler:

Our biological evolution to all intents and purposes came to a standstill in Cro-Magnon days. Since we cannot in the foreseeable future expect the necessary change in human nature to arise by way of a spontaneous mutation, that is, by natural means, we must induce it by artificial means. We can only hope to survive as a species by developing techniques which supplant biological evolution. We must search for a cure for the schizo-physiology inherent in man's nature, and the resulting split in our minds, which led to the situation in which we find ourselves.[9]

This is a view of biology shared by psychologists – 'Our prime duty is to serve evolution, to keep life varied, exploratory, and open-ended'[10] – and cyberneticians – 'We should no longer look to the philosopher-*qua*-philosopher for guidance in practical and everyday matters, or in ethical and social questions. Instead, we should look to the scientists to see what it is that science provides by way of guidance based on previous experience, and in terms of the purposes which people have.'[11] A faith as enduring as this must have a moral motivation.

Sometimes this is explicit:

We have not yet met a case where we have had proper experience and yet failed to agree. We can, therefore, only believe that proper experience will probably lead to unanimity in the acceptance of ultimate ethical criteria, just as it has led to unanimity in other cases.[12]

This is a moral philosopher talking, but one who believes in the philosophy of science. Other philosophers directly grant moral attributes to scientists:

The scientific temper can be psychologically conducive to an ethics of generalized benevolence. The scientist tries to find laws of nature which apply anywhere and anywhen, and he will therefore be attracted by a moral outlook which places the interests of all men, whatever their caste or creed, on an equality. He will even be attracted, beyond a merely humanistic ethic, to consider the interests of other species of animal.[13]

'The society of scientists,' says a physicist, 'must be a democracy.'[14] To preserve their integrity scientists must withdraw from the 'pervasive moral distortion, a readiness to use any means for its own ends, which warps the machinery of modern government'.[15] Through the concept of 'mental health' psychiatrists save us from individual 'moral distortion' as they aid 'good interpersonal relations with oneself, with others, and with God'.[16] As the priest and the moral philosopher have declined in importance in our society, there has developed an 'emphasis upon the medical element in anti-social behaviour ... as an expression of the unique prestige enjoyed today by the medical profession'.[17] Sometimes it claims a moral overlordship. Sometimes, in concert with social scientists, 'it assumes that it represents, at least in principle, a closed system, capable of yielding definite answers to practical social problems without reference to moral and metaphysical beliefs'.[18] In either case it is unwilling to accept that its solutions are at all controversial and writes off its critics as uninformed, if not insane.

The dominion of 'medical fatalism which equates the revolutionary and the malcontent with the psychological invalid, and regards "adaptation" and "morale" as gods to be bowed down before'[19] has been challenged by academic figures like Alex Comfort and Barbara Wootton and even by some psychiatrists. But its most implacable foe, convinced 'that the greatest menace to world peace, to the general well being of all people, to the education of our children, to the sanctity of our Churches, and to the administration of justice in our courts, is the head shrinking cult of psychiatry',[20] which exists 'to undermine the morals of a nation, to seek to eradicate its churches and to promote sexual promiscuity',[21] is a cult which promotes scioethics and sciomorality in a yet more dogmatic, bizarre and controversial form. This is the Church of Scientology of California,[22] which grew out of L. Ron Hubbard's *Dianetics, The Modern Science of Mental Health* (1950), *Scientology, Handbook for Pre-clears* (1951) and *Science of Survival. Simplified, faster dianetic techniques* (1951), and whose headquarters is now in Britain. Its origin is a world obsessed by the Bomb, the Cold War, personal analysts, Eastern mysticism and scientific (or pseudo-scientific) jargon. To its founder has been attributed[23] the interesting background of electronics engineer, psychologist, nuclear physicist, ethnologist, philosopher, explorer, scriptwriter, science fiction writer, novelist, horticulturalist and naval officer.

From this experience and from the wisdom of the Vedas, Buddhism, Taoism, Greek and Enlightenment philosophers, 'old-time faculty-psychology of 400 years ago',[24] nuclear physics, lie-detectors, Freud and Commander 'Snake' Thompson, he has created Dianetics ('man's most advanced school of the mind')[25] and Scientology ('knowing how to know'),[26] 'a precise and exact science, designed for an age of exact sciences'.[27] To an anxious world it advertises Certainty.[28] Scientology is 'a new science capable of handling man' which 'can and does do exactly what it says it can do'; with it 'man can prevent insanity, criminality and war'.[29] It 'carries forward a tradition of wisdom which concerns itself with a soul and a solution to the mystery of life' and includes 'those things of which one can be certain'.[30] One of these is: 'In the mest (matter–energy–space–time) universe ethics seem to be a liability, honesty is all but impossible, save when armed with force of vast magnitude. Only the strong can afford to be ethical, and yet the use of strength begets but the use of strength ... In one's own universe, on the other hand, honesty, ethics, happiness, good behaviour, and justice all become possible.'[31] So the aim is, as in Buddhism, to help the 'reactive mind', based on stimulus-response, to lose its negative reactions and unconscious memories and then to disappear. This is done with the help of an 'auditor' and an E-meter.[32] Thus 'cleared' of the dross not only of this lifetime but of the whole existence of his 'thetan' (soul), the individual has 'a high survival and success potential and is more at cause over self and environment, than unwilling effect'.[33]

To the ancient East and modern America scioethics and sciomorality owe other debts. Some of the resulting cults have, like scientology, from time to time claimed to be religions. Partly this has been an attempt to escape criticism or prosecution, taxation or rating, but there are wider implications. Some of their techniques to gain mystical experience, notably yoga or drug-taking, are by no means new and form part of certain ancient religions. Indeed, it could be said that religioethics, especially of Eastern origin, is a branch of scioethics. The ancient Hindu *Atharva Veda* called cannabis, the source of marijuana, the 'liberator of sin' and 'heavenly guide'.[34] Among the Amerindians sundry hallucinogens, of which the best known is mescalin, the sacrament of the Native American Church, are used for religious and moral purposes. Sometimes they are taken to 'expand'[35] or 'reveal' the mind, laying it open to new knowledge or moral insights. Sometimes they are held to be aids to good moropractice. Thus the Shamans of South America used the seeds of a plant, Datura, as a sort of 'truth drug' to elicit incriminating hallucinations from thieves; while the Jivaro administer it to wayward children so that spirits of the tribe will come and rebuke them in their visions. Recently many white Americans have taken to L.S.D.-25,[36] a synthetic originally made in Germany and growing in popularity throughout the world. In its honour two clinical psychologists, Timothy Leary and Richard Alpert, formed first the scientific International Foundation for Internal Freedom, and then the religious League for Spiritual Discovery with its celebrated other-worldly, or non-worldly, creed: 'Turn on, tune in and drop out.'

Britain has contributed one of these 'scientific' cults, whose headquarters is now in America. Inspired by the success of scientology and communicators with unidentified flying objects, or 'flying saucers', and by Aetherius, an Intelligence or Cosmic Master from the planet Venus, in 1954 a former cabby and oil-company employee George King was told to 'PREPARE YOURSELF! YOU ARE TO BECOME THE VOICE OF INTERPLANETARY PARLIAMENT'.[37] Since then it has transpired that the universe is governed by a hierarchy emanating from the 'ONE' and our solar system by twelve Perfects on the planet Saturn. Because of their wisdom they choose and are obeyed by the Cosmic Masters. They believe that 'the great sin' is 'ignorance' and would have us 'control . . . the inside elements', 'become self-illumined Masters of our lower aspects of Being . . . to draw nearer to the Divine Spark of God within' and 'pre-determine the result' when we finally judge ourselves in the Hall of Judgement by changing ourselves now.[38] Saturn also offers us 'the great science of Shape-Power',[39] which is to be used in building five temples that will be sources of spiritual energy and faith healing for a world whose magnetism has been disturbed by 'wrong thinking and wrong action'. Meantime these energies are radiated to earth by spacecraft from the various planets and reflected by the faithful periodically gathered on the tops of mountains. Christians are reassured to find that Jesus was another Cosmic Master from Venus, mystics have the comfort of *karma*, and lovers of gadgetry have a battery of tape-recorders and radionic apparatus which acts as a 'safety valve' during the transmission of 'Pranic Energies'.[40] So that an enthusiast can tell readers of an Underground magazine that the society is 'honestly laying foundations on which we can build a New World'.[41]

Whether based on orthodox science or the bogus scientism just described, scioethics claims a universality of derivation lacking in the systems it seeks to supplant. For it is the ethical wing of what Wells called the 'unifying influence of the mechanical revolution'.[42] Religion, irreligion and politics grow out of special conditions which determine their nature, distribution and viability when circumstances change. Though claiming universality they have never in fact been able to achieve it; for there is a limit to their ability to adapt without evolving into a new system, and to the capacity of those empires that embrace them to become, in a literal sense, world powers.

The great 'world religions' have become international, but no single faith has gained the allegiance of the world or even of a majority of its peoples. The irreligious ethical systems have succeeded even less in securing active support, and what followers they attract are united more by their anticlericalism than by their positive programmes. Many political movements are purely local or nationalistic in their appeal; while those, like Socialism and Communism, that claim universality have already demonstrated that as they grow they fracture, both ideologically and organizationally. In all these systems of ideas and ethics the world-views of particular people gain dominance, and substantial groups take them up because they offer a solution to some particular problem that happens to be dominant in their lives and/or their consciousness: corruption, hopelessness, tyranny, instability, poverty, injustice. Science, on the contrary, does not invoke special names or advertise the solution of special problems. It claims to spring from the common humanity of man, to irrigate areas that are truly universal, to flow over all ideological and political boundaries.

Scioethics begins with no *a priori* assumptions about the world or man, does not depend on any esoteric acts of faith or commitment, inspiration or intuition, mysticism or proselytism, formula or programme. As a behavioural psychologist put it recently, 'instead of traditional values like justice and freedom' it employs 'the scientific values of controlled experiment'.[43] This new technique of 'knowing' is universal in application and its findings are accepted only when they are universalizable. Here then is the first authentic tool to discover the nature and origins of morality. Using the same technique man devises sciomorality: an objective, authenticated, universal system based on human needs everywhere. Heaven and earth may pass away, but as long as men survive anywhere in a space-capsule they have in science the seeds of a new beginning. Sciomorality does not claim to be absolute in the old sense of unchanging. It does not rely on some once-for-all revelation but evolves and matures as the frontiers of knowledge expand. From interpersonal relations sciomorality spreads to interracial, intercredal and international *rapport*. The old religious and political hostilities seem strangely irrelevant in a world where communities are no longer isolated and where knowledge is available to all. No more can one group claim privileges on the grounds that to it alone has been vouchsafed wisdom or inspiration or education. Through social science we now study the needs of man in society; through psychology, his individual emotional drives; through technology, how to satisfy these needs and drives.

We can no longer inflict injustice through ignorance; people can no longer think that what is foolish is right. Trial by ordeal or the torture of heretics becomes untenable when we undermine the metaphysical or religious plinth they were built on. In the past, political systems were based on conceptions of class or tribal or national inferiority, and wars were justified in the name of inherent superiority. Sometimes strife broke out accidentally because states did not know what their neighbours were thinking or feeling and misjudged their intentions. Today science has questioned many anthropological assumptions that underpin politics, while the cybernetic revolution has let loose information gathering, storage, retrieval and transmission on an unprecedented scale. We now know many of the causes of conflict inside the individual and society; while on the international front we have a 'hot line' and other instruments to put heads of state in contact to resolve uncertainties and misunderstandings in diplomatic relations. With the aid of the machine-tool and the electronic brain, the all-consuming drudgery of repelling natural enemies like fire and flood, famine and thirst, disease and predatory animals, is falling from our backs. The harsh, unloving demands of the struggle for survival in a pre-scientific world disappear, and man can devote his energies to the things of the spirit, to moral speculation, to the ennobling leisure-time pursuit of art and creative hobbies, to forward planning and prophylaxis against moral as against physical disease. Matters which were formerly left to chance and which led to recurring crises are now the creatures of human control. As one scientist puts it,

It is, in principle, scientifically discoverable how far the maintenance of private property or of marital fidelity may contribute to the most general end of universal happiness, and thus warrant acceptance as intermediate ends.[44]

In this atmosphere of precision, predictability and stability, free of the arbitrary plateaux and precipices of morality based on one or other of the older ethical systems (that after periods of great rigidity suddenly change through some new revelation, party line or *coup d'état*), moropractice has a better chance of flourishing.

There are many interesting differences between the attitude to science today and that of a century ago. Then the orthodox feared that its discoveries would undermine dogmas and religious organizations. In many ways this has proved true of literal belief in creeds, church membership and direct political and moral influence.[45] But the faithful who endure, neatly compartment their minds and cheerfully accept both science and religion. Last century the apostles of science really believed it was the messiah of a new age and would solve the moral, as well as the physical, problems of the world. Today there are few who sing this litany. The concern is not simply over the death of 'traditional morality', where unbelievers mingle with believers among the bereaved. This is seldom now blamed on science as such. In the past religionists feared that those who admitted the Copernican theory in astronomy or Darwin's theory of evolution would blow up the Garden of Eden, original sin, redemption and its moral consequences; but only a handful of fundamentalists support this view today. It is rather that those who looked to scioethics for an enlightened sciomorality, and those who looked to that for secure moropractice have been disillusioned. Worse, many – even among scientists – have come to fear, even to hate, science itself or its technological progeny as a new Moloch demanding not only worship but human sacrifices. The disenchantments are both theoretical and practical.

While goodness, beauty and truth may be related in the minds of philosophers and theologians, and it may be questioned whether goodness and beauty can survive long in a climate of systematic lying, the three do not necessarily go together. In the early days of its brief career the Nazi regime produced unquestionably artistic propaganda like Leni Riefenstahl's 1936 film epic *Triumpf des Willens*. Equally, creations painstakingly devoted to truth have lacked beauty and ultimately failed to produce goodness. One recalls Oscar Wilde's quip about the story which was worse than immoral because it was badly written.[46] In personal terms we all know clever rogues and stupid rogues, and the clever rogues are rather more to be feared. The mere act of 'knowing' is not enough. In the first place, there is the philosophical problem of passing from an 'is' to an 'ought', which has been dealt with before. And there are more serious anxieties from the moral standpoint. Scioethics grew from the assumption that knowledge was an end in itself, that it was a moral imperative, that the pursuit of knowledge gave a dynamic to the good life, that the knowledgeable were virtuous and the ignorant vicious or at any rate worthless. There is a widespread belief today, for which solid evidence is slim, that criminals are on the whole high-grade mental defectives. Even if undisputed statistics from the world's prisons were to be gathered, this would still apply only to followers of those antisocial activities formally designated as 'crimes' and to felons who get caught. For many commentators the gathering of 'statistics' is the worship of a new god, and not infrequently a false one.

Knowing about the world is not the same as knowing the world, and knowing about man is not the same as knowing or understanding him. Increasingly people are coming to see that, at least from the moral standpoint, science is a means and not an end. The gathering of information may suggest to us what next to gather in the pursuit of knowledge; it does not tell us what we ought to gather, what it will be useful or helpful to gather, or how to use the knowledge to benefit mankind. Scientists have not turned out to be moral proconsuls. In seeking insight into human problems few people today tackle the dreary jargon of psychological and sociological texts. They are more likely to turn to an Elizabethan–Jacobean poet-playwright, whose scientific inaccuracies have been gleefully exposed in countless learned tomes. This is one reason why senior pupils are turning away from the sciences and towards the arts at a time when the physical achievements of science are growing ever more spectacular and, for those who understand them, exciting.

In its higher reaches, as distinct from its technical estuary, science bubbles in air that is keen with imagination and intellectual speculation; but this has not enhanced its ethical reputation among scientists or non-scientists. When he learned that the cut-and-dried atomic world of Dalton had given way to the picturesque sub-atomic world of Rutherford-Bohr, the Existentialist writer Albert Camus exclaimed:

I realize then that you have been reduced to poetry . . . So that science that was to teach me everything ends up in a hypothesis.[47]

Now that this new model is acknowledged to be pure speculation and the implications of the theories of relativity, indeterminacy and uncertainty are known to well-read non-scientists, the 'knowledge' of science is seen to be more debatable and less absolute than had been thought. Even in the physical realm there are rival theories on such fundamental matters as the origin of the universe, the properties of distant space, the nature of light, the formation of the earth; and controversies grow in intensity as one passes to the biological, psychological and sociological disciplines. Purely 'objective' measurement is found to be impossible, and even if this were not so a mass of measurements is meaningless to the human mind without a hypothesis to string them all together into a coherent whole. So science turns out, after all, to be subject to the same individualistic biases[48] and interpretations as the philosophy it was intended to replace.

Each scientific discipline has come to concentrate on its own allotment. To explain the general intentions of scientists and try to link the allotments a 'philosophy of science' has been evolved. Even this has no direct connection with morals, though it has a more plausible claim in that, like moral judgements, it is concerned with a total situation and not the jigsaw fragments of each separate science. For the 'prescriptions' of science are not necessarily the same as moral 'prescriptions'. They tell us what will achieve certain technical results, but scientists cannot, as scientists, tell us what should be our aspirations and order of priorities. Morally, science reveals the present and does not illuminate the future, except in the 'negative' sense of giving us warnings of the likely result of our conduct. Sometimes science shows us things that are wrong in our thinking or our actions; but it is often easier to show what is wrong than to say what is right or to decondition what has already been conditioned. In other words, scioethics finds it very hard to elaborate a consistent sciomorality. Indeed, most scientists believe today that scioethics is itself illusory.

They take the view that science is ethically neutral, amoral. To such an extent that scientists are themselves accused of being amoral. The Hippocratic Oath has not stopped doctors from participating in bacteriological warfare, and no comparable oath has been required of other scientists despite the exertions of Bertrand Russell, Albert Einstein, Josef Rotblat, Hyman Levy, the Pugwash conferences[49] and the newly-formed British Society for Social Responsibility in Science.[50] Scientists have proved as incapable as anyone else of 'reconciling ethical feelings with ethical doctrines'[51] and the general public, with more or less justification, has come to believe they are as uninterested in this question personally as they are disinterested professionally. Understandably, those scientists of whom this is not true retort that in matters of public policy members of the public are agents and they are instruments that cannot be expected to accept vicarious moral responsibility. They simply do what they are paid to. But, urge opponents, this was not held to excuse war criminals. There would, perhaps, be wider sympathy for scientists if they always seemed to play a neutral role, modestly disowning, in the words of the progressive educationist A. S. Neill, knowledge of 'anyone wise enough, good enough, to mould anyone's character'.[52] In fact they seem often to become moral jurists, juries, judges and prison officers. This is especially true of the social and psychological sciences.

Here available data are so vastly complex and the necessity for selection so obvious that working hypotheses, on which social work and psychiatry are based, are obliged to ignore whole chunks of material. What is selected is then interpreted. All this is personal. In theory, it is subject to confirmation by other workers in the field so that idiosyncrasies cancel one another out. In practice, the weight of orthodoxy tends towards conformism. For science has produced its authorities, its dogmas, its sacred texts. It has known its frauds (Piltdown man), its pious hopes (the Lamarckian theory of the inheritance of acquired character-istics), its myths (the notion of phlogiston as a 'substance' emitted when things burn). Sometimes these have been used for political purposes: the Lamarckian theory in Stalinist Russia, the theory of evolution to justify genocide in Nazi Germany. In the section on Positivism we saw the reactionary effects sociology could have. More often there is the risk of false analogies. Referring to Hobbes's *Leviathan*, Waddington observes:

The attempt to consider human evolution in animal terms led to the aberrations of Social Darwinism. Comparisons between human society and animal organisms are no more satisfactory.[53]

At the present moment undue weight is probably being given to analogies between human society and a posse of gorillas. On one hand scientists are accused of straining after novelty; on the other, of working on the conservative assumption that whatever is, is right. Despite their supposed involvement in student unrest the latter charge is probably juster. One heterodox psychiatrist declares:

Society highly values its normal man. It educates children to lose themselves and to become absurd, and thus to be normal.[54]

Of schizophrenia he says, 'The judgement that the diagnosed patient is behaving in a biologically dysfunctional (hence patho-logical) way is, we believe, premature, and one that we shall hold in parenthesis.'[55] Despite their theories of humility before the facts and the evolutionary nature of scientific growth, scientists are no more willing to change their intellectual and operational habits than anyone else. The very specialization on which their progress has depended renders them prone to distorted views when any holistic judgement, as in moral matters, is to be made. A psychologist has recently urged his colleagues, now equipped with batteries of bleeping machines, to take a 'great leap backwards' to the 'string-and-cardboard psychology of our forefathers, when experimenter and subject faced each other in a warm, friendly relationship'.[56]

The main anxiety over science is not simply that it has failed to yield a viable scioethics or that its sciomorality has proved irrelevant to human needs and moropractice, but that it has brought to light facts and into being technologies we might have been better without. Scientific investigation, which was to have demonstrated the essential unity and equality of mankind, has increasingly come to demonstrate differences. Racial colour, once attributed to environmental factors like sun or diet, is now seen to be genetically determined. To the same origin are referred not only physical but intellectual, emotional and moral factors, though the extent and manner of operation are still debated. It has been shown that the animals we like or dislike are those that look more or less like us;[57] depth psychology reveals that we are unconsciously more prejudiced than we appear on the surface; anthropology lights up hierarchies and class divisions even in the most primitive societies. But most disturbing of all has been a realization that 'advanced' communities, which imagined they had gained a moral superiority, proportional to their hardware, have unleashed a technology they seem powerless to control, whose minions have scaled new heights of savagery.

Concentration camps, mass exterminations, world wars, and atom bombs are no 'relapse into barbarism', but the unrepressed implementation of the achievements of modern science, technology, and domination.[58]

Knowledge has abundantly turned out to be power, megadeath power. We have been brought closer together without becoming friendlier and our tensions have multiplied. So has our population. Death control has proved easier than birth control, just as every technique depending on mass action has surpassed those needing individual attention. Certainly there is the possibility of compulsory sterilization by state intervention, but democracies are understandably wary. The only use of eugenics on any big scale has not been for the 'perfection' or even the improvement of man but for the extermination of unpopular minorities.

War, rather than creative research, has been the prime stimulus of scientific advance.[59] In its pursuit we have forged instruments that have increased as well as those which have reduced uncertainty in military calculation. Yet these are one and all assumed to be more reliable than the unaided human intelligence. For the users of technology tend to accord it an infallibility its inventors may once have claimed but rarely pretend to today. So, while the 'hot line' comforts, misinterpreted signals on a radar screen pose a constant threat to world peace. When hostilities do break out, weaponry shows new potentialities. Most obviously it has a destructive power and ability to endanger future generations never before encountered. From our viewpoint its most notable feature is its impersonality. Face-to-face fighting is psychologically and morally responsive. It allows submission signals to be given and received; after a certain time it builds up satiation and moral revulsion at slaughter. Press-button warfare does not. Millions can be killed without any moral feelings stirring in the killer, or any feelings at all save delight at the efficiency of some lethal toy. Today the difference between death and megadeath is two syllables of nonchalant speech.

The explosion of ideas has likewise become too great for a single person to comprehend. What first excited now tends to deaden or disturb. The problem of unmanageable bigness laps around us like the processes of a giant amoeba, yearly widening the gulf between the individual and the state, the non-expert and the expert, one generation and the next. New situations develop before we have adjusted to the old, and so many unfamiliar moral decisions present themselves we long to sink into the amorality of the world itself or the scientific tools that probe it. Even 'life' and 'death'[60] have lost their old meanings, and we are bewildered by moral choices – the keeping alive of foetal monsters or the vegetating victims of accidents, disease and age, the transplantation of hearts and later perhaps of brains or heads,[61] artificial insemination donor (A.I.D.), even in time the celebrated test-tube baby – where once nature took its course, freeing us from responsibility. There is every prospect soon of being able to dictate the sex of our children; but while this will foil chance production of unwanted boys or girls, with their individual problems, it may well cause male imbalance with graver social problems. Labour-saving machinery has itself caused concern. As the Luddites long ago feared, it has led to fully automated factories, offices and transport containers, which will in the end create massive redundancy, especially in those sections of the population lacking imagination for executive planning or creative leisure. Data banks [62] and electronic gadgetry are a growing threat to our privacy, while our capacity for polluting the earth and depleting vital resources daily mounts. In treating illnesses like severe depression by prefrontal lobotomy (leucotomy), doctors may actually impair our capacity to form moral judgements. Little has been done by them, or by psychologists and sociologists, to improve it. They have not discovered 'universally acknowledged' moral truths or views on private property and marital fidelity. Man has not emerged as a god but looks rather more like a thing. Or like a collection of things dismantled for investigation. Can they ever be put together again?

8 Endoethics and Endomorality

When Camus discovered that science had dissolved into poetry, he drew three consequences: 'my revolt, my freedom and my passion'.[1] André Gide wrote existentially[2] about an *acte gratuit* or unmotivated crime committed for the sense of liberation it gave, a murder without a cause by a rebel without a cause. Similarly motivated, or unmotivated, was the hero of the James Dean film,[3] typifying a whole generation of fictional – and all too often real – tearaways in revolt against society, however constituted; aliens to the world and the underworld, to overground and underground movements; devoting their lives to the pursuit of 'kicks'. Though for the most part bookless, if not uneducated, they do in fact have an ideological heritage over a century old. Their spiritual ancestors are those who proclaimed that, as the individual's only sense of 'authenticity' is in his own consciousness, so he is the only valid source of moral authority.

In the 1840s, as the Romantic Movement was washing away the last grey matter of the Enlightenment, three important writers were in revolt against established intellectual and ethical systems. One of them, Proudhon, became well known in his own lifetime as the founder of modern anarchism. Another, Sören Kierkegaard, was ignored in his lifetime but is now hailed as the father of existentialism. The third, Max Stirner, is still largely unknown outside his native Germany, though some of his ideas influenced Nietzsche and through him Nazism. For Proudhon science and reason were valid. The trouble was they had not been properly applied. Threatening the old regimes was republicanism, but its source was a vague *res publica* (the public thing) and its political content therefore meagre. 'Even kings are republicans.'[4] He believed that 'the authority of man over man is inversely proportional to the stage of intellectual development which that society has reached' and called for 'scientific social-ism'.

Property and royalty have been crumbling to pieces ever since the world began. As man seeks justice in equality, so society seeks order in anarchy. Anarchy, – the absence of a master, of a sovereign, – such is the form of government to which we are every day approximating.[5]

As such, anarchism might have been dealt with in the chapter on politics, either in its own right or as a division of one or other of the chosen sections. Historically it has close associations with socialism and communism. Out of it grew Nihilism, one of whose exponents, Peter Kropotkin, criticized 'collectivists' for wanting to abolish capitalism but retain representative government and an unequal wage system. So he announced:

We shall build on new foundations, those of Communism and of Anarchy, and not those of Individualism, Authority, and State's Charter.[6]

But he was friendly with many English Radicals and Bradlaugh claimed the nihilists were 'not socialists' but were 'striving for political freedom and a constitutional form of government'.[7]

If the anarchists believed that politics grew out of individual freedom – but not economic freedom – they were less confident of the origin of morality. Most of them chose to ignore ethics as an abstract discipline, though their censure of the existing structure of society was largely moral. Stirner was prepared to follow anarchy to the end and thus created not only Individualist Anarchism but also endoethics.[8] Hitherto, he complained, ethics had been based on collectivist abstractions, religious, irreligious, political, philosophical.

What is not is supposed to be my concern. First and foremost, the Good Cause, then God's cause, the cause of mankind, of truth, of freedom, of humanity, of justice; further, the cause of my people, my prince, my fatherland; finally, even the cause of Mind, and a thousand other causes. Only *my* cause is never to be my concern.[9]

However described, all the acceptable causes were, in his view, religious, and were often so-called: the 'religion of love', the 'religion of freedom', 'political religion'.[10] Thus ethics and morality trailed behind religion, promoting worthless ideas like chastity and selflessness. Truth, morality, justice and light were regarded as 'sacred'; rationalists censured Christianity for things that were 'unchristian'; while 'he who attacks morality itself gets both to deal with'.[11] All this is humbug. God himself is represented as a supreme egoist. In a godless world man must pursue his own egoism. The individual is 'unique'. Stirner's final message is bleak:

If I concern myself for myself, the unique one, then my concern rests on its transitory, mortal creator, who consumes himself, and I may say: All things are nothing to me.[12]

Such views are likely to appeal to rather unclubbable people and to prove fissiparous in any organization they may succeed in establishing. Claiming derivation from Stirner is a small body in Paris[13] calling itself *Les Amis de Jules Bonnot* (the Friends of Jules Bonnot, leader of a French 'Bonnie and Clyde' gang). Other descendants, whom Stirner would almost certainly have disowned, are latterday demonists. Best known of these was Aleister Crowley, the 'Great Beast', who believed in 'the law of the strong'[14] to support the law of the self. Two of his 'commandments' are:

Do what thou wilt shall be the whole of the law.
    Thou hast no right but to do thy will. Do that, and no other shall say nay.[15]

Though 'love under will'[16] is the law, 'man has the right to kill those who would thwart these rights'.[17] In the same tradition is the American Church of Satan,[18] whose founder declares:

Basically the principles of Satanism are contained in the first words of Faust's Homunculus, 'I live, therefore I must act.' We're here, and we'd damned well better make the best of it and not look beyond this life.[19]

His *Satanic Bible* reverses the Sermon on the Mount and urges: 'Be simple animal man, indulge your appetites, hate your enemies with a whole heart, and if someone smites you smash him.' Not only are cults of this sort regularly aired in glossy magazines and trendy 'current affairs' radio and television programmes throughout the world, but there seems much truth in the Satanists' claim, 'What we advocate is what most Americans practice.'

Lenin observed that 'anarchism has failed to give anything even approximating a true solution of the concrete political problems, viz. must the old state machine be *smashed*? and *what* should be put in its place?'[20] The same is true of moral forces. For Crowley such hardly existed. And for Stirner? While rejecting morality he believed his views brought 'moral' benefits. Arguing for the promotion of selfishness as the basis of telling the truth, he insisted that 'everyone would easily understand how by lying he fools away that confidence in him which he hopes to awaken in others . . . Nobody believes a liar even when he tells the truth.'[21] If the matter had been put to them many of the collectivist anarchists might have agreed, but on the whole they seemed to accept socialist or communist politicoethics and politicomorality, or a sentimental version of Christoethics and Christomorality. In moral, as in other matters, the hippie-anarchists of the modern youth movement have no settled or well-articulated views. Nor do they enjoy the sympathy of the American Satanists, who dismiss them as 'weak freaks'.

Other movements, or rather trends, are really based on endo-ethics and endomorality. Within the humanist movement are upholders of 'individual morality', whose text could be the line of Karl Popper's: 'It is I who must decide whether to accept the standards of any authority as good or bad.'[22] Crossing all ideological frontiers without discovering a common spring of morality are the existentialists. Those of a religious bent can quote St Augustine: 'Love God and do as you like.'[23] To this Kierkegaard added a similar analysis to Stirner's: that only man's personal consciousness, his own unique feelings and will are real to him. It is his 'existence', then that of other people and things, which is important and not his or their 'essence', which is dis-covered, if at all, later. The rationalists only stultify man, while the scientists chop him up and lose his will. Nothing better comes from politics. 'The idea of socialism and community cannot save this age.'[24] Ethical theories are pointless. Only by a personal discovery of God do we know what to do, and this we can gain only by a 'leap of faith'. Atheist existentialists do not want or need this prop, though it is less certain what they do rely on.

The most obvious objection to endoethics and endomorality is that individuals do not grow up in isolation but in some sort of community. All the evidence suggests that in those rare cases where this is not so no moral sense develops at all. It might even be called perverse to use words like 'ethics' and 'morality' in a purely personal context. They surely involve our relations with other people. Now, 'endoethics' and 'endomorality' (from the Greek *endon*, within) are words I have coined, and the more full-blooded of the individualist anarchists do not lay claim to them. Yet there is in the writings of Crowley an uneasy bravado, as if he is conscious of not living in a moral void. When we come to the existentialists we find great attention given to morality, and often to moralizing, but we are still awaiting a consistent ethical theory in their writings. In 1946 the atheist Jean–Paul Sartre announced that existentialism was 'a humanism'.[25] Those who do not follow him in this usually call themselves Jewish or Protestant or Catholic existentialists. So perhaps after all they derive their ethics and morality from some irreligious or religious tradition outside existentialism. There is, however, the danger that people without these traditions will hop on the existentialist bandwagon and seek to justify any excess of 'moral' relativity. It is interesting to note that the movement has flourished during and immediately after major wars, with the irrationalism, anxiety and demoralization they represent. (That they cultivate *camaraderie* and selflessness is largely a myth of old soldiers and romantic novelists.) The egoistic capers of Crowley will be regarded by most as an amusing aberration or a sick joke rather than a sinister threat, but egoistic behaviour in this century has become a matter of grave public concern. Endoethics and endomorality may be illusory, but the actions of those who treat them as realities are not.

Part Three
Nucleoethics and Moral Influences

9 A Fresh Look

Readers who have patiently gone through the last section will, if it has achieved its purpose, have lost confidence in the power of ethical theories to explain man's moral motivation or produce a universally valid moral system, and of moral systems to promote universally desired moropractice. These theories are based on world-views which it is not the purpose of this book to evaluate, though I am bound to say I find some of them more plausible than others. But none of them, in my submission, has any relevance to human moral needs. On balance, for practical reasons to follow, their effects are likely to be morally detrimental. All of them are concerned with ideas which are interesting; which have been, and will no doubt continue to be, the answer to many an intellectual's prayer; which, however deplored or deplorable, it would have been futile to try to abort. Some of them, while claiming universality adduce little or no 'evidence' which any lawyer or scientist would accept, and even boast of their appeal to intuition or faith, whereby they cease to be amenable to either acceptance or refutation.

It may be that they fulfil some deep psychological need of the individual believer. In the limited sense in which 'want' has been used earlier, people believe what they want to believe.[1] Mental illness can often be regarded as an escape to a phantasy world from the individual's unresolved problems in this one; and ideological commitment, especially of a fanatical and exclusive sort, may represent this tendency within the range of normality. According to the general climate of opinion, state of knowledge or social need, one particular ideology may gain an ascendancy in one community at one time. As his knowledge or his circumstances change, the individual may himself be converted from one ideology to another, while ideological shifts are visible in society at large wherever there has been prolonged research. Sometimes this involves a reversion to an earlier idea, rediscovered and reformulated. There are, additionally, notions which have been discredited and seem unlikely to return, and it would be perverse to deny an evolution of knowledge. But intellectual notions may be incidentals and not essentials in our attitudes to the world and other people, infinitely varied, highly personal and unlikely ever to gain universal assent.

If that is so, it is clear that any ethical theory based on a specific ideology is not drawing on all the relevant data of human experience, and any moral system that may be deduced from it is at best valid for believers in the ideology. It is important to stress 'at best'. After the fashion of devotees the foregoing chapters dealt with world-views as if they lived in isolation in a social vacuum. Obviously they do not. It is much to be doubted if there has ever been a community so small, isolated, closed and populated entirely by unimaginative conformists, that there was unanimity of belief within it. In our own societies the individual is bombarded by a variety of contradictory and mutually exclusive views on every possible subject. The most dictatorial state cannot entirely eliminate travel, heterodox books or stencilled broadsheets, foreign broadcasts picked up on transistor radios, underground political movements or churches; and is powerless to deal with the person-to-person transmission of ideas, experiences, memories and dreams. Even if it should become possible, as some claim, to pass on uniform memories through chemicals in drinking water, it appears unlikely that those responsible could ever agree among themselves on a consistent philosophy in a world context, or that a single individual could ever gain such a position of power. If he did, he would himself be the product of an amalgam of world-views absorbed in his own lifetime.

World-views that 'promote morality' may turn out to have little or no connection with ethics. Their content is often intellectual rather than moral. They tell us what we ought to think rather than how we ought to behave. Moral systems put forward in their name are not really derived from them but have some other source. But where there is some real connection they may still have no relevance to the lives of individuals or even to whole communities. To a greater or lesser degree they are ideal rather than practical, static rather than dynamic, general rather than particular. Inevitably they deal with people and situations as abstractions, simplifications; they arise from some body of thought which, whether or not it claims to be absolute and unchanging, is in fact codified under particular circumstances and on certain assumptions and then assumed to be valid for different circumstances and in spite of contrary assumptions; they are more concerned with issues and trends than with problems and particularities. Sometimes they are better adapted to relations between nations, classes or other groups of people than to interpersonal relations. Sometimes a concentration on interpersonal relations or individual satisfaction ignores and distracts from the achievement of social justice.

To illustrate a few of the above points we may take the example of a widespread moral injunction, 'Thou shalt not kill',[2] derived from an equally widespread ethical view, by no means confined to religionists, of the 'sanctity of life'. Clearly this is generally laudable. No one would be happy if the contrary view prevailed: that life is worthless and it does not matter what you do to it. But the embargo on killing is really of little help. Outside communities of Jains and one or two other Hindu, Buddhist or Christian sects, nobody takes it literally. Of course, we say, it doesn't apply to killing other animals, or killing people in self-defence, war and capital punishment – in some kind of order of descending acceptability. By 'kill' we are asked to understand 'murder'. This is a little more practical. But war crimes tribunals and general courts are still called on to decide such matters as Geneva Conventions, *mens rea*, minimum force required to overpower, and other subtleties not at once apparent in the simple injunction. Everything depends on how 'murder' is defined by the appropriate court, and this is often a political or legal matter rather than a moral one. Can the individual be expected to be an expert in these disciplines? If he is not, is his ignorance itself immoral or criminal or both? But suppose we overlook the difficulty of definitions. We find that in passing from 'kill' to 'murder' we have undercut our original ethical ground. For if we justify manslaughter in a variety of circumstances, we clearly do not hold *life* to be 'sacred'. Something else has become 'sacred': oneself (killing in self-defence), national integrity (war), public order (capital punishment). If abortion be deemed a form of 'killing', further difficulties arise. Moral decisions are much more complicated than we were led to believe by the moralists or the moral philosophers.

Most of those who have stressed the 'sanctity of life' have not believed it themselves. Very often they have justified killing in ways the unenlightened human being would be unlikely to adopt, for reasons which do not occur to the lower animals: holy wars, ritual sacrifices, witch burning, heresy hunting. And so with other ethical ideals and moral absolutes. By concentrating on pleasant-sounding phrases, stressing their 'positive' approach to the world, luxuriating in idealism, moralists ingratiate themselves with followers and potential followers, undermine the position of critics and rationalize their own motives. Not only have the grand ethical abstractions done little to promote morality and less, as we shall see, to promote moropractice, they have often proved actual disasters. When it has not been simply maudlin, 'universal love' has been the vehicle of ferocious paternalism and self-righteous possessiveness, colonialism and imperialism. 'Patriotism' is, as Samuel Johnson long ago observed, 'the last refuge of a scoundrel'.[3] In the name of 'duty' every cruelty has been justified and every decent impulse silenced. 'Honour' has taken the most dog-eared leaves out of the books of patriotism and duty. More calls for 'sacrifice' have sounded from palaces and been answered in hovels than any other cant known to man. 'Adoration' and 'veneration' have been used by the old to restrain the young from copulation, masturbation and other simple pleasures.

I do not deny that in many of these ethical abstractions there is a kernel of truth from which we can all take nourishment. The fact that in the right atmosphere their note awakens a response that harmonizes with universal feelings cannot be ignored. But in so far as this response is universal it is spontaneous. It does not need to be elicited. Nothing can in fact keep it back. Ethical theories and theoreticians are morally redundant. My point is that where these feelings are universal they are most likely to be in tune with the biological needs of man for solidarity, security, mutual respect, affection. Now, spontaneous feelings are not necessarily moral, just as the first answer that comes into our heads is not necessarily the right one. But they are not to be ignored lightly. A craving for food may be pathological; perpetual anorexia (loss of appetite) undoubtedly is. Today doctors are more willing to admit than a few years ago that desires for particular kinds of food are often a good indication of bodily requirements. It is the same with moral feelings. Like farm animals they are more tasteless when caged and force-fed.

When people are whipped up by ideological clamour into unnatural states of activity – and it is possible to do this by various techniques – the outcome needs to be examined carefully. I suggest that it is more likely to be disadvantageous than advantageous to the human race. No doubt the organizers of the more 'successful' crusades, pogroms and religious or political witch-hunts were gratified by the results. To them it was a splendid illustration that people were not entirely sunk in 'materialism' and 'decadence', but were able to respond imaginatively to a moral 'challenge'. It is often said today that we must give young people more opportunities for 'idealism' and 'inspire' them to 'service'. This is not only nonsense but dangerous nonsense. There are plenty of opportunities for idealism, for old and young alike; and all over the world they are constantly being taken, with minimal fuss, by those genuinely interested. People can be brainwashed or rabble-roused or intoxicated into activities normally alien to them, but they cannot be truly inspired as a propaganda exercise. 'Inspirational' exhortations, like 'inspiring' music, may be quite meaningless to those who do not understand or emotionally respond to them. Increasingly it is obvious to young people today that most of those who talk of Alexander, Hercules, Hector, Lysander, great names and 'idealism' are themselves busily looking after number one, have some axe to grind and need to be watched. Unostentatious example is the most effective pedagogic tool, however distasteful it may be to demagogues. What young people need to be taught is not idealism – which is either unnecessary or dangerous – but realism. They need knowledge of what the world is really like, what are its problems, what are its dangers, what are the techniques that have proved useful in coping with similar situations in the past. Cynicism is stultifying if it becomes the perpetual sneer. So is scepticism if it believes nothing. But if these attitudes produce a sense of realism that takes nothing on trust, especially when it is high-sounding and conspicuously 'noble', they will in the long run prove desirable.

Biologically we have moments of activity and rest according to need. States of hyperactivity are seldom biological – unless they are pathological. They can be induced by the grand vision, the consuming passion; but for every such vision or passion as solidifies into a work of creative genius, a thousand erupt into violence or fanaticism. Especially is this so when there is some more or less hidden reward like post-mortem blessings for participation in a crusade or *Jihad*. At best 'idealism' leads to overoptimistic expectations, whose failure to materialize produces bitter disillusion and reaction. In political terms one thinks of the more grandiose 'five-year plans' in the second and third worlds, John F. Kennedy's 'new frontier', Lyndon B. Johnson's 'great society' and Harold Wilson's 'technological revolution'. Originally they were all spelt with capitals; now they hardly rate spelling at all. This is not to say that these regimes have not known their successes or that the statesmen concerned were not men of a certain sincerity and ability, but their achievements are overshadowed by the collapse of their castles in the air. It is said we have not had enough political idealism. The truth is we have had too much. What we need is more informed *Realpolitik*.

It is the same with the great social problems of the world. Where they have been recognized as moral issues they have been assigned to the moralists or the theologians. Poverty has been explained as the fate of those who will not work or were born inferior or were wicked in former lives or are made to suffer now before being rewarded in heaven. Among the idle rich, smitten with conscience from time to time, it is the occasion for them to indulge in periodic charity, gain a good opinion of themselves once more, and look forward to some earthly or heavenly award as philanthropists. Large numbers of peoples neither in tangible need nor in idle luxury, who do not regard themselves as better off than they deserve to be and are not called on to vote for or against poverty or to administer charity, tend not to regard the issue as a moral one at all. The result is that practically nothing throughout the world has been done to tackle it. If the approach had been a social one, even a biological one, poverty would be seen as not just a sign of failure, a distasteful mockery of civilization and human know-how, but a source of rancour and instability. Likewise, public expenditure on social provisions like contraception,[4] abortion, welfare workers, child psychiatrists, youth employment officers and the like might be fostered by talking less in idealistic terms and more in the realistic language of the cost to the community where they are not provided, when unwanted children, delinquents, criminals and misfits flood hospitals, prisons and other repair agencies. Many of these social provisions have been bedevilled not only by a failure to make them moral imperatives but by the attitudes of certain religious groups which have declared obstruction to them to be in the highest degree moral. Thus many people have been led into actions or inactivity which would never have appealed to them as social animals but gain a new dimension in the name of 'idealism'. We need to drop from the rarefied heights of ideology to the plains of biology.

This then is nucleoethics. Not scioethics based on some abstraction like the noosphere or evolutionary destiny, but a recognition that morality rises from the needs of man as a social animal and that these are complex variables. Why 'nucleoethics'? Because I am proposing it in a nuclear age when the risks of ideological miscalculation are greater than ever before? Partly. But the name is more direct than that. Its root is *nucleus*, a kernel; its modern analogy, the Rutherford-Bohr atomic centre of tightly packed but identifiable particles, some charged, some uncharged, all held together by powerful forces but capable of disintegration under special conditions. It represents the paring away of shells of illusion, of fibrous layers of happiness and other principles, of all-encompassing ideologies that give the world a neat casing with a glossy exterior, so that we can reach the real kernel of man in society. There is no mystique about it to rival the ideologies that have promoted ethics hitherto. It is not an ideology itself; it recognizes that all past and present ideologies have been moral failures however they may otherwise have succeeded, regards this statement as an observation and not as the formulation of a new ideology, and thinks it most unlikely that any future ideology could have a moral triumph. Though prediction is dangerous, it is hard to conceive of the emergence of any world-view – as distinct from a new church, political party or scientific theory – radically different from those we have hitherto known. Nucleoethics has some ideological consequences. It does not postulate the death of ideology, but forecasts that none will ever become universal and a basis for world morality or comprehensive and a basis for personal morality; that there is no corpus of morality the preaching or teaching of which will make people better; that moral awareness as an aspect of life is a function of environmental influences and individual potentialities, multicentric in its points of growth and forming part of a normally indivisible psycho-physical continuum; that moral infections must be treated empirically by the moral antibiotic that proves effective in each case. These influences, growth points, infections and antibiotics will now be outlined.

Those attitudes which belong to nucleoethics have been churned over many decades and matured in recent years. It is tempting to relate them to our *Bomb Culture*,[1] and doubtless this has played a part. But it is easy to exaggerate its effect. The feeling that we have unparalleled anxieties to cope with and dangers to avert can be observed in each generation. When one considers the extent of the contemporary stockpile of nuclear weapons and chemical and bacteriological agents, it is certainly plausible to state that the dangers facing us today are unmatched; but it may be questioned to what extent they have entered the consciousness of more than a small minority. A fair proportion of this group are 'natural' drop-outs, who would feel themselves alienated from any settled society, however loving, peaceful and sympathetic it might chance to be. At the same time, there are a number of socially active, well-informed people who are gravely disturbed by the lethal potency of modern conflict. Nevertheless, a preoccupation with possible disasters is always a minority interest.

One of the features of division of labour is the handing over to 'specialists' and 'experts' of responsibility for worrying about such threats and reporting to the rest of us from time to time. Though this has its obvious defects, it enables us to get on with our own jobs and preserve our own sanity. An obsession by ordinary people with universal hazards is often a way of escape from their personal problems[2] and may result in a paralysing neurosis that is as ineffective in finding solutions as outright apathy. Now, some may say that these anxieties and neuroses – if that is what they are – are a peculiar feature of our own age and this is responsible for the crisis of authority noted at the beginning of this book. Perhaps. I find little evidence. The majority of people seem to pursue their daily lives in more or less confident calm. In the United States the boom in psychoanalysis is as much an index of affluence as of anxiety; and what sense of insecurity there is, which is probably growing, comes from social problems like Negro and student unrest that have no direct connection with armaments, war scares or technology at large. I do not wish to play down the fear factor in today's arms race, but believe we lose sight of the day-to-day anxiety that used to beset our ancestors confronted by savage beasts, the uncontrolled and unexplained forces of nature, disease, hunger, arbitrary and often hostile spirits of the night, the dead, forest, mountain, fire.

But, supposing that *Weltschmerz* (world pain) is a dominant factor of our times. Why should it lead to a collapse of authority? Why should that lead to a challenge of moral authorities? What has happened to morality while this has been going on? We know that anxiety, such as that which results during war-time, may well serve to strengthen authority, political and religious. For reasons given earlier this does not necessarily promote moropractice, though it may lead to a redefinition of *mores* and *immores* which conceals the true extent of criminality and delinquency. For example, murder and robbery are masked by 'legitimate' killing and commandeering of supplies at the front, while at home minor crimes are less likely to be reported and detected than during more settled times. In such circumstances ordinary democratic processes are actively or tacitly set aside, patriotism and church-going flourish. But this is where anxiety is the product of some physical event like a hot war. The anxiety of our own day has, it would appear, a mental source. Few of those who complain of it are, as far as we can see, physically suffering, nor is some economic, military or other disaster likely to overtake them tomorrow. In this vague situation an appeal to traditional authorities seems less relevant. Furthermore, it may in many cases be said that it is the collapse of those authorities, though dimly apprehended, which has provoked the anxiety in the first place. The remaining chapters in this part of the book will deal with some of the reasons for this collapse without its producing, despite the jeremiads, a collapse of morality itself. The last part will deal more fully with moral prospects.

We may begin with two of the questions asked at the start of the previous paragraph. It is unlikely that a collapse of authority in society, as earlier set out (not to be exaggerated because it was concentrated), leads to a challenge of moral authorities. Rather the reverse. Though unrest usually leads to agonizing talk that these authorities will be undermined if it continues, their erosion is already far advanced. For it is the weakening of traditional institutions, whose job it is to provide stability and authority, that habitually activates any tendency to social anarchy. The causes of this weakening are complex, but they are usually matters of personnel or faith. That is, either the apostles of the system discredit it by their activities, or it becomes incredible. In all the systems discussed, both factors can be observed today. But world-views have always attracted unworthy disciples and strained the belief of some, while it could be said that there have been few periods in history when theologians, theoreticians and politicians were more conscientious. What is true is that they are more exposed and so more vulnerable. Basically it is the systems themselves that have become incredible. Partly this is because of their internal contradictions, already outlined. Partly there has been the expansion of new ideas or a new look at old institutions which, while not directly repudiating these systems, has subtly sabotaged them.

One of the features of modern life is its anti-intellectualism: suspicion, dislike or boycott of intellectuals; according status to those who do or those who own and not those who know; impatience at theories which do not bring obvious material advantages. It is all very distasteful, especially to poor intellectuals, and in certain respects, notably cultural, may have been damaging to society. But it is part of an attitude that 'actions speak louder than words',[3] that knowing *what* instead of *how to* is of little interest outside the ivory tower, that the extinction of intellectual mammoths and the invention of plastics in our society have made ivory towers obsolete. Replacement of scholars and mystics by businessmen and engineers has not been the disaster for the masses that 'creative' communicators have made it out to be. This mood was, in the usual way, pioneered by men of ideas, by 'intellectuals' if you like, but they were intellectuals outside the mainstream of the older disciplines and the ethical theories we have discussed. Not surprisingly, their influence turned out to be 'subversive'. Of one of them it has been said that he 'applied his talents and his longevity to wrecking the educational philosophy which had been built up through twenty-five centuries of classical and Christian experience'.[4] Also not surprisingly, the movement originated in the land of 'know-how', the United States.

From the Greek *pragmata* (acts, affairs or business) Kant evolved the adjective *pragmatisch*. The English 'Pragmatism' was coined by Charles Sanders Peirce and his Harvard friends in the 1870s and reached the public in an article 'How to Make Our Ideas Clear'.[5] From the start the pragmatists were concerned with communication and the meaning of what we say. In this they are related to the logical positivists and linguistic analysts. A statement like 'Ferric oxide consists of iron and oxygen' depends for its truth on what names chemists have decided to give to three materials and what happens when ferric oxide is heated in a laboratory with limestone and coke. But Pragmatism claims to deal with more difficult intellectual statements, 'that is, of those upon which reasoning may hinge'.[6] It differs from Positivism in that it accepts 'scholastic realism', 'retention of a purified philosophy' and 'the main body of our instinctive beliefs'.[7] We are led to intellectual inquiry by an uneasy feeling that our existing beliefs are wrong. What we then use is the Pragmatic Principle:

Consider what effects, that conceivably might have practical bearings, we conceive the object of our conception to have. Then our conception of these effects is the whole of our conception of the object.[8]

If the practical effects deduced from our new ideas accord better with our experience than those deduced from the old, we revise our views and accept some new 'truth'. That relieves our tension. But at the back of our minds we know that in the future further adjustments must be made; so we do not have any notion of absolute truth. Rejecting the possibility of infallibility, we commit ourselves to 'Fallibilism'.

Disciples of Peirce and people who have never heard of him but like the 'pragmatic' approach have made his theory increasingly pop, so that in later life he adopted a new name, 'Pragmaticism', which was 'ugly enough to be safe'[9] from adoption and perversion. One disciple, F. C. S. Schiller, called his pragmatic theory 'Humanism'; another, John Dewey, to whom was attributed the 'wrecking . . . of classical and Christian experience' referred to above, chose 'Instrumentalism'. William James, who first popularized and jazzed up Peirce, had quaint metaphysical views of his own about 'pure experience' and 'radical empiricism' that need not concern us. What is important is that he used Pragmatism so as to be 'tough-minded with regard to any question of natural fact, and tender-minded with respect to morals and theology'.[10] He thought he could give a common-sense explanation of all the tricky statements made by religious and ethical theorists, which, as we have seen, the tendency is now to regard as having either a mystical meaning or no meaning at all. His formula was:

The whole meaning of a conception expresses itself in practical consequences, either in the shape of conduct to be recommended or in that of experience to be expected if the conception is true.[11]

Religious beliefs and moral codes were justified if they made people happy and we should not make any further inquiry into their 'truth'. Peirce did not believe that happiness was a 'practical consequence' and thought these questions were beyond the scope of Pragmatism. Though he was himself a freethinker James was trying to rescue traditional attitudes. Dewey, on the other hand, thought Pragmatism quite dissolved the ground of religious belief and the 'moral law'. Because he advocated 'participatory democracy' and was for many years the honorary president of the American League for Industrial Democracy, from which the militant Students for a Democratic Society originated, he has been blamed for the recent wave of student unrest, although his views were far from anarchic. Indeed, he once said:

Let us control or regiment things in order to make men free.[12]

As popularly understood, 'pragmatism' has come to mean that truth is 'what works' or 'what is convenient' or 'expediency' and is the favourite toy of party politicians. As such it is regarded as amoral or downright immoral, and it could certainly have these consequences. By this criterion the only objection to Belsen and Dachau would be that they failed in their intention to preserve the Third Reich and achieve the 'final solution' of the Jewish 'problem'. But if we set aside these latter-day distortions of the theory, we can see that it is a useful tool in deciding many practical and moral issues, that its subversion of traditional dogma has often been healthy. Today we do not have – or need not have – abstract views of conduct. The important question to ask is: What are its practical consequences? Let us take the question of premarital sexual intercourse. To the religionist this is a sin because it is against the putative will of God or the teachings of the church, and represents a defilement of the body, which is 'the temple of the Holy Ghost'.[13] It is also immoral because it is against the natural or moral law and the conventions of respectable society. The pragmatist knows nothing of these objections, save by hearsay. He merely asks: Will the activity cause personal or social benefit or harm?

Practically everyone will agree that the production of unwanted children and the transmission of venereal diseases are harmful both socially and personally, and if these are inevitable consequences of intercourse very strong arguments must be given to justify freedom. It would, for example, have to be shown that sexual deprivation led young people into aggressive crime and nations into militarism, and these were worse than unwanted children and V.D. If, however, by contraception, hygiene and antibiotics the practical ill-effects of intercourse can be avoided, the situation is entirely different. If the practical ill-effects of abstinence can also be avoided – by, for example, pep talks, sport, cold showers, surgical or chemical intervention to sublimate or remove sexual urges, or masturbation or some other sexual outlet as an alternative to intercourse – the question becomes socially neutral, or not a social question at all: that is, it involves an action which does not have either beneficial or harmful social consequences. If the practical ill-effects of abstinence cannot be avoided, then premarital intercourse becomes a social good. But, the moralist urges, there are the relations between the couple to be considered. Women, it is said, go to bed only with the men they expect to marry, so premarital intercourse represents some sort of masculine fraud. Now, it may be true that some men hold out false promises of marriage to some women, but the moral issue then is one of fraud and not of sex. In many, probably most, cases the woman no more anticipates marriage than the man. The moralist is not, however, lightly put down. Whether or not the couple realize it themselves, he argues, premarital sexual intercourse, save perhaps after a firm engagement, leads to promiscuity, which makes it impossible to form any lasting relationship in later life. Not only is this a moral consequence for unfortunate future partners, the disruption in family life that results will cause psychological problems for the children which may have social consequences; while even the affianced will lose mutual respect and have marital difficulties later.

In recent years there has been an interesting shift, among the upholders of purity, from religious, to abstract moral, to social grounds, a shift which itself testifies to the impact of pragmatism. Claims that premarital sex unsettles marriage can be judged pragmatically. It is true that in every indulgence immediate pleasure may be followed by regrets and if these flow profoundly enough they will erode the banks of morality. Yet very often this happens because the individual has been educated to regard the action as 'wrong' and so productive of a 'guilt complex'. If the views of society and education change, the complex and regrets do not usually arise. A pragmatist is not particularly interested in the utilitarian happiness principle even if he follows James in regarding happiness as a practical consequence for the parties concerned. Rather is he likely to consider that on balance it is easier in a democratic society to control conception, venereal disease and education than biological urges, so he directs his attention to changing the views of society.

In great practical and moral issues like warfare there is scope for pragmatism. The idealist has tended to have two reactions to nuclear weapons. His first reaction was to denounce the 'balance of terror' as an 'obscenity' and overlook the very unpleasant effects conventional warfare has had. Naturally he was influenced by thoughts of the greater destructive potential of the new bombs; but it is arguable to what extent an offence is morally qualified by its size, though sanctions against it may well be.[14] Then he reached, one suspects, a new verdict. This was not advertised, but thereafter the Campaign for Nuclear Disarmament declined. Perhaps, after all, the bomb would be a deterrent and war in a nuclear age would become 'unthinkable'. So neurosis led to complacency. Meantime pragmatists like Herman Kahn ('Dr Strangelove') in his 'think-tank' at the Hudson

Institute continued to think the unthinkable, and played 'war games' not only with conventional weapons but also with nuclear weapons advancing up the rungs of 'escalation'.[15]

While man retains his aggressive impulses and politicians find they can stifle internal criticism by finding an external foe, while there are autonomous nations that can achieve, or think they can achieve, their ambitions by war, there will be nothing unthinkable about it, whether or not there is agreement not to use certain weapons. Nor will calling warfare 'immoral' help, for in all past conflicts there has been no dearth of moralists to find that the current struggle is morally neutral, or even praiseworthy. With our modern techniques, however, we must recognize that war poses a biological threat. As social animals with a will to live we need to turn from the idealists and the moralists and seek the advice of the pragmatists. One possible solution is chemical treatment with 'anti-hostility agents'[16] or electrical control of the aggression centre in the human brain. This suggestion will provoke outraged cries against interfering with human 'freedom' or 'dignity', as if the alternative of war promoted these excellent qualities. Naturally there are serious reservations about such interventions; but they are pragmatic ones. We must first be satisfied that creativity, 'divine discontent', our power to respond to and resist real threats to our survival are preserved. Other pragmatic solutions, involving the formation of an effective world peace-keeping force and international court (on foundations already established) or world government (which has long been a dream), must be investigated. What we cannot do is unlearn the technical knowledge we have gained. Nor is there much use moralizing about all men being brothers. Were not Cain and Abel brothers?

11 Technology

The most conspicuous product of science is technology. 'The world of the machines begins,' according to the communicator Marshall McLuhan, 'to assume the threatening and unfriendly countenance of an inhuman wilderness even less manageable than that which once confronted prehistoric man.' As a lover of the middle ages he believes that scholastic philosophy gave us 'an intelligible map of man and creation'; its by-product technology merely 'offers immediate comfort and profit'. As the 'medieval spirit of religious intensity and moral duty' still motivates it, there is 'much conflict of mind and confusion of purpose in producers and consumers alike'.[1] We have married a *Mechanical Bride* who may ultimately satisfy or devour us:

A single mechanical brain, of the sort developed at the Massachusetts Institute of Technology by Professor Norbert Wiener, when hitched to the telepathic mechanism of Professor Rhine, could tyrannize over the collective consciousness of the race exactly in comic-book or science-fiction style . . . From the point of view of civilized values, it is obvious that, as our powers of crime detection have advanced, the power to define vice or virtue has declined. In the same way, as market-research tyranny has developed, the object and ends of human consumption have been blurred. Knowhow has obliterated the why, what, and when.[2]

It is certainly right, as we saw in the chapter on scioethics, that we should not turn to science and scientists to solve the moral dilemmas of the ages, and that we should consider the social effects of technological advance before planning decisions are taken. For experience shows that once government, local government or private industry has undertaken massive invest-ment projects it is virtually impossible to scrap them on social grounds alone. Noise, pollution, smog are not just aesthetically distasteful to twentieth-century Pre-Raphaelites. In that they induce mental illness and physical diseases like cancer in innocent members of the public, wilful production of them must be regarded as a moral issue. Our knowledge of silencers, neutralizing agents and air filters is just as great as that of noxious processes. We simply will not take the trouble or incur the expense of prevention. And so with a wide range of domestic, industrial and road accidents. In many cases safety devices are known but for commercial reasons are not fitted or used. Workers on piece rates or bonus schemes may be just as guilty as manufacturers. The flesh indeed is willing, but the spirit is weak. For all these reasons it is idle to shrug off the effects of technology as purely technical. While shrinking from iron as 'the best and worst servant of humanity', able to 'bring death more speedily', Pliny the Elder added, 'Let the blame for such death be brought home to man and not to nature.'[3]

The world of machines need not be less manageable or as threatening and unfriendly as the wilderness that confronted prehistoric man. To most non-intellectuals, immediate comfort and profit are not only more intelligible but more satisfying than the medieval map of man and creation. Nor can it be said that the moropractice of today's industrialists is, by any reasonable standards, worse than that of medieval monks and friars, priests and popes. Whether or not mechanical brains will ever be feasible with all the complexity envisaged by M.I.T., Rhine's 'psycho-kinesis' (P.K. or the control of matter by mind) has been shown lacking in laboratory credentials.[4] Our difficulty in defining vice and virtue has no direct connection with the techniques of crime detection; while human consumption has always involved both essentials and those non-essentials we can afford and be per-suaded to buy, whatever the tyranny, or even in the absence, of market research. But if know-how has not obliterated the why, what and when, it has greatly influenced them. By its prolifera-tion in recent years it has undoubtedly been one of the influences undermining metaphysics and the old ethical systems. Indeed this is the thing that some people most hold against it.

The technologist is more concerned to ask why certain processes create certain products than why man should use these products, let alone why the species exists at all. It is when man is largely unable to manipulate the world that he asks questions about his and its ultimate reality. Intellectually individuals in all civilizations are peculiarly led to problems of this sort and peculiarly fertile in the answers they give. But however they may have enriched metaphysics, they have given little clarification to ethics and less to an understanding of natural laws. On the contrary. This book has attempted to show that by giving wrong ethical answers they have promoted foolish moral codes and *mores*. When man discovers the techniques of modifying his environment, he gives little attention to teleology (the study of 'purpose'[5] in the universe). Any great obsession today with this medieval preoccupation, outside the ranks of professional philosophers and theologians, might even be called a neurosis, if 'neurosis' be defined as unproductive worry over issues whose solution is both unlikely and irrelevant to the business of living. Giving attention to the details of the physical world is prejudicial to religious pursuits, if only through a worldly diversion of human interests and – in the enthusiast – passions. This is regardless of the questioning of dogma and scriptures that the scientific method directly promotes. It is also prejudicial to ethical speculation. On this account, no doubt, modern observers regard the technological revolution with greater alarm than mankind's growing interest in the acquisition of consumer goods would itself warrant. Technology becomes, for them, not just amoral but immoral.

What is morality, however, if not a concern for the day-to-day matters of human relations? In fostering manipulation of the environment along certain lines, technologists may promote wants rather than needs, things rather than people. But this is not intrinsic in the process. If properly channelled, practical concern is of greater moral value than ethical speculation or ideologizing about Man, a creature made in the image of God or of moral philosophers and having no existence outside their fancies. Theologians and metaphysicians tend, on the whole, to live comfortable lives serviced, according to their society, by men or machines. From this vantage-point they can afford to look down on the 'materialism' of lesser mortals, who have to struggle for their own little luxuries. In their professional lives they take the fullest advantage of electronics and the rest of the battery of industrial development. From scorning print technology, which few writers have found so advantageous, McLuhan has passed on to adoration of television technology, which, he enthuses, 'encourages unification and involvement'[6] and restores us to the solace and virtues of a medieval village. Now, this dichotomy of the communications media, with savage scorn for one sector and unstinted praise for the other, seems to me utterly perverse. But it is at least a recognition that technology itself is simply a tool which is morally neutral and can be employed for vicious or virtuous ends. These ends are the responsibility of everyone, scientist and non-scientist. Deriving from his expertise, the additional responsibility of the scientist is to advise us in advance what practical consequences may come from new inventions, though he may be as unable as anyone else to foretell all the social effects. So regular assessments must be made by the whole community, which should show the same biological adaptation in changing unsatisfactory technologies as the individual does in abandoning food that does not agree with him. As a modern writer has put it, 'Instead of rape technology we must have seduction technology, persuading nature to help us.'[7]

Before we become utterly despondent about machines and turn into latter-day Luddites, we should consider what some scientists have pointed out. The first is the German chemist Justus von Liebig, speaking in Munich a century ago. This was perhaps the hey-day of scioethics and sciomorality, but his observations are valid whatever one thinks of the scientific world-view:

The development of culture, i.e. the extending of man's spiritual domain, depends on the growth of the inventions which condition the progress of civilization, for through these new facts are obtained . . . The progress of Greek civilization was dependent essentially on the change of slave-labour into free, a transformation not supposable without the employment of natural forces, applied to labour-saving machines . . . Only the freeman, not the slave, has a disposition and interest to improve implements or to invent them; accordingly, in the devising of a complicated machine, the workmen employed upon it are generally co-inventors . . . The improvement of established industrial methods by slaves, themselves industrial machines, is out of the question . . . Future history will describe the victories of freedom which men achieved through investigation of the ground of things and of truth, victories won with bloodless weapons and in a struggle wherein morals and religion participated only as feeble allies.[8]

Of all the machines whose cold flesh has pressed chillingly against us, the most dreaded, since Mary Shelley's *Frankenstein*, is the robot. When there flickered no mechanical brain more sophisticated than a cash register, the most heinous consequences of this development were foretold. It was vaguely feared that computers would escape from rules and conditioning in a way human beings find largely impossible, and defy their programmes and programmers. Not only is this a groundless phantasy, the study of electronic brains has given us considerable insight into the functioning of our own. If this has provided tools for potential dictators and brainwashers, it has also equipped us to understand human 'systems', including moral processes. Only the determined pessimist supposes that this knowledge will inevitably be exploited for ill, that the biological resilience of man in confronting dangers and snatching worried prey out of the jaws of death, in turning knowledge, however dubiously and disastrously acquired, to ultimate account, will fail him now. On the contrary, as a science-fiction writer argues,

It may well be from ultra-intelligent robots that we will learn all the things that we have failed to learn despite the best efforts of our various religious and holy men.[9]

From the computer will come 'the possibility of breaking . . . the whole notion of a social order based on work . . . deeply embedded in the Puritan tradition'.[10] Then we could, if we chose, reverse the tendency towards 'planned obsolescence', which is largely a device to maintain the profits and employment to provide money for different classes of people to buy the short-lived products of other machines. But if there were no need to count new pence for new purchases, many would enjoy the novelty of frequent change. A 'throwaway' technology need not imply, as the frugal Puritan suggests, a throwaway morality. Yet the world of machines is unlikely to satisfy the emotional needs of all. One psychologist has posited two general classes of people: those who turn to the 'exact sciences' to escape from people and those who need the arts 'to take refuge from things in people'.[11] To combat the effects of 'mechanization' in Soviet life a Russian chemist[12] has developed a drug to banish black and blue moods. In the last section of this book we will look further into the moral implications of computer and drug technologies.

In regretting that 'we no longer have a rational basis for defining virtue or vice', McLuhan declares:

And the slogan 'Crime Does Not Pay' is the expression of moral bankruptcy in more senses than one. It implies that if crime could pay, then the dividing line between virtue and vice would disappear.[13]

Crime and its relation to morality will be considered in a later chapter. At this stage it should be noted that 'Crime Does Not Pay' is interpreted in both a moral and a material sense. From the one standpoint it is asserted that 'satisfaction' in the performance of a criminal act is outweighed by subsequent feelings of guilt and shame or fear of being found out. From the other, the financial rewards of crime are held to be surpassed, over a lifetime, by the fruits of honest toil. Neither consideration is to be dismissed in McLuhan's lofty way. If crime were not accompanied by disquieting feelings it would be nothing but behaviour met by arbitrary accusations without moral implications at all, and the institution of sanctions, whose purpose is mainly psychological, would break down. If substantial numbers of people derive satisfaction from what their community defines as 'crime', this suggests grave defects in education or a mislabelling of 'criminal' activity.

On the material side, it is nonsense to assume that a pay-off for criminals obliterates the boundary between *mores* and *immores*, though it may influence the populations of the two paddocks. What it implies is that criminals are better organized in their pursuits than society is in their detection and punishment. This may represent a failure of social will or some degree of political anarchy which reflects a moral *malaise*. It may simply be that one side rather than the other is exploiting technology more effectively. Would the British Great Train Robbery have been attempted if huge numbers of negotiable banknotes were not transported in trains devoid of security arrangements? It would be nice to think that everyone cherished the law and that persuasion could alone prevent crime. In a

significant number of cases, however, this approach is not working and has never worked. If crime does pay financially its
practitioners increase. Nor is it necessary or desirable to go to
the other extreme and initiate police violence on the Chicago
pattern, a tactic which always escalates. What is necessary is to
come to terms with technology and see that law-enforcers are
better equipped than law-breakers. Though machines are
morally neutral, they can, if only negatively, aid moropractice.

12   Admass

From technology comes production in an ever richer flow. But the flow would soon stop unless consumption opened sluice-gates at the other end. So modern society devotes much of its energies to facilitating consumption. Even with enough purchasing-power, people will not buy without wants and needs and the knowledge and impulse to satisfy them. This is obviously true of capitalist countries, which are often indicted as a conspiracy to create wants and pass them off as needs. But the socialist countries stage a similar operation. As expressed by Anastas Mikoyan, who studied American production methods and was put in charge of Russian foreign trade and canned goods,

The task of our Soviet advertising is to give people exact information about the goods that are on sale, to help to create new demands, to cultivate new tastes and requirements, to promote the sales of new kinds of goods and to explain their uses to the consumer.[1]

Whatever the formal structure of a country's economy, production cannot begin before the collection of a wide range of information about techniques, raw materials, labour force and likely markets. Whenever a country has skimped on this – and the Soviet Union has from time to time – the results are both ludicrous and wasteful. It is estimated that in the West 'information costs'[2] are some 10 per cent of the final price of a commodity. Sales-promoting advertising is five times cheaper. Of the advertising budget, some 70 per cent is given to what the economist Alfred Marshall called 'constructive' and the rest to 'combative'[3] or brand-image promotion.

The impression has grown that not only may combative advertising be nothing but shadow-sparring for which the consumer pays, but that it is by its very nature immoral. In some circumstances perhaps it is; but 'propaganda' was not invented

by Madison Avenue, or even by politicians, but by the church
It was the way the faith was 'requiring to be spread'.[4] A modern
Jesuit has defined it as 'any attempt to modify opinions, attitudes
or actions by non-coercive means. Most often it is an *organized*
effort aimed at influencing a *group* by means of mass *communication*'. It becomes 'unethical', in his view, when it seeks to
impose false opinions and attitudes or elicit immoral actions, or
presents false motives or a balance between reason and emotion
which is 'not proportional to the change intended'.[5] The admen
broadly accept this analysis and claim to function, on the whole,
virtuously. A modern exponent equates virtue and efficiency:

The more informative your advertising, the more persuasive it will
be.[6]

By 'bitter experience' he found that advertising cannot 'foist an
inferior product on the consumer'.[7] True, as Phineas T. Barnum
observed, 'you may advertise a spurious article and induce many
people to buy it once'. But 'they will gradually denounce you
as an impostor'.[8] With righteous indignation advertising agencies
point out that they have professional organizations which
enforce codes of conduct, and that their concern for morality is
so strong that the promotion of pharmaceuticals is called 'ethical
advertising'. This plea is not to be taken too seriously. But if the
big drug houses persecute truth today, their tortures are nothing
to those of Dr Bloggs's Herbal Panacea in the virtuous days of
Queen Victoria.

Whatever the admen say will not stifle their critics. No word
is more laid, like a lash, on the back of modern society than
'admass'. It is the chastisement wielded by socialists and social
workers, intellectuals and artists (including many who are well
paid by the industry), teachers and theologians and moralists of
all ethical persuasions. J. B. Priestley coined it:

This is my name for the whole system of an increasing productivity,
plus inflation, plus high-pressure advertising and salesmanship, plus
mass communications, plus cultural democracy and the creation of the
mass mind, the mass man.[9]

It is especially loved by non-economists who forget that the
opposite of inflation is depression, communicators expert at
selling themselves, democrats who have never been able to face

up to their patrician dislike of democratic 'values', lovers of the people who hate the masses. Its financial side was turned by J. K. Galbraith into *The Affluent Society*, where

The even more direct link between production and wants is provided by the institutions of modern advertising and salesmanship. These cannot be reconciled with the notion of independently determined desires, for their central function is to create desires – to bring into being wants that previously did not exist.[10]

Experts question to what extent it is psychologically possible to 'create desires' in any fundamental sense. Galbraith and his supporters mean more than that on being told something is on the market people will go out and try it. The implication is that mere knowledge would not have influenced them and the admen have exercised improper persuasion; that the victims of admass are induced to desire things no rational man would conceivably covet and which he would probably be better without; that this manipulation of others is immoral in both its operation and its effects. No one should gain this position of power over his fellows, much less those whose intention is to inculcate 'materialistic values', the pursuit of affluence, the neglect of things of the spirit. Now, this amounts to an ethical theory: that people gain their standards, bad and presumably good, through the conditioning of vested interests. One logical consequence might be a joint advertising campaign by property-owners against theft. But the admass theorists seem to believe that exerting influence on other people is itself wrong, however good the end, and that it is easier to persuade people to do foolish than sensible things. It is the doctrine of original sin and the serpent, without much hope of being 'born again'.[11]

In one form or another this theory is widespread. It is the sophisticated version of 'them' against 'us'. Politicians are another set of all-purpose villains. Like the chosen chief of old who was sacrificed for the expiation of the tribe, they are the whipping-boys for our accumulated dissatisfaction with one another. Nationally and internationally things go wrong because the decent instincts of ordinary people are warped or crushed or simply ignored by their rulers. If only the 'man in the street' could take over the reins of government, all would be well. So the theory goes. Unfortunately, it is as mystical as those considered in the second part of this book. Politics is the aggregated wisdom and the aggregated virtues and vices of the people who support it. The politicians' nastiness is our nastiness. It is the same with advertising. The advertisers' cupidity is our cupidity. Though they may, if skilful, persuade us to try new ways of satisfying our basic needs of food and fuel, our hidden desires for possession and status, those needs and desires are not created but are imbedded in our natures. So are our social urges, our spontaneous sympathy for the afflicted. Advertisers cannot create these, but they can use them. A good campaign is as effective in persuading us to give to a particular charity as in inducing us to spend on a particular product. Rather more of our national budgets and advertising accounts are spent on products for ourselves than on charities for somebody else; but this is because we are by nature selfish. This has nothing to do with the machinations of admass. It is biological. The survival of the species depends on the survival of groups and mutual support of their members; more fundamentally still, it depends on the individual looking to his own welfare. He can do this better than anyone else. Looking after other people is a worthy secondary aim, but relatively inefficient.

The building of machines is a technique. In itself a technique is morally neutral. It is what the machines are for and what harm or good their products may do which bring in a moral component. Advertising is also a technique. It may promote something which is good or something which is bad. Here is a moral potential half of which is often ignored. Yet the technique of advertising seems to most people to be somewhat different from that of building a machine. In both cases the intentions and the results (which need not coincide) can be good or bad. But engineering method does not quite seem the same as psychological method, which is what advertising depends on. Are devices like subliminal pro-jection (assuming it to be as effective as some claim), depth motivation and – to mention things that dictators, if not ad-vertisers, have tried – electrodes, chemicals, torture, deprivation–satisfaction 'brainwashing', and message bombardment during sleep justified, however noble the intentions or lofty the attitudes one is trying to establish? The question is more complicated than at first appears.

Many moralists who would unhesitatingly censure these methods use highly dubious persuasion techniques for their own purposes, usually religious. Though their apparatus may be minimal, they are chiefly dealing with youngsters whose minds are still to a large degree plastic, and whose factual memories and moral experiences are limited. These too are individuals, with human dignity to be respected and personalities to be treated uniquely. It will perhaps be retorted that they are legally and morally dependent on adults for nurture and guidance; that we must tell them what to do and think, or at least what not to do and think, in their own best interests as well as our own. This has a certain plausibility. But so has the argument that antisocial individuals or nationalities of any age group need 'aversion' or 'motivational' therapy. In both cases the possibility of abuse is a consideration which joins whatever moral objections to manipulation there may be. A clever minority might promote its sectional interests in a way which would curtail or eliminate criticism and thus foster or ensure acceptance by the majority. With the best of motives 'brainwashing' of the young might well appear more harmful biologically than persuasion therapy on criminals. For while there is no agreement among adults on what ideology is most acceptable, and in a rapidly changing world it yearly becomes more disadvantageous to try to imprint on impressionable youngsters the obsolescent creeds of their elders, in every community there is a fair measure of consensus on behaviour that is most unacceptable. When the tumult and shouting on fringe issues like drugs and sex has died, liberals and conservatives combine to censure murder, rape, robbery and fraud. It is best (most effective as well as aesthetic) if criminals return to better ways spontaneously. Otherwise 'persuasion' may prove more effective and humane than incarceration and other forms of compulsion.

While 'admass' suggests to the intelligentsia amorality rather than moral neutrality (whose difference is psychological) and vice rather than virtue, to the masses themselves it is one of the forces which have broken down the old ethical systems and compounded nucleoethics. It has thus brought the two meanings of 'the good life' closer together. Despite occasional nods in favour of the Puritan ethic and caution over the obvious 'treat yourself; you deserve it' type of advertisement, it has persuaded most people that the pursuit of a more relaxed, comfortable, cosmopolitan, labour-free, creed-free, news-served, entertaining life is not something to be shunned but to be welcomed. Against this encroachment of affluence – or hankering after it, on an unprecedented scale, among the have-nots – bishops and moralists have protested in vain. With improved communications it becomes clear to all that they do not themselves lack the trappings of the good life. Indeed, after a secret courtship their gloomy message has been joined to the media in a joyous white wedding. When radio began, the churches feared that religious broadcasts 'would be received by a considerable number of persons in an irreverent manner, and might even be heard by persons in public houses with their hats on'.[12] Today they reserve their best pews for the television cameras and bishops discuss Jesus with pop stars or anybody else the producer can entice along. In a world of electronic communication, what price intuition or mystical awareness? This phenomenon is not confined to the West. There must by now be few Indian *gurus* who have not interrupted their meditations to go on barnstorming, arc-lit, amplified tours of the fleshpots of Europe and America or welcome celebrities on sabbatical at their ashram-hotels.

Though the by-products may often be unedifying, admass has been of enormous benefit to man as a communicating animal. It has brought to his attention snippets of the rich and varied life of the human species round the globe. Bombarded with strange, if not new, ideas, the old enclosed systems are untenable; the old intolerances come to seem absurd and probably dangerous. Among young people, that section most exposed to universal communications, there is a greater acceptance of differences, variations of dress, appearance, habits, hobbies, race,[13] than among their elders. True, there is a disturbing intolerance of free speech to be found among revolutionary students, but this probably reflects a desire – misguided, in my opinion – to maintain other forms of tolerance more quietly championed by middle-aged supporters of 'civil liberties' and the 'liberal' press. Increasingly we shall be educated and re-educated several times in our lifetime. This is a disturbing idea. It cuts across the 'seven ages of man',[14] the old hierarchies and established positions in

227

life on which we had come to depend for emotional security. But man is almost infinitely adjustable when required.

Dependence on an ordered, stable world of narrow compass made it difficult to cope with the inevitable upsets and imbalances when two cultures or empires or races or religions came into contact. Contact automatically led to conflict. Today there is more contact than ever before and so more conflict than ever before. But whereas in the past it was acute, today it is sub-acute. This is the best indication that, for all our anxieties and festering prejudices, we are gaining control of our passions. We are influencing and being influenced, persuading and being persuaded, preaching and being preached unto, permitting and being permitted. Often it seems that there is little real tolerance, that all that is happening is that law and order and values are breaking down. In retrospect, however, this time may be seen as one of flux, where established values are indeed breaking down, but new, more tolerant values are rising in their place. With admass has come a concentration on such things as status symbols, with a great growth of theft and violence in their pursuit; and it is right for us to be alarmed. But the concomitant rise of senseless vandalism among the young may ultimately prove a healthy reaction. If we can come to terms with automation, leisure, resources and the population explosion, so that goods are in real abundance and lose much of their fascination, we shall yet win through to a new order and a new security.

228

13 Bureaucracy

The growing tendency towards 'creeping socialism' in capitalist countries, state capitalist 'revisionism' in socialist states, 'paganism' in Christian nations, 'Christian values' in pagan lands, in short, the whole disintegration of pure ideologies and ethical analyses, may be attributed to the psychology of pragmatism. But psychology is, unaided, slow in growth and erratic in action. That movement towards universalization and eclecticism which we have called, in its moral implications, nucleoethics, has gained impetus and direction through its association with an important unit of the power structure of modern society, the bureaucracy. The precise extent of its influence is disputed. In the estimation of the American writer C. Wright Mills, bureaucrats are dwarfed by *The New Men of Power* or *The Power Elite*;[1] while a lecturer[2] at the London School of Economics, Ralph Miliband, has recently reasserted the Marxist view that in capitalist society' most bureaucrats are themselves drawn from the capitalist class and manipulate affairs in its interest. In America faceless foundations,[3] in Britain discretionary trusts, are simply tax-havens for the rich. Yet it can hardly be denied that bureaucracy is expanding throughout the world.

Questioning certain Marxist presuppositions, Max Weber contended that technology grows up side by side with an industrial bureaucracy trained to administer it, whatever the politicoeconomic system in which it develops. Into the language of this new sociology have burst such vivid phrases as James Burnham's *Managerial Revolution*,[4] Robert Michels's 'iron law of oligarchy',[5] William H. Whyte's *Organization Man*[6] and Bertram M. Gross's 'organized polyarchy', 'iron law of multiple oligarchy' and 'administrative revolution'.[7] Their relevance is not simply to the world of big business. Indeed, the political 'transition of a predominantly competitive economy into a predominantly organized economy' has been one of the chief creators of bureaucracy, while 'the rule of the few becomes particularly marked in those mass organizations which, more than other movements, are essentially devoted to democracy'.[8] This admission by a legal adviser to the Social Democratic Party in the Weimar Republic is extenuated by the need for secret tactics in the proletarian struggle. 'Wage slavery' was given by Lenin as 'the reason why the functionaries of our political organizations and trade unions are corrupted – or, more precisely, tend to be corrupted – by the conditions of capitalism and betray a tendency to become bureaucrats, i.e. privileged persons divorced from the masses and standing *above* the masses'.[9] Even after the revolution, during the dictatorship of the proletariat, there would be 'a certain form of state', but he did not want 'a special military and bureaucratic apparatus'.[10] The fact remains, however, that in socialist countries such an apparatus has flourished more even than in Western democracies, and a communist journalist reports that 'in the U.S.S.R. a privileged bureaucracy rules supreme'.[11] One recalls that last century the Tsar was 'powerless against the bureaucratic body; he can send any one of them to Siberia, but he cannot govern without them or against their will'.[12]

We need not concern ourselves with the precise relationship between the modern 'manager' and the old-time 'civil servant' who might as an individual have massive power or none at all. Corruption of the French and Russian civil service was named at the time as the primary cause of two great revolutions, and the subsequent hope of reformers and revolutionaries throughout the world was that governmental bureaucracy would, if not 'wither away', at least shrink. It was for libertarian as well as economic reasons that Victorian Liberalism called for 'retrenchment'. But the experience has everywhere been contrary. As 'democracy' has spread – measured by the yardsticks of one-man-one-vote, female suffrage, universal education and the like – bureaucracy has grown. Partly this is the result of the population and information explosions and the complexity of modern life. But in a series of serio-comic analyses of the British Civil Service C. Northcote Parkinson has shown that this growth may have scant connection with productivity. In 1957 he elaborated Parkinson's Law: 'Work expands so as to fill the time available for its completion.'[13] As the armed forces and the colonies have dwindled, those civil servants administering them have mushroomed. If the rate were to continue, half the population would be engaged in public administration by the year 2145, and all of it by 2195. Similarly throughout the world.

In socialist countries, where accommodation and the supply of luxuries are regulated by factors other than purchasing-power, and where the basic salaries of bureaucrats are also high, there are prudential reasons for joining them. Apart from the gaining of security in times of high unemployment, these reasons do not, on the whole, operate elsewhere. Marcuse has described public and private bureaucracy as the 'incarnation of the general will, the collective need', and regrets that, 'since it keeps, at least in the advanced industrial countries, society going under improving conditions and with better satisfaction of needs, the rationality of opposition appears even more spurious, if not senseless'.[14] Yet bureaucrats can hardly be motivated by satisfaction at public appreciation. If they do in fact take up 'public service' in its literal meaning, if their lives really embody the 'general will' and 'collective need', they gain slight recognition. Almost universally 'bureaucrat' and 'bureaucracy' are pejorative terms.[15] A sometime senior British civil servant has designated his former colleagues as 'generations of public school–Oxbridge amateurs, capable in their own conceit of administering anything or anybody, without needing any training or specialized knowledge, and able to get away with anything by secrecy and sticking together', who have an 'inbuilt tendency to regard all Britain beyond Watford and Slough as the last crown colonies'.[16] *Mutatis mutandis*. Industrial managers in Britain may come from a slightly broader background, and in other countries recruitment is differently oriented, but bureaucratic attitudes or assumed attitudes are a constant and the public response is uniformly hostile.

There is no evidence that as men bureaucrats are guilty of more moromalpractice than anybody else. Usually they are in the position of Caesar's wife, with a bigger obligation to private virtue. What concerns us here is their impact, if any, on public

231

virtue. As a body they tend to be conservative, supporters of conventional *mores*. Though usually in the tradition of one ethical view rather than its rivals, these habits really represent an amalgam of influences derived from many subcultures, religions and – in all but one-party dictatorships – political interests. More than an established church, the presidium of a one-party democracy, the monarchy or the flag, a bureaucracy ensures continuity. Churches may be disestablished, party lines changed, monarchies abolished, flags replaced; but bureaucratic government goes on. Rarely does anarchy reach the grass-roots. In countries where there are alternative, and alternating, governments, one socialist and the other not, elected for seven or six or five or three years (the abandoned democratic dream of the nineteenth century was one year), there would be intolerable confusion for the electorate without the stabilizing influence of a civil service, politely pointing out to each new administration how the future is imprisoned by the past, how limited its options really are. Nor is this of purely academic or political interest. It has moral implications.

Moropractice can grow only where there is some stability of moral codes. Delinquents tend to come from homes where from the earliest years they have been allowed to run wild, or where one parent imposes one set of rules and the other another, or where both parents arbitrarily change their own rules according to mood; so that the child develops with no notion of a moral code at all, or no stable one. Within certain limits children are more adaptable than their parents, and the moral, like the intellectual, attitudes of most individuals are not fixed till about the age of twenty-five. Children grow under the influence of their contemporaries, teachers and others besides their parents. If the external moral environment is too different from that of the home there will be further confusions; but if each setting is self-consistent they tend, like chameleons, to take on the right protective coloration for each background and not suffer irreparable damage. As new knowledge and needs arise, moral codes change. These changes seldom bring the older generation into conflict with authority, but they do bring it into conflict with the views and *mores* of the young, who have grown up with, and as teenagers accepted, somewhat different systems. With a measure of tolerance all round, these conflicts can be peacefully resolved or at any rate ignored. By its very nature morality is multicentric and we cannot make it uniform. But the universal desire for uniformity – so long as it is our own code which is accepted – suggests a limited tolerance to adjustment in the system and a biological need to preserve overall stability. In the arena of public life this is what bureaucracy affords, and its corruption or inefficiency is the corruption or inefficiency of society itself. That it should be universally reviled is another index of our need to find a scapegoat for our resentment at the regimentation of our lives. That it should never be effectively attacked is a recognition, albeit unconscious, that we are social animals with basic interests in common and a dependence on stability.

Like a colony of coral polyps, bureaucrats may flap in opposite directions but they all serve a common system. Here is their basic loyalty. Ensuring its survival is the source of their secrecy and their clannishness. Perturbed by their general lack of accountability, their critics claim that they are the immoral mechanics of vicious politics or the amoral lubricants of self-starting machines, and censure their 'red tape' and jargon. Their communications are characteristically short and dry, drained of emotion and moral judgements. Whatever private hopes and fears, loves and losses they may have are set aside. No wonder they are thought to have no ideology and no values save the need to keep the system going. In a sense this is true. But what they have really stumbled upon and helped to shape is nucleoethics. This they have used in their own way for their own purposes. They find it useful in the ministry and other bureaucratic offices, but they have never wondered or cared whether it might have uses in the outside world. Their intentions are entirely selfish. Yet if the organism they serve has a sociobiological function – and I submit it has – they deserve more gratitude than they get.

14 Law

As the late Renaissance set about codifying the laws of nature, so it gave special attention to the origin and purpose of the laws of man. The European feudal system, which was then breaking down, functioned rather like a multiple *gens*; that is, a hierarchy of units each based on more or less unquestioned obligations, duties and filial obedience such as one would find in a family or small community where everyone knew everyone else and deferred to traditions, customs and the rulings of fathers and elders, with little thought of their derivation or the means of enforcing them if challenged. As one modern jurist has put it,

To the medieval mind . . . law is primarily reason, and its promulgation is less essential. In fact for most 'laws' there was scarcely any definite 'sanction' whatever, but they were none the less laws.[1]

It sounds idyllic, and Pre-Raphaelites have looked back on it with nostalgia. To the emergent modern world of the sixteenth and seventeenth centuries, however, its operations seemed far from idyllic. From the resulting struggles for change and counter-attacks by established authority came the great legal theories which are influential today. For man, the social animal, has always had a biological need for law, and there has never been a regime, however despotic, which has not been able to produce, when required, its political theorists and legal apologists, who claim to know how to make people better or at least stop them from becoming worse.

After the manner of theorists from as far back as the ancient Greeks, but with the need to particularize in the light of their own situation, protagonists on both sides appealed to 'natural law'. The reformers invoked it to justify change. 'Positive' law, or the legal relations that obtained, was seen as the corrupt institution which perpetuated the power of oligarchies and autocracies, denying to the mass of the people the rights they held under natural law. The laws of nature were also appealed to by Hugo Grotius, the 'father of international law',[2] over the heads of warring nation-states in an attempt to resolve conflicts between autonomous legal systems. In the estimation of the traditionalists, however, law was more concerned with duties than with rights. The democrats were simply giving natural law their own definitions, artificial and perverse. Had not all the theologians demonstrated that the laws of nature were the laws of God? Had the Almighty not established in authority patriarchs and kings? Their actions were not to be judged by ordinary standards. Indeed they were not to be judged at all, as they ruled by the 'Divine Right of Kings'.[3] Among those who held this view there was some dispute over whether authority flowed from the divine reason, as Thomas Aquinas believed, or the divine will, as Duns Scotus and William of Occam contended; and hence whether it was recognized by human reason or, in the words of Paul, came to 'the Gentiles, . . . written in their hearts'.[4] Nevertheless the reactionaries had, as usual, the easier option. All they had to do was stick together and assert that the government and the law were as God intended. For some time this policy successfully deferred change. When it did come it was usually bloody.

Once established, the new regimes acted as if they were direct continuations of the Garden of Eden. The United States Declaration of Independence declared that the 'Laws of Nature' were 'self-evident' and human rights 'unalienable'.[5] Enshrined in the French Declaration of the Rights of Man and Citizen were 'imprescriptible natural rights'.[6] But it was one thing to speak of rights and another to define them. Spinoza asserted that when a person followed the laws of his own nature he was acting 'in accordance with the highest natural law and the justice of his action is proportionate to his power'.[7] On the face of it this seemed to justify totalitarianism; for not every critic of the past was a political liberal. Whether liberal or conservative, monarchical or republican, however, the new thinkers had to find some basis for law and order in society. If there were no apostolic succession from Jesus or Moses, or tablets divinely carved in stone, how was political and moral authority justified? To meet this need a 'social contract'[8] was invoked.

The complex literature on this subject need not detain us. Its complexity arose from the difficulty of explaining who were the contracting parties, what was the state of 'society' before a contract was entered into, how it could be changed, what – if any – were its penal clauses, and who enforced them if it was broken. It was simplest to assume the parties were the governed and the government, though this idea could not explain the origin of government in the first place. Thereafter what happened was a matter of power politics. In Britain, for example, there was assumed to be an 'original contract between King and people' by the breaking of which James II 'endeavoured to subvert the constitution of the kingdom'.[9] This was the formula used by the Convention Parliament to justify the Bloodless Revolution of 1688. Gradually the view of Richard Hooker prevailed that the contract was formed among all the individuals in the state. According to Rousseau this brought into being a 'collective moral person'[10] which negotiated, with the people, the setting up of a sovereign authority. Absolutists like Hobbes, and to some extent Locke, handed over to this authority supreme power which only a revolution or emigration could break, but Rousseau saw its dangers and wanted a renewable contract.

When the Pilgrim Fathers emigrated to America in 1620, they announced:

We do solemnly and mutually, in the presence of God and of one another, covenant and combine ourselves together into a civil body politic.[11]

Being suspicious of supreme powers and judiciaries that were tools of the ruling class, they demanded a citizens' militia rather than a standing army, the right of the individual to carry firearms, and the election of judges (with the later exception of the Supreme Court). In this way 'the people' were to be not simply the source of power in an abstract or mystical sense, but were to exercise it collectively. The system worked bravely when it came to asserting independence from British government and law, but it soon cowered before lynching parties, *vigilantes*, political 'fixers', demagogues and gangs with city hall and county court connections, bringing democracy itself into disrepute. So that, in the United States and elsewhere, despite populist protests from time to time, there has developed a widespread acceptance of 'big government' and proliferating national law as the only way of bringing antisocial elements to book.

If the clauses of the social contract have been questioned, so has its conception. The first clear criticism came, as with so much other sensible iconoclasm, from Godwin:

No consent of ours can divest us of our moral capacity. This is a species of property which we can neither barter nor resign; and of consequence it is impossible for any government to derive its authority from an original contract.[12]

Just before this Kant had shown that 'pure reason' was as incapable of discovering the truth about nature and natural law as it was unable to reach God, but 'practical reason'[13] gave us moral insight into human rights. As G. D. H. Cole put it, 'From Cromwell to Montesquieu to Bentham, it was the practically minded men, impatient of unactual hypotheses, who refused to accept the idea of contract.'[14] For them it was 'a mere fiction'.[15] The jurist John Austin, who codified their views, saw law springing from the 'command' of the sovereign and nothing else.[16] This view need not be repressive. On the contrary it can be highly progressive politically and morally. It was the basis of the great spurt of Benthamite legislation in mid-Victorian England, using statute law to blanket common law, i.e. the law of custom and judicial decisions, which conservatives like Sir William Blackstone had regarded as the 'perfection of reason'.[17] The command view of law has been taken over by the Soviet Union. In 1919 the governing body of its Commissariat of Justice declared law to be 'a system (set of rules) for social relationships, which corresponds to the interests of the dominant class and is safeguarded by the organized force of that class'.[18] On this principle the 1918 Constitution sought to avoid the 'artificial separation between the executive, the legislative and the judicial powers' practised by bourgeois constitutions, and 'to concentrate all these functions in one central organ'.[19] When classes disappeared so would the law. Gradually Soviet orthodoxy changed. In 1932 Andrei Vyshinsky, then Deputy Public Prosecutor, observed:

Law is the aggregate of rules of conduct – or norms: yet not of norms alone, but also of customs and rules of community living confirmed by State authority and coercively protected by that authority.[20]

In other words, even if classes disappeared, the law would not.

After two decades of Stalinism and arbitrary extermination, this cosy definition of the role of State authority has received some chilling blasts. But the idealistic formulae of 'natural law' and 'social contract' find little favour with political theorists today. It is true that the Universal Declaration of Human Rights was launched in 1948 as a 'recognition of the inherent dignity and of the equal and inalienable rights of all members of the human family',[21] and that 1968 was proclaimed Human Rights Year. Yet the resultant document and activities (or lack of activities) do not represent any coherent world-view but a blend of aspirations derived from many countries, muddled and sometimes mutually exclusive. Capitalists are wooed in article 17 and socialists in article 22. There is free expression enshrined in article 19 but 'honour and reputation' are protected in article 12. One part of article 26 supports the 'full development of the human personality' of children; another gives their parents a 'prior right to choose the kind of education that shall be given' to them. National sovereignty is upheld in article 21 but subordinated to the United Nations in article 29. What is most interesting is that language peculiar to one ideology or another is avoided and there is a pragmatic attempt to satisfy as many conflicting interests as possible. On this account alone it is not surprising that no nation has implemented more than about two-thirds of the thirty articles. 'Social contracts' have fared little better. They suggest the abstract and unworkable rather than the concrete and practical, and are uncongenial to the modern mind. Yet some conception of them lingers on along the pragmatic lines sketched in Britain's first republican journal in 1817:

The laws are, in fact, the conditions of THE SOCIAL CONTRACT; the People submit themselves to the laws, in order to enjoy the right of making or changing them.[22]

Whether or not there is a contract, a republic or a monarchy, an absolutist or a democratic view of government, law always, to some extent, represents a highest common factor of citizens' beliefs and practices. Though it never forgets the vital interests of the ruling class, from which most judges and jurors are in fact selected,[23] and though there is 'a certain inability to perceive the lawyer as someone to whom the ordinary person has easy access'[24]

– in this he has been likened to the Ritz Hotel – courts of law usually make some pretence to be courts of justice. On a command interpretation of the law there is no explanation or any real possibility of constitutional or international law. For how can an absolute power command its constitutional existence or accept limitation of its jurisdiction by other absolute powers? Yet the tendency is for constitutional and international law, agreements and codes to grow. Considerable changes may be made in the legal system after a *coup d'état* and judges are not inviolate but can be replaced, yet a substratum of law survives the most dramatic political upheavals. The fortunes of Rhodesia's Unilateral Declaration of Independence since 1965 have to some extent hung on the malleability of her High Court judges as they switched allegiance from the British Governor to Ian Smith.

As modern society has grown more complex so administrative law and tribunals have proliferated. In all this, law appears to have affinities with bureaucracy. It cuts through the barriers of established ideologies and ethical systems and allows creeds and subcultures some measure of mixing. Thus it is one of the components of nucleoethics. Like bureaucracy it also arouses the innate hostility of ordinary people, though even members of Utopian communities have been glad on occasions to apply to it against their colleagues. To the reformer it promises change by statute, which makes it more accessible and accountable than bureaucracy. Through it *laissez-faire* capitalism and 'social Darwinism'[25] receive some check and equity and social justice some recognition. To such an extent that in 1859, anxious at the 'increasing inclination to stretch unduly the powers of society over the individual', Mill declared that 'a large portion of the morality of the country emanates from its class interests' and should not bind the individual; that 'the only purpose for which power can be rightfully exercised over any member of a civilized community, against his will, is to prevent harm to others'.[26] In the form that it was not the business of the law to enforce morality, this argument gained increasing sympathy in academic legal circles. But not among practising lawyers. Asserting that 'vicious habits . . . set a bad example to people at large' and that 'vice is a bad thing from which men ought by appropriate means to restrain each other', and citing many examples of the entry of moral considerations into indictments, verdicts and sentences, James Fitzjames Stephen declared that 'criminal law in this country actually is applied to the suppression of vice and so to the promotion of virtue to a very considerable extent; and this I say is right'.[27] After a brief flutter the controversy subsided. In 1959 it broke out again with heightened passion.

Two years before, the Wolfenden Committee on Homosexual Offences and Prostitution had reported that 'there must remain a realm of private morality and immorality which is . . . not the law's business'.[28] Patrick Devlin, a High Court justice like Stephen, had submitted quite liberal evidence himself and accepted the committee's central finding that 'homosexual behaviour between consenting adults in private should no longer be a criminal offence'.[29] Soon he 'had in mind to . . . take other examples of private immorality and to show how they were affected by the criminal law', but study replaced his 'simple faith' that further law reform was necessary with a firm conviction 'that I was wrong' on the central issue.[30] So in 1959 he delivered a lecture advocating 'The Enforcement of Morals': 'A recognized morality is as necessary to society as, say, a recognized government . . . No society can do without intolerance, indignation, and disgust; they are the forces behind the moral law . . . There are no theoretical limits to the power of the state to legislate against treason and sedition, and likewise I think there can be no theoretical limits to legislation against immorality.'[31] At once a storm broke out on both sides of the Atlantic. Foremost of Devlin's opponents was the jurist H. L. A. Hart, who believed that 'you will find no English judges making speeches in public on the liberal side, i.e., in favour of relaxing the criminal laws which enforce morality'.[32]

In protesting against 'moral populism'[33] Hart identified four questions on the relations between law and morality: (1) the influence of morals on the development of the law and vice versa;[34] (2) the place of morality in legal definitions; (3) the possibility and forms of moral criticism of the law; (4) legal enforcement of morality. If the law were to try to 'enforce morality' it could operate in four ways: (1) threaten punishment; (2) punish offenders; (3) prevent offences by removing their source; (4) enforce court orders. The point was, however, should

240

it try? Hart believed that certain backward-looking statutes obliged this intervention but that the common law had long since escaped medieval orthodoxy, Puritan intolerance and Methodist enthusiasm in moral matters. Then came the *Ladies' Directory* case.

The first result of Wolfenden was the Street Offences Act of 1959, which drove Britain's prostitutes off the streets. Whereupon an enterprising Soho publisher[35] produced a magazine which obligingly stated where they had gone and which ladies offered what professional services; and was duly prosecuted and convicted. The case was fought through to the House of Lords. Counsel for the appellant argued that there was no common law misdemeanour to corrupt public morals and so 'conspiring to corrupt public morals' could not be indictable. 'Pungent statements'[36] from the bench in old cases were simply *obiter*. Most notable of these was Lord Mansfield's observation in 1774: 'Whatever is *contra bonos mores et decorum* the principles of our laws prohibit and the King's Court as the general censor and guardian of the public morals is bound to restrain and punish.'[37] One of their Lordships thought this role had since lapsed but his colleagues disagreed. Hart and his fellow liberals gasped at the words of Lord Simonds, a former Lord Chancellor: 'When Lord Mansfield speaking long after the Star Chamber had been abolished said that the Court of King's Bench was the *custos morum* of the people and had the superintendency of offences *contra bonos mores*, he was asserting, as I now assert, that there is in that Court a residual power.'[38] Most of his colleagues agreed.

With the growth of religious toleration it is a long time since the law has tried to standardize *mores*; but what of morality? How does the man on the Clapham omnibus relate the two? Usually it is thought that a moral person is one who obeys the law. Usually he does. But a hypermoral person might feel that the law supports things alien to his conscience and that it is his duty in these cases to defy it. He may, for example, consider that his taxes are being spent on an unjust war and refuse to pay them, thereby breaking 'positive' law in the interests of what he would call a 'moral' law or 'critical morality'.[39] At war crimes tribunals the issue is a practical one. Generally, however, friends urge on hypermoral rebels both prudential and commonsensical reasons for conformity: the chaos that would result from purely subjective interpretation of legal obligations, the disadvantage to us all if we were to discover that our rights were held as lightly as our duties, and the possibility in most cases of changing laws and public policy by making out a social case for reform. Communally accepted law brings stability to our lives. It codifies what in the last analysis we can expect of others and what they expect of us. Even under a tyranny, where law may be held to be perverted or improperly constituted, most parents and educators would agree that it is the business of moral training to inculcate respect for the law (unperverted and properly constituted). If people, on the whole, get the sort of government they deserve, so, except for relatively short periods, they get appropriate laws; and however much they complain the majority of citizens usually accept the broad outlines of law and law-enforcement in their community. They believe, in effect, that morality should enforce the law. Where disagreement prevails is over the question of whether the law should enforce morality.

Now, most people in any one society agree that certain immoral acts are also crimes and merit the full rigours of the law. But what of torts where the liability is technical rather than moral, and 'transgressions' that are more common or more controversial or generally regarded as less serious? Firm opinions are often held but firm adjudications rarely given. With their customary thoroughness the Germans have sought codification. Section 826 of their B.G.B. code[40] states that anyone who violates 'good morals', or the sense of equity and justice of the whole community, must pay indemnities for damage to another. When questions of 'morality' are decided courts always claim to be acting in the interests of the 'whole community', whatever the percentage which happens to agree with them. When they really uphold 'equity'[41] and 'justice' there can be little ground for complaint. But the feeling has grown that the law's idea of 'morality' and that of many citizens may be very different. A modern jurist, Glanville Williams, sees views on morality divided between the utilitarians, who are empiric, and traditional moral intuitionists, who are formalistic. Attitudes to the criminal law he describes as libertarian or authoritarian. The two divisions may, but need not, coincide. Authoritarians are those who 'believe in authority in moral matters. They tend to assert their own morality against that of other people, and they expect this morality to be backed by the law.' Today they are cautious:

Moral authoritarianism is no longer often overtly defended. It is generally concealed, and generally when these debates take place they take place in terms of utilitarianism. Even those who defend the traditional attitude towards, say, abortion, homosexuality or mercy-killing, will try to find utilitarian grounds.[42]

This debate about 'permissive legislation', variously related to the individual or the local authority, is no new phenomenon. Over a century ago a libertarian article with this title was published in a radical weekly.[43] A few years later Richard Harte brought the debate into the centre of the sexual field:

Physiology tells us that chastity is natural until the age of puberty, unnatural after that age . . . Such sexual intercourse after the age of puberty, as is neither hurtful to the individual nor to society, is a perfectly justifiable thing, and . . . to take steps to prevent conception is as legitimate as any other attempt of man to secure his happiness by modifying the action of natural causes.[44]

A recent index of the 'permissive society' was the Arts Council proposal 'that the Obscene Publications Acts of 1959 and 1964 should be repealed'[45] and a parliamentary initiative to effect this reform should be sought. From a Conservative member of parliament came the promise of a counter-lobby. The change, he declared,

is revolting to me and, I am sure, the overwhelming majority of decent British people. It is a further slide into the disgusting mire of permissiveness, squalor and pornographic filth of recent years.[46]

At the same time the then Chancellor of the Exchequer, who had when out of office supported much permissive legislation, including an earlier liberalization of the obscenity laws, observed that 'the permissive society', 'always a misleading description', had been 'allowed to become a dirty phrase':

A better phrase is the 'civilized society', a society based on the belief that different individuals will wish to make different decisions about their patterns of behaviour, and that, provided these do not restrict the freedom of others, they should be allowed to do so within a framework of understanding and tolerance.[47]

In a survey of these trends *The Times* observed:

Abortion, divorce, obscenity – all the ingredients of the permissive society – these are areas where governments and party leaders are customarily hesitant to tread. No doubt they will remain so for some time yet, but if these seem to the public to be some of the most important political questions of the day then the political parties will not be able to stand aloof for ever . . . Politicians will have to concern themselves more and more with such questions as the relationship of law to personal conduct and with the policies that are necessary for a decent and harmonious society.[48]

It went on to mention the problem of 'the preservation of privacy in an age of computerized records'. From failure to recognize this problem we are now passing to consideration of legal and technical ways in which preservation can be achieved, and it is suggested that 'invasion of privacy'[49] should become a new offence. The anxiety is that personal data from our doctors and tax inspectors, from ministries, local authorities, social workers, schools, universities, places of employment and law courts, will all be fed to centralized computer banks, where they could be read off by anyone with electronic access, legitimate or otherwise. Certain safeguards will no doubt be found. But it is equally certain that privacy will be increasingly invaded, whatever computer firms promise or the law decrees. One way of minimizing unfortunate consequences for the individual will be the development of a new tolerance for *immores* by spreading throughout the community something of the unshockability and understanding of a good social worker or novelist.

The authoritarian case does not rest on emotive statements alone. Lord Devlin is a convinced Christian who believes that 'the law must base itself on Christian morals'[50] on the grounds of both their virtue and their historical role:

I reached the conclusion that the criminal law of England was based on the moral law, although in many respects it had lagged behind it for there are many sins which are not punishable as crimes . . . Real crimes are sins with legal definitions. The criminal law is at its best when it sticks closely to the content of the sin . . . The criminal law is shaped by the moral law; the quasi-criminal is based on it; the law of contract is the legal expression of the moral idea of good faith; the law of divorce formulates the permissive relaxations from the moral ideal of the sacramental marriage.[51]

One of the Arts Council recommendations in connection with the obscenity laws was:

No encouragement should be given to the concept of the State as *custos morum* with its corollary that merely to shock is a criminal offence.[52]

It had received submissions from a Cambridge professor of Law, R. M. Jackson, who strongly criticized the *Ladies' Directory* decision:

It is, however, a somewhat astonishing doctrine these days to say that in the last resort the way we can behave, the things we can read, look at, hear and presumably enjoy, are subject to Big Brother wigged and gowned on the judicial bench.[53]

Many libertarians say that not only should law leave *mores* alone, it should steer clear of morals. Yet on closer inspection it seems doubtful whether, outside a handful of anarchists, anyone really wants this. There are, as we have seen, divers crimes that most people would regard as infringements of their moral code, or of which their ancestors took this view. Just before proclaiming 'I think that there is very general recognition today of the value of toleration', Glanville Williams admitted 'I think one may say that the demand of mass opinion still tends to be for conformity'.[54] Putting the two statements together one may say that where people conform they are not tolerant and they are tolerant where they do not conform.

It is a matter of common observation that many 'reactionaries' are authoritarian in matters of sex, censorship and punishment, but libertarian in matters of income, welfare, parental rights and private education. On the other hand, 'progressives' are libertarian in the first field and authoritarian in the second. That is, one group wants the law to intervene to ensure conformity in sexual behaviour, culture and penology but thinks it should do nothing about unequal incomes, the unemployed (simply lazy, in their estimation), the treatment of children as chattels by their parents, and all decisions over schooling. The responses of the other group are exactly reversed. What one section regards as a question of taste or convenience the other regards as a question of morality. It is my submission that if people feel strongly enough that something is a moral issue they will expect others to recognize similar obligations; they will not be content with the usual moral sanction, disapproval, but will demand the full sanctions of the law.

Behind many political campaigns, 'reactionary' or 'progressive', are moral views. The anti-obscenity lobby really believes that, in the words of the Obscene Publications Act of 1959, such matter will 'tend to deprave and corrupt'.[55] Their opponents do not, on the whole, take a stand on any absolute issue of cultural freedom – 'publish, and the consequences be damned' – but do not consider that literature depraves and corrupts or that evidence to this effect is ever presented in obscenity trials. In matters of 'state intervention', which underlies the Welfare State, and compulsory, followed by 'comprehensive', education, there are equally strong moral issues. As Lord Beveridge, the architect of the Welfare State, expressed its philosophy:

The greatest evil of unemployment is not the loss of additional material wealth . . . There are two greater evils: first, that unemployment makes men seem useless, not wanted, without a country; second, that unemployment makes men live in fear and that from fear springs hate.[56]

Similar motives infused the Webbs and other pioneers. For practical men of affairs there were the economic arguments, based on lost production (but not always taking account of productivity), and prudential fears of 'hunger marches' and riots. But the formulators were also inspired by a moral feeling against avoidable human degradation. And if it can be said that some measure of welfare provision is today accepted by most political parties in most countries, and that to provide this every earner of money is levied in some way, against his will if need be, it is probably true that from recognition of these practical and moral aims has emerged their underpinning by the law. If in questions of personal behaviour that have no effect on other people one way or the other, save the questionable and utterly subjective one of 'shocking' or 'disgusting' them, 'moral authoritarianism is no longer often overtly defended', it seems unlikely, as Glanville Williams suggests, that people no longer believe in authority. Rather is it that most people have a reduced view of what constitutes morality. What was once a moral issue is now an aesthetic one, or is simply done without any thought of values at all.

This is, of course, a process which has long been in existence. Part of the function of the original Roman censor was to regulate dress in the interests of 'public morals', and this concern has persisted to our own day. Apart from sheer bloody-mindedness it was based on moral evaluations. An ostentatious appearance might arouse envy and provoke robbery; a display of female anatomy might arouse *libido* and provoke rape, or at any rate marital infidelity. To some the sheer evocation of 'undesirable' thoughts was itself immoral. Gradually the belief is spreading that thoughts cannot be exactly predicted, that in so far as they can they cannot be controlled, that in the absence of stimulation similar thoughts arise spontaneously, that it is bringing law into disrepute to apply it to matters it cannot regulate. Down the centuries each new change of fashion has been launched to murmurs of admiration from some and howls of outrage from others. Traditionally this has been seen as the battle between the forces of darkness and the forces of light – or vice versa. Today we know rather more about the psychology of difference: that many actions and words will arouse wildly different responses. These will be physiological or ideological, according to the individual. From these diverse sources comes nucleoethics. Out of these diverse responses a highest common factor of reactions emerges. These are what the community as a whole accepts and on which it is likely to legislate if it thinks this practicable. The process is an ancient one. Only recently have we understood its psycho-biological function.

It is here that the question of whether morality is positive or negative arises. Williams asserts:

The inheritors of the nineteenth-century liberal tradition argue that enforced morality is not morality at all and that in so far as morality has to be enforced on social grounds, it should be reduced to the minimum necessary for social cohesion.[57]

The assertion needs qualification. I have already put forward the paradox that people's behaviour is determined by a mesh of circumstances but that in one sense they do what they 'want' to. Short of physical manipulation of their limbs they cannot be 'forced' to behave in a certain way, though threats can increase the probability. Short of electrode stimulation of their brain they cannot be 'forced' to think in a certain way. In their effect on the mind, threats may even be counter-productive. Before the authoritarian schoolmaster the stupid child grows stupider. In all these ways, therefore, 'enforced morality' is impossible. But the argument that it is 'not morality at all' is a loose expression of another viewpoint. This states that whatever is inspired by 'negative' considerations like fear of punishment is only the morally neutral exercise of obeying the law; that genuine morality consists of 'positive' attributes like generosity and courage which cannot be legislated for. If this were literally true, however, morality could not and would not need to be 'enforced on social grounds', and only persons who happened to have 'positive' or outgoing personalities could be regarded as moral. This is surely more perverse than the opposite view, which gives credit for morality to those who obey the law because they are cowards. Fortunately we can rely on a large measure of spontaneously helpful behaviour in people, but there is a lot of 'spontaneous' behaviour we wish to deter. For this reason we bring in not only the techniques of moral education but also the sanctions of the law, especially in a 'negative' form: 'The rule that you are to love your neighbour becomes in law, you must not injure your neighbour.'[58]

The first objection of the passionate libertarian is that if we cannot artificially create good responses we cannot artificially deter bad ones. In our present state of knowledge this is broadly true. But I have already suggested that we are on the dangerous ground of mental inquisition when we worry too much about 'responses'. It must finally be behaviour that concerns society. By this criterion it is undoubtedly true that we can promote the good by morally neutral means or even by means that a purist might deem dubious. The military and civil honours system, the Duke of Edinburgh's Award Scheme for young people, and the whole armoury of perks and prizes in every institution work on the assumption that incentives bring results. A Zacchaeus cannot be turned into a Zealot or a Shylock into a Good Samaritan, but people can be encouraged in devotion to duty or acts of philanthropy beyond their own expectations. The real motive may not be 'philanthropy' but a selfish hope of status or flattery. Yet the end-product is the same. If this is so, then the psychology of restraint must be of equal interest. Behaviourists like H. J. Eysenck have shown that the efficacy of incentives or restraints largely depends on the individual. Introverted children respond better to one, extroverted to the other. In educational terms this means praise or blame. The same alternative is relevant to adults. But if neither seems to work, is punishment justified? Eysenck appears to think not. He quotes animal experiments. One series with rats in a T-maze suggests that non-specific 'punishment' stimulates learning. Another with dogs in two compartments suggests that double 'punishment' makes learning impossible. He gives more attention to the second finding, which he deems relevant to the treatment of recidivists:

Punishment, under certain circumstances, can 'stamp in' the behaviour we are punishing, rather than stamp it out.[59]

These experiments are, however, completely arbitrary. The 'punishment' they involve is a pattern of electric shocks unrelated to any training process wherein human, rodent or canine approval and disapproval could be displayed. Thus the situation is not a moral one and the 'punishment' cannot be associated with any conception of 'wrong-doing'. If human punishment is applied in the same arbitary way it too will do harm. But modern penology seeks to avoid the arbitrary.

Whatever views are taken of the relationship of law to morality, penological theories and discoveries throw light on moral thinking. As the concept of 'diminished responsibility' has grown, so has demand for more humane prisons. There is now some attempt to provide educational and vocational training, psychiatric investigation, probation services, suspended sentences and parole, better relations between the 'screws' and the 'cons'.[60] More often fines or attachment of income replaces gaol sentences. Special efforts are made to disgorge prisons of their female inmates. In most respects therefore the institutions are more aesthetic than previously. They are also doing better business, particularly in males, while the law courts still cannot cope with their turnover. It was expected that as society and law became more complex, 'offences' (as distinct from 'crimes')[61] would proliferate. What was not anticipated was that crimes would grow as fast. From this observation comes much of the moral anxiety of our time. For we seem to have weighed every theory and found it wanting.

The mystical conception of expiation was, outside religion, largely abandoned long ago. Retribution and deterrence took its place. At one time it was usual to speak of both as 'retribution'; but only in the case of the 'cat' for assault or hanging for murder was it really retributive. Usually the punishment was more severe than the crime, so that by 1810 in Britain there were 222 capital offences, most of them trivial by modern standards. The motivation, explicit or implicit, was deterrence. Societal retribution merely matched the 'retribution' the criminal had himself exacted, all too often, for some real or imagined grievance in his own past, and confirmed him in his antisocial activities and determination not to get caught again. To authority, capital punishment and transportation had the blessed simplicity of removing one human problem while hopefully deterring others. Apart, however, from the fact that conspicuous injustice made the situation morally intolerable for many jurors, so that they refused to convict, it was also an inducement to someone detected in a minor crime to stop at nothing to escape, since a major crime brought no greater penalties. Realism and liberal concern combined to reduce the number of capital offences to thirty-seven by 1837. Traditionalists forecast disaster which did not come. But criminals did not, in their gratitude, abandon crime, and by 1863 Stephen was asking for flogging to be made more severe. Today flogging and capital punishment have all but disappeared in Britain,[62] but the idea of deterrence has not. Though liberals dispute its value it seems, particularly with mob crimes like race rioting and football hooliganism that from time to time gain a vogue, to have uses. The liberal alternative is reformation, linked with permissiveness. With the young, the sensitive and the supported it has worked well. With the old, the insensitive and the friendless it has not. To the vicious tear-away the kindly judge with the 'you've been a naughty boy' manner is regarded as 'soft' in the head as well as in the heart. Sternness is all he understands.

Just as the developing child responds worst of all to moral instability in the home or school with no set pattern of expectation, so the criminal fraternity is unlikely to be helped by penological instability in society. This results when starry-eyed idealists, who have never met a crook or even a tough schoolboy, alternately quell and cower before birchers and hangers whose own delinquency has always been hushed up by their public school, family lawyers and corporation accountants. In this conflict neither side will budge from the position that its methods have universal validity. The penology of nucleoethics is not that stability should come from standard techniques, but that there should be different techniques for different personalities and consistency in dealing with each individual throughout his life. If half the money given to traditional 'law-enforcement' were given to personality testing and assessment of human needs, thus supplying 'early warning systems' in schools and advice throughout life, the results could be impressive. Another break with tradition I would recommend is abandonment of the sanctity now accorded to the rights of natural parents. While they are, ideally, the best nurturers of their children, many are far from ideal. The legal status of suitable foster parents and the social status and staffing of children's homes should be raised to make these attractive alternatives. Since so much delinquency is familial – genetic or environmental – compulsory sterilization must at some time become a legal sanction. The right to breed is no more absolute than any other right, and its curtailment would be rather less oppressive than denying light and liberty to habitual criminals, love and prospects to their children, or life and limb to their victims. Already this is quietly practised on mental defectives without benefit of legal process.

The old dream that law would wither away has proved nugatory. Even Marcuse has been forced to admit that 'the rule of law, no matter how restricted, is still infinitely safer than the rule above or without law'.[63] With foresight we can use it to aid moropractice.

Part Four
Nucleoethics and Persomorality

When the earth ceased to be regarded as the physical centre of
the universe, Man did not become, in his own estimation, merely
a form of life in a corner of the Milky Way. On the contrary,
frenetic attempts began – and have persisted to this day – to
demonstrate that he was himself the psychic centre of the
universe, so that his hopes, his fears, his need for 'salvation',
his moral awareness, his 'extra-sensory perception' transcended
astronomical limitations and gained a cosmic significance. No
sooner did the heart lose its dominance (relatively, not absolutely,
as current reactions to heart transplant operations show) as the
seat of the soul, than the pineal gland or the brain offered
domicile. Despite the growing success of neurophysiology and
neurosurgery, mental processes were still regarded as independent, in some sense or other, of physical events in the brain.
When, in recent years, cyberneticians suggested that there were
striking parallels between brain function and that of electronic
machines, not only the clergy protested that as far as man was
concerned there was a 'ghost in the machine'. This harking back
to a mystical past was in part sentimental and in part political,
but perhaps its prime impulse was moral:

Metaphysical systems, as constructed in traditional philosophy,
often serve the function of expressing a moral outlook. Moral attitudes, sentiments, interests and needs are rationalized and related to
other aspects of human thought. Thus Cybernetics develops a
mechanistic-materialist philosophy of mind as a support to scientific
materialism; man is regarded as something analogous to a highly
complicated robot.[1]

This new attitude to man, which cyberneticians could take in
their stride, flourished among scientists in 1954, 'at a time when
the sub-science of Bionics (the study of living systems with

specific reference to the construction of cybernetic artifacts) was in full flood. Because of excessive idealism, and a consequent failure to fulfil its promises, Bionics went into a ten-year slump from which it is now however beginning to emerge again.'[2] Not, however, among the general public.

In a popular sense psychology is more concerned with how man thinks he thinks than with how he thinks. There are, moreover, biological reasons why he should see himself as special, unique, fired with a personality that eludes and elates, that exudes and inhales wonder. Indeed man is biologically special, unique and wonderfully personable. Yet this belief in the cosmic preciousness of human life has not prevented its wanton dissipation in war and famine and persecution. For the corollary to the claim that life or thought is mystical is that it can be mystically renewed. Grandiose views of man have hidden, like layers of shellac, the true grandeur of his image, and we will learn more from an analysis of the pigments than from a lantern lecture by the moralists. Paradoxically, a functional study of the human brain will enhance rather than diminish its status. How many people command the resources, the respect or the loving care of a computation centre, a computer or, for that matter, a first motor-bike? Yet the human brain is capable of immeasurably more operations than the largest computation centre known today. It is not therefore with any contempt that we should hail the new investigation of man as *res cogitans*, a thing that thinks.

To say that the brain is a computer has long been a truism, for everyone knows that it can compute, however slowly by digital standards. In the world of politics, domestic or national, it has long been fashionable to speak of 'calculations'. There has however been little effort, or desire, to follow through the implications of this terminology. Most people continue to think of computers as enlarged comptometers capable of only the simplest operations and completely dependent on human operators. For a time they were called 'electronic brains' but they were not regarded as anything more than sophisticated versions of the calculating machine invented three centuries ago by Gottfried Leibniz. Few, if any, universities use computer technology as an introductory course to neurophysiology, and I know of no attempt to work out data processing and programming implications for morality. Yet it is over two decades since Alan Turing wrote with 'Promethean irreverence' of 'intelligent Machinery'[3] and affirmatively answered the question 'Can a Machine Think?'[4] By implication he was giving the same answer to 'Is Man a Machine?'[5]

People who may cheerfully concede that the gut is a filtration plant, the liver a chemical factory, the kidney a disposal unit, even the heart a pump, are unwilling to concede that the brain is a computer which regulates every intellectual, affective, aesthetic and moral experience. This is no surprise. It is part of the paranoia which, until 1828,[6] insisted that the waste product urea could be produced only by living tissues. Many biological concepts – purpose, drive, *élan vital*, entelechy, Gestalt – have mystical overtones. Yet if we strip the mysticism from them we find parallels to the functioning of a machine, 'created' in specific circumstances to do a specific job which is relevant only in the context of other jobs and has no ultimate significance. Universal teleology can be reduced to an inter-related complex of day-to-day problem-solving.

As organisms grow from the simple cell into something more complex, different types of cells evolve to take on special functions, as in human society. Most cells are not now directly exposed to the environment or directly concerned with reacting to it, but all depend for their survival on these operations being successfully carried out. In this way receptor cells to detect danger, and effector cells to move the organism away from it, arise. Linking them and connecting each receptor–effector pair with other pairs are co-ordinating cells which determine the magnitude of the response. This is the structure of the simple reflex machinery. So, for example, temperature and pain receivers record dangerous (and unpleasant) heat or cold and pain, thus activating nerve cells which in turn trigger off muscle action to get out of the way. As the organism gets more complex still, it tries to avoid the trauma involved in repeated trial-and-error by developing cells to memorize the experience and other receptors to recognize the danger through associated impulses. Hot things produce a wide range of electro-magnetic radiation, some of which can be seen, and may burn with a tell-tale smell. In this way we learn to give the minimum of work to our temperature and pain receptors and thus cause the minimum of damage to our cells. These increasingly refined processes result from mutant cells in mutant organisms whose better survival value passes on genetically from generation to generation until their descendants have established a biological dominance. The process is organic, but the Greek *organon* means an instrument.

Perhaps the oldest property of life is its power of reproduction, derived from the long spiral molecule, desoxyribonucleic acid or D.N.A., which lies in the nucleus of every cell and along whose double helix are various side-chains which act as information stores. During reproduction the helix divides, each half acting as template for a complementary spiral molecule, ribonucleic acid or R.N.A., which synthesizes new cellular material, and then for a twin to complete the original molecule and preserve its information. Higher animals that reproduce sexually have specialized cells whose D.N.A. (genetic) material remains divided until they link up with cells from another individual to form offspring with the potentialities of both parents. In this way the gene pool, which comes to contain some interesting mutants, is continually stirred up and oxidized. Thus life can die but cannot stagnate. Cybernetically it can be defined as a 'self-replicating information system'.

A living thing's most obvious property is that it responds actively to the environment through its receptors, effectors and the nervous tissue that connects and co-ordinates them. This is analogous to the 'hardware' of a computer and, because of the dynamism of metabolism, its essential 'software'.[7] In this lie both the basic data and the basic programmes of the individual's life, which exist from the moment of birth. His mind is not, as Locke and other early empiricists believed, a *tabula rasa*, or clean sheet. It has the predetermined capacity not only for reflex and instinctual responses that are common to the species but for more or less active emotional responses to its internal and external environment, that are unique to the individual. The baby's 'machine code',[8] which is genetically determined and so, save for identical twins, unparalleled throughout nature, is the basis of his persomorality. Yet it has close links with those of his own family and, at a further remove, with those of the whole human species. So that, unless there is a gross impairment, it is able to respond to 'assembly languages',[9] verbal and non-verbal, from parents, teachers and other adults, and from peers. In this way the child is 'socialized'.

Yet he is socialized in terms of, and subject to the overriding constraints of, his 'machine code'. This is what psychoanalysts call the *id*. Here the basic drives are codified, appetites perceived and satisfactions sought. Primarily they are associated with survival (individual, familial and posthumous, in decreasing order). Except when the system, and thus the organism, breaks down to be consumed by a 'death wish', they are both personal – what gives each of us from birth a 'sense' of identity, even before the concept of the 'self' is formed – and universal, uniting us all in a common purpose. But, especially in times of scarcity, common purposes can produce conflict and universality can provoke aggression. Our personalities may change with the state of our physiology, but the idea of our own person is the thing that is most real to us. This is the centre of our wants and our 'will', our moral will, our will to live or our will to die. Through this mechanism we always do what we 'want' to. All the later programmes connected with conscious emotional and intellectual development, through which we add 'purpose' to 'will' and ego to *id*, must be translatable into this code if our computers are to accept them, if morality is to become moro-practice. Inspired by the self it is essentially selfish. People may, and do, give lip-service to altruism. The technology of our brains, however, gives scope for nothing better than enlightened self-interest.

How this is induced is a cybernetic problem. Information of all sorts is continually pouring into the brain. Unprocessed it is meaningless. At the periphery the maximal number of nerve fibres are activated by every stimulus through the overlap of sensory areas for neighbouring receptors. This redundancy fortifies the stimulus and guards against the misinterpretation of chance events in a single fibre. But it would be intolerable if the brain had to cope with an endless barrage of redundant signals. So relay systems maximize the information content of incoming impulses. At all levels there are connections on to the centre and back to the periphery. By this use of servo-mechanisms[10] part of the electrical impulse is fed back negatively to effectors which act to reduce the original stimulus. So constant small adjustments to the environment are made, mostly unconsciously, and a fairly stabilized pattern of nervous stimulation results. Probably servo-mechanisms exist inside the brain, just as D.N.A. is an information store inside its specialized cells as inside any other. But the process of human programming and information storage and retrieval is highly complex and still imperfectly understood. Simplistic claims that specific memories can be implanted by injection into the brain of nucleic acids, that learning can occur by playing recorded lessons during sleep, and that control of another individual can be gained through hypnotism, brain-washing adults (using conditioned reflexes) and subliminal advertising, are to be treated with extreme caution. So are most claims of moralizers.

The baby is born with a full complement of neurons. Unlike the connective tissue cells around them, and most other body cells, they do not reproduce themselves. As they die they are not replaced, so our resilience and our mental functions tend to decline after middle age. Yet while the baby's brain is at maximal potentiality it is at minimal achievement. 'A large remnant of the random behaviour of infancy remains in the adult. All of this suggests that the cortex of the infant is an unorganized machine, which can be organized by suitable interfering training. The organizing might result in the modification of the machine into a universal machine or something like it.' [11] In this way the baby makes sense of his environment intellectually and morally and eventually makes his own intellectual and moral impact on it. What he does is related to what he is, and both to his experiences. Partly these are pedagogical and preceptive Overwhelmingly they are practical and experiential. What he is told – in catechisms and injunctions – may be reproduced in words; it is not reproduced in actions unless the words fit in with his sensory experience of the world, unless it seems fundamentally a sympathetic and secure, co-operative and just place to be in.

In the early years of life the nerve connections of the cortex appear to be largely random. Before reaching the synapse, or junction, with its neighbours each fibre breaks up into processes which link up with many cells, and each cell receives impulses from many sources. A single cellular discharge is thus unlikely to reach the threshold value and provoke a response in any of its neighbours. Only fortified impulses achieve this result. If they are repeated, stable pathways are formed; for unused nervous processes, like other unused tissue, atrophy while used ones develop, especially in youth. These pathways are emblazoned by 'positive feedback'[12] which derives from many sensory sources that show a positive response to particular actions in a random pursuit of trial and error. They are formed slowly; so man is a slow but stable learner. At first this learning is non-verbal. When the senses reach a certain level of development, however, symbolic logic – the logical way in which symbols are found to correspond to reality – embraces, but is never confined to, verbal forms. What is usually called 'thought' is a sequence of words, logically related to one another and, through cortical connections with the autonomic nervous system[13] and endocrine glands, to feelings. For the articulate, words are a powerful catharsis. Whatever other qualities they may have, violent individuals are often found to be inarticulate. Without words we are subhuman. No wonder the ancients regarded the very name of God as sacred.

Even when the infant understands indicative language, it fails to understand commands. And it is interesting to note that these are the years of which he later has little or no recollection. Memory is not simply the recalling of data. It is the restimulation of pathways that are concerned with the processing of data worth recalling and the formation of programmes to utilize it. The popular sequence of awareness–will–memory is exactly reversed. From the manipulation of new data and its integration with previously stored data we both memorize the material processed and contrive programmes, in conjunction with established programmes, for action. Much of this activity seems to occur during sleep, probably the secondary or 'paradoxical' phase of sleeping, when our muscles are relaxed and our brain is hot with blood. Then our central processor is 'off-line',[14] undisturbed by the daytime flood of new data, unengaged in the daytime operations of living. Herein lies the advantage of not immediately deciding a problem that can be deferred but 'sleeping on it'. This insight has been made possible by a new theory of dreaming, devised by an experimental psychologist and a computer engineer.[15] As police interrogators long ago discovered, personality disorders soon develop with deprivation of sleep; not, as is still widely believed, because the brain needs rest but because it then does its essential work of assessing, storing or, by a 'destructive read',[16] abandoning information. 'The dream serves primarily as a "memory filter" ';[17] 'dreams which are experienced (i.e. brought to conscious level and thus remembered) are *interrupted* dreams'.[18] On this assumption Christopher Evans has warned that 'sleep learning' would be dangerous, even if possible; that certain drugs, like barbiturates, may produce a level of sleep too deep for optimal dreaming; and that psychedelic drugs, which produce 'waking dreams', may disturb the true dreaming process and incorporate trivia in our cortical programmes. Within cells impulses are transmitted electrically but at synapses chemical reactions occur. The transmission agents, serotonin, adrenalin and acetylcholine, are chemically similar to these hallucinogenic drugs and to dimethoxyphenylethylamine (D.M.P.E.), which is found in many cases of non-paranoid schizophrenia. Most dreams, like most hallucinations, are of trivia, though repeated ones may be connected with unresolved problems. I would suggest that, while the Freudian interpretation[19] of dreams is needlessly flamboyant, sleep may open up peripheral memory stores which are normally inhibited by conscious responses to painful memories. For, when we are awake or 'on-line', programmes lead to activity the beginning of which we call 'will' and the observation of which, on our computer's display terminals,[20] we call 'consciousness'. Through stimulation or inhibition the brain is enormously responsive to both internal and external challenges, so that we become not 'moral' in a mystical sense but biologically 'effective'. With understanding of ourselves and our environment, of growing up and education, the effective may also be, in the best sense, moral.

Theologians protest that computers acquire their programmes from men while men conceive their own programmes. This is a misunderstanding. The primary programmes from both come from the manufacturer (as far as free will is concerned, it matters little whether man is formed by natural processes or by God). From these and fresh data, in both cases secondary programmes are elaborated by 'choosing' one of a set of alternants according to the results of the first computation; and, while the operation is deterministic, the end-product may not have been determined, or foreseen, by the programmer. Edinburgh University's[21] FREDERICK (Family Robot for Entertainment, Discussion, Education, the Retrieval of Information and the Collation of Knowledge) will be goal-directed in a similar way to Little Johnny. During the early years of life the secondary programmes – the do's and don't's of social living – are grafted on to the primary programmes for personal survival. They are not simply imposed from outside, though sanctions play as important a part in the process as incentives. Unimaginative sanctions (authoritarianism) may seem to work when the child is completely dependent but break down when he is not. For the secondary programmes that determine his social attitudes do not properly develop. No harmonious relationship exists between outside injunctions and emotional experiences; no spontaneous, unconscious social attitudes – as spontaneous and unconscious as the personal impulses that constitute his inborn primary programmes – develop in his creative early years. Instead, a conflict of programmes, alternately docile and hostile, evolves; and psychoanalysts, called in to breakdowns – of relationships, self-control, inner peace – speak of a conflict between the ego and the superego. What has happened is that the business of living calls for problem-solving at the day-to-day or tertiary level; but these tertiary programmes lead to a satisfactory solution (not necessarily the 'right' solution in any intellectual sense, but a solution which enables further trial and error to take place and does not provoke undue guilt in oneself or hostility in others) only if there has already been laid down a more or less consistent pattern of primary and secondary programmes. Any system can break down under overwhelming challenge, but an unintegrated system cannot cope with minimal change. It follows that children need stability and love especially in their early years, and that negligence at this stage cannot afterwards be compensated for by big pocket-money, child guidance experts or moralizing headmasters.

Save for gibbering idiots all individuals form secondary programmes of a sort and are not entirely without morality; though people whose programmes are immature, eccentric or erratic may seem 'amoral'. Those religious, philosophical or political systems that purport to create 'new men' hope, in effect, to create secondary programmes when it is too late or to create them in the wrong way. Sometimes they try to ignore man's primary programmes. They represent him as a wretched creature and forget that people who do not respect themselves are unable to respect others. Sometimes they pour into him injunctions and parables that are unrelated to his life and are thus rejected by his computer. In forming tertiary programmes that work, he needs adequate operational data; but intellectual or 'moral' material has no necessary connection with forming either secondary or tertiary programmes, and a glut may invite total rejection or negative responses. Indoctrination may join emotion to implant unsuitable programmes which later cause conflict and psychological damage or lead the individual into quixotic adventures like holy wars for which he lacks information and manageable feedback. Done in the name of altruism, these adventures are in fact effected by appealing beyond the humanity of secondary programmes to the egocentricity of primary programmes, the primitive desire to fashion the world in our own image. Ultimately disillusioned, he turns to a directly contrary system (usually another form of religious or political authoritarianism) and another set of quixotic adventures. Throughout, conduct that he would normally have thought outrageous or criminal he justifies in terms of the programme. Indeed the programme is its own biophysical justification. On this assumption, then, moromalpractice is less common than is usually supposed. It arises from a tertiary programme that consciously runs counter to secondary programmes. Because the individual tends to run at a 'steady state' emotionally, the resultant conflict has to be resolved. Short of mental illness there has to be a programme change. Mostly it involves the tertiary programmes, which are more recent and likely to be temporary because based on casual experience; though sometimes an overwhelming personal event – which is much more likely to be traumatic than thaumaturgical – can have more impact than a lifetime of education.

Forcing people to do 'positive' things they do not really feel an impulse towards can be equally counter-productive. Paying a 'duty call' on granny when you really think her a detestable old crone will rouse only resentment in the caller and, unless granny

264

is utterly insensitive, discomfiture in her. During the visit there need be no crisis, for most of us can, for a time, curb what we say if not what we feel and how we look. When, however, we are drunk or overtired and our tertiary programmes are in a mess, verbal curbs disappear. Afterwards we say we didn't mean it. In truth it is exactly what we meant. So, in any meaningful sense, it is redundant to have commandments like 'honour your father and mother'. If they are honourable we do it automatically; if they are not we cannot. Yet the censure of thought lives on as a moral imperative in a world that refuses to put mentality before sentimentality. Commitment to mentality means giving the fullest opportunity to the individual to develop according to his own needs and the changing patterns of society. Secondary programmes that are too precise and too dependent on contemporary *mores* impede flexibility in the future.[22] Enforceable rules ideally coincide with the highest common factor of perso-morality and exclude matters which do not concern the community at large or where there is no general agreement. Within the personal computer, thought must be recognized as a vital electrical process which imaginatively follows out scenarios for action as a prelude or, if an unpleasant abreaction[23] occurs, a counter to action itself. It is only by having the idea of murdering our children or our parents that we can develop, through shock, the negative idea. Otherwise we would kill them on impulse when they annoyed us. In our thoughts and our dreams our computers flicker over alternatives. They may be gross. They are not immoral. Only actions are immoral. From both social and anti-social thoughts come social programmes that pay off emotionally. As a professor of psychiatry at the University of California recently told the American Psychiatric Association:

A thought of infidelity a day (without guilt) keeps the psychoanalyst away.[24]

Camus has said that life is not a problem to be solved but an experience to be savoured. Rarefied speculations about eternity, past or future, destiny, terrestrial or celestial, purpose, human or cosmic, are all very well for those with the leisure and taste to pursue them, but should not be fed into the moral computers of man as material suitable for secondary programmes. All the evidence suggests that if they are not implanted at this impressionable stage they will not normally arise to modify tertiary programmes through spontaneous reaction later. Nor is it desirable that they should. Ethical speculators have no monopoly on virtue. If they display any psychological characteristic preferentially, it is likely to be neurosis. To each fresh generation they pass on anxiety over the questions for which there are no answers and the beginnings of things for which there are no ends.

It is often said that the thing which is uniquely human is this capacity for speculation. If so, it could be the thing that will bring the disaster forecast by the pessimists. The history of evolution is of succeeding species gaining a particular quality which made them dominant in one epoch and vulnerable in the next. Man has fretted about the problem of life as a by-product of his capacity to puzzle out the problems in life. With an unusually long phase of dependence on his parents he can be fed a wider range of knowledge and components of secondary programmes than other animals, and so advance geometrically from generation to generation. But the advance need not be up. This is one of the myths of the scioethicists. It would be perverse to say that all man needs to do is follow his instincts. In that way he would not have found answers to the physical hazards of life that have overwhelmed many other mammals. But too great an overlay of secondary programmes and conditioned responses on the primary store of instinct can warp and distort and lead to disaster. We may thus come to believe in the literality of myths: that life is a blessing, regardless of its quality or its quantity, its burden to the individual or its cumulative invasion of biological living space; that 'just wars' are always better than compromises or, alternatively, that non-resistance to aggression is always right; that beliefs are more important than behaviour and to be defended at all costs.

Adults help young children to recognize the rights of others (though peer pressures may well be more important), but then proceed to wreak havoc by imposing roles. Boys are to be manly, tough, chivalrous, unsentimental, aggressive (but not to fight on school premises); girls are to be lady-like, delicate, dependent, sentimental, soft (but not to lose the hockey match). The extreme of silliness was yesteryear's war of chivalry or duel for a lady's 'honour', and the lady's simulated fainting dead away at mention of a naughty word, whose meaning she might not have been expected to recognize. So men and women could never feel at ease in each other's company and women entered marriage utterly oblivious of sex. It is less so today and the moralists are shocked. Recently the chairman of the British Health Education Council, Lady Birk, called for replacement of 'differing voices' that 'propound differing philosophies' by 'a consistent and far less inhibited and less hypocritical approach to the content and context of sex education',[1] and the moralists were outraged.

To them morality is a fixed and elevated thing to which we should all lift up our eyes even if we break our necks; it has nothing to do with the ground of knowledge or the ground of our being. With their rigid segregation of value judgements and judgements of fact, the philosophers have aided this trauma. Yet history and anthropology combine to show that morality, albeit retarded by the moralists, changes with the advance of knowledge. Whether it goes up or down depends on the ingredient analysed and the taste of the analyst. Today the prevailing mood is one of pessimism and morality is said to be going down. I see no more grounds for pessimism than for optimism. In day-to-day matters I would say there is improvement. Increasingly we are aware that morality springs from the social situation and our experience of it, from the felt needs of ourselves and the observed needs of others. If our impulses do not conflict with our observations, who should intervene? Short of marked genetic change our impulses show a statistical average that does not change from generation to generation. Our observations change as our knowledge and understanding change, and as far as our ideological blinkers will let us see.

Take sex as an example. When there was no knowledge of conception or contagion it was relatively free. As the mechanisms of procreation and infection were understood the possible effects of actions could be better calculated. Fear of unwanted pregnancies and venereal disease became a part of human experience and the obvious means of checking them – chastity – a moral duty. Today we are on the point, it would seem, of overcoming these hazards and a new freedom is open to us. But to many the means of chastity has become an end, and instead of welcoming the new techniques they deplore them as an incentive to vice. This response is misconceived. No mere technique can act as an incentive without an underlying motivation. Psychological evidence suggests that sexual needs and tastes, like those in food and clothing, are almost infinitely varied. Some individuals are naturally frigid, others naturally promiscuous. But the traditionalists have caught on to something which is actual, and for them alarming. Many who are conditioned into being chaste are not frigid; their needs are not being satisfied; their personalities are not being fulfilled; or if they are, they are burdened with subsequent guilt.

Anxious to appear respectable most of the liberals go on preaching one thing and practising another; but as young people are educated more and more they see more readily through subterfuges of this sort and gain a generalized cynicism, about their elders and society, which cannot be creative. Some liberals go so far as to say that 'premarital sexual experience need not necessarily be wrong'. What they should say is that for many people – probably most – it is a jolly good thing, part of the normal experimentation of life, whether it be auto-, homo- or hetero-erotic. For while sex is usually a part of marriage, marriage need not be a part of sex. After marriage the psychological expectations of the partner become a factor to reckon with.

Probably they are less demanding (and the ties may be weaker) in group than in monogamous marriage. After the birth of children their need for security is another ingredient. New decisions may very well be reached. From outside the personality of the individuals concerned and the intricacies of their situation, no one can know what behaviour will or should result. It is the prime job of society to feed as much data as possible – of psychology, contraception, medicine, social security and the rest – into the human computer, where they will combine with the intrinsic factors of innate and childhood programmes. If the latter have not been scrambled by inconsistency or distorted by regimentation, the computer's solution should be acceptable to both the individual and others. But only if they do not have doctrinaire expectations.

Sex is only one of the platforms from which we might profitably sing the old music hall song: 'A Little of What You Fancy Does You Good.' Another in the news is obscenity–pornography. Not for the first time. There can be few libraries without at least one volume that has at one time or another, in one place or another, been the subject of an obscenity prosecution. While such works may titillate they also instruct. They throw open landscapes of the mind for exploration, survey and settlement. But many who take obscenity in their stride go rigid before pornography. Despite alarmist fears of avalanches of filth, there are probably very few citizens with pornographic libraries or any hard-core pornography in their possession at all. Nevertheless most men have on occasions been shown the latest treasure a friend has brought back from Denmark or Sweden (or perhaps Soho), and derived pleasure from it. Is any harm done? It would, I submit, on first principles be neurotic to fling the filthy thing away. We read about wars and murders every day. They are a part of life and on any balanced judgement considerably more 'obscene' than dirty books. But this is not the reaction of the moralists. Pornography is, in their estimation, always and absolutely evil. They would, of course, have a point if we were to drop everything and take the first plane to Copenhagen or Stockholm. It is necessary to have a sense of balance. One traditionalist paper has given a warning to those who wish to repeal the obscenity laws, that 'they play with fire'. A back-lash will set in. 'Such movements, usually led by unreasoning zealots, enforce (whether anybody likes it or not) public order and rigid morality.'[2] The warning may be sound. There have been alternations of licence and rigidity before. But the 'licence' has, in the past, usually had a clandestine back door or a brazen front one and has allowed itself to be seen as 'immoral'. The inevitable response has seldom been the spontaneous reaction of affronted individuals but the simulated horror, soon accepted as 'natural' by all concerned, of ideologists. What will increasingly be a feature of the new permissiveness is insistence that it is, in every genuine sense of the name, a 'new morality', continually renewed; that unreasoning and unreasonable restrictions are themselves wrong.

A yet more contentious issue – which splits the 'progressives' down the middle – is 'drugs'. Properly, drugs are anything in the pharmacopoeia. Many are life-saving. Some are not physically necessary but to certain individuals have become psychically necessary. Of these some – notably the most fashionable, alcohol and tobacco – are organically harmful. These are not however what are meant by 'drugs' in the 1970s. The word denotes certain hallucinogens, narcotics[3] and stimulants. A few of them can be obtained in huge quantities on prescription, by respectable matrons and businessmen, as slimming pills, anti-depressants, sedatives, tranquillizers or analgesics, and in specialized psychiatric treatment. The rest are available on prescription to 'addicts' but are otherwise illegal. It would take us too far to go into the medical and legal implications of each of them, though general observations can profitably be made. The paternalistic desire to save people from themselves may be a kindly, is often an officious, and is usually a forlorn hope. While young children and mental patients need special protection because they lack knowledge or the capacity for judgement, the rest of us are entitled to the facts and to no more. There are chemicals, including some 'drugs', which are poisonous and should be labelled as such. There are others, like the agents of chemical and bacteriological warfare, whose production it would be best to ban by international agreement. And there are those which appear to do little harm in small quantities, though they may cause physical or psychological problems of dependence in large amounts. On these there tends to be more hysterical speculation than sound research. This is one of their difficulties. Another is the transitional stage of society in which we live.

With only partial automation, work is still a social need as well as an obsession of the Puritan ethic. Anything which renders work impossible and entails sponging on one's fellows can be described as an illness which should be treated or an indulgence which is sinful or antisocial and should be punished. It is hardly surprising that society grows exasperated at those who refuse treatment and demand public maintenance. Their numbers have been exaggerated by the police but they exist. In the not too distant past, countries like Britain feared underpopulation, whereupon marital responsibilities became important and drugs which caused impotence or sterility or instability gained an antisocial status. Little fear of underpopulation need exist today, yet the idea of settling down and raising a family remains a respectable norm. In the future, scientific developments are likely to bring such radical changes to the realms of work and population that a moral revolution, involving drugs, may be demanded. With full automation we should have to persuade governments, trades unions, employment and probation officers and ordinary citizens not only that work (other than social work) was not a virtue but that a desire for it was a positive neurosis. We would then need to look to those who had found ways of pleasurably filling in a ceaseless whirl of leisure without recourse to vandalism, punch-ups, larcenies and other familiar diversions for bored young people. Flower Power, which today seems debased or silly, may be a dynamo of real strength for tomorrow.

Similarly, any breakdown of the monogamous family unit geared to breeding may be advantageous in a world of teeming life. Into the headlines of the 1960s burst accounts of organ transplant operations. The publicity and hysteria which glow in their slipstream have origins other than medical interest. There is understandable anxiety over the writing-off, as it were, of one individual so that another can gain his spare parts. To that is added a superstitious regard of 'life' itself, a horror that bio-chemical processes should be allowed to cease even if no consciousness or other higher faculty is projected from them. A similar attitude is directed at those who are using drugs to try to change the normal biochemistry or consciousness of the body-mind continuum. Yet we are on the fringe of discoveries that will make L.S.D. trips or pot-smoking or heart-transplants of marginal impact upon living processes as we know them.

Apart from the brain, liver, testes and ovaries, our organs tend to perform relatively simple mechanical or chemical functions. This is especially true of the heart, where plastic replacements may ultimately prove more useful than tissue transplants. But more fundamental are biochemical advances. From knowledge of cellular ageing may come the means of constant rejuvenation. The test-tube babies of *Brave New World* are just around the laboratory corner. For years there has been the dream, which may yet be realized, of bypassing altogether the genetic lottery of fertilization and reproducing desirable individuals at will from the development of undifferentiated plenipotential cells. All the cells from any one person have similar genetic contents, modified for their specialized functions. Certain of the cells in newly forming scar tissue are, however, thought to be capable of wide differentiation according to need and thus to resemble embryonic tissue. By the time biochemists are able to culture and develop these into a separate organism or 'clone', it should be possible to effect changes in the body's D.N.A. or R.N.A. molecules and thus modify cellular synthesis internally. Geniuses, it would appear, can be both born and made.

By the use of drugs we can already release the intolerable hold of the superego on the ego and the *id* of a depressed and guilt-ridden individual; but we run the risk of removing moral responsibility altogether. The brain is a complex and delicately balanced mechanism and we intervene at one point only at our peril. Within it are contained all the checks and balances not only of the individual's lifetime of education and experience but of the whole evolution of life upon earth. That is why some of today's caution over mind-changing drugs and operations is justified. Their effects could be more catastrophic in, say, a car driver than acute alcoholism. But already, in the privacy of one's home, they have their uses for the anxious and the neurotic, the fugitive from life, or the jaded mind in search of adventure. In the future when the whole neural mechanism is understood – and it does not seem impertinent to forecast this – it may be possible to intervene chemically with knowledge and precision and balance. Earlier in this book I advocated, in the light of present understanding, resolving conflict between the superego and the *id*, which undoubtedly exists in our society, by educational and social changes that would modify the superego. This is clearly the easier option. In the future we may have another possibility: chemically changing the *id*. Yet unless we are mature enough to achieve the former we would be most unwise to attempt the latter.

Persomorality is grounded finally in society. Germinating in man as a social animal, its roots bind society together. But the two sets of needs, personal and societal, must be focused by two eyes from slightly different viewpoints to give a three-dimensional picture. Those who felt the previous chapter was a transcript of science-fiction fluttering from the windy heights of sciomorality may equally feel that it pursued the personal gratification of lay-abouts, or of mad scientists, without regard for social imperatives. Mad scientists in league with mad politicians are, I concede, the greatest hazard of our day; and we will do well to consider messing about with our genes more suspiciously than tinkering with the atmosphere or agriculture. By the gradualist, problem-solving methods we have recommended there are, however, grounds for going straight to the genes as soon as our biochemistry is sufficiently refined. There are known genetic diseases like haemophilia and phenyl ketonuria involving the blood or metabolism and bringing death or insanity, and tendencies to aggression coming from an extra Y chromosome in men. A 'negative' solution of these genetic problems must be welcomed. But any 'positive' genetic programme to, say, raise intelligence before studying emotional or moral concomitants could create serious problems.

It is, after all, very recently that the problems of the gifted child (who had always been thought blessedly free of them) have been studied, and few solutions have yet been found. We know, too, that some of the most valuable evolutionary changes have come from biological sports, randomly developing, which any overall genetic control would eliminate. Conversely, genetic manipulation could increase 'random' change on statistical lines; but as many phenotypes, or resulting individuals, might turn out to be monsters and have to be destroyed, grave moral anxieties would result. Creatures so superior to present-day man as to constitute sundry new species would result, and as our morality – with some extension to domestic animals – is a species morality its biological roots would be cut and a Frankenstein's-monster conflict or concordat would supervene. The problems of induced genetic evolution are immense. As we still have so much technical knowledge to use and social insights to assimilate, and as the accelerated growth of evolution in the modern epoch has come from psycho-social expansion, it is premature at the moment to make genetic interventions. Whether it will ever be opportune is a matter for further research and assessment. Man has hitherto shown himself infinitely adaptable to new knowledge. We must look to its and his continuance.

Even supporters of theism and historical determinism agree that human understanding can change history. What it behoves us in this age of fast-changing knowledge and moral needs to appreciate is that human adaptability must accelerate. The real, not the assumed, role of morality as a cohesive force in society should be identified so that each new generation is not indoctrinated with the mistakes and misconceptions of the past. Already certain aspects of scientific humanism are redundant, yet many countries are still programming their children with the bygone formulae of old-time religion. Public figures and private citizens who have abandoned creeds pay lip-service to moral systems that are meaningless in their absence. As immense moral and social problems confront us, adults sit and fret over whether little Johnny is reading trashy comics, saying naughty words or playing with himself. The pattern of life and death is not a liturgical drama but a biological imperative. In the past, individuals were born and morally programmed, contributed to new knowledge and died, before their secondary programmes were too out of date. As they aged, their increase in experience and perhaps in wisdom just balanced a declining adaptability to new conditions or a wilful resistance to change. In the future, there will be progressive survival of the elderly combined with a reduced proportion of the neonatal. This seems certain, even without dramatic breakthroughs in cellular chemistry or family planning propaganda. The population will thus gradually age, becoming further removed from its period of active education and youthful resilience, further alienated from the younger generation, further resentful of its greater freedom and sex life and prosperity. It is for these reasons that the speculations of the last chapter are not purely visionary but, whether practicable or not, have a practical moral purpose. And they give additional justification to the proposition that moral instruction should be as realistic and minimal as society can manage with.

I have great confidence in the ability of the untrammelled human being to live peacefully with his fellows. Great but not unlimited. The assumption is, moreover, apocryphal, as the individual is not untrammelled. He is subjected not only to the conditioning processes of society but to the irritations and provocations of its injustices. What to the affluent is 'irrational' behaviour is not irrational to the deprived. If this book has given more attention to society's conditioning than to its injustices it is not because the one circumstance is more important than the others but because it is, in my submission, largely ignored. It is also of universal relevance, whereas injustices are many and varied and depend on local political circumstances. Many of these were outlined in the chapter on politicoethics. There are just two general points that might be made here. Nationally we should aim at a level of automated productivity that will ensure the necessaries of life to everyone without work. What inventing, hand crafts, arts, luxury production, salesmanship and human engineering citizens engage in beyond this, and what disbursements of income, goods or services are made for them, would be matters for political decision by democratic processes inside each country. Internationally we should start as soon as possible, using especially the electronic media, to extend the child mind from its orientation to family and school until he feels himself a citizen of the world.

This development would, one imagines, parallel a strengthening of the United Nations and the creation of some sort of world government. But this aspiration would not clash with the national independence just outlined. All the evidence of nationalism, separatism and tribalism in the modern world renders any thought of a monolithic world-state impracticable. Probably it would also be undesirable. If a loose world order can effectively outlaw war as a method of solving disputes, and bring some order to international trade and currency crises, it will serve a most useful function. National governments will then be like regional governments writ large, preserving their own languages (at least as second languages), customs and traditions. This dual aspiration is far from realization but is not a pot dream. Technological knowhow exists for one. World trends like the ecumenical movement in religion and supranational military, economic and political blocs forecast a climate of opinion for the second.

Yet, as the chapters on scioethics and politicoethics sought to show, technological and political changes seem unlikely of themselves to solve the great problems of aggression and greed that afflict us. In a world where sporting fixtures increasingly lead to fatal rioting no one can be complacent. It is true that closer examination of these trouble-spots usually shows underlying religious and political tensions that would largely vanish if aggressive ideologies were to decline. But it would be rash to predict that even then rioting would vanish. Herd identification with sporting teams and the viability of aggressive ideologies after rational arguments for them have collapsed, suggest an inherent aggression and partisanship in man. Ethologists attribute these to his primate ancestry and suggest that he is stuck with them. But primate studies show very different pictures in the jungle and in the zoo. Enclosed, confined, thrown endlessly upon one another's company, animals display a marked upsurge in aggression. Man may not have free will but he is less constricted than a menagerie ape. If he reacts more fiercely to frustration, it is because he has higher expectations of life and is more persistent in chasing them. These are rational aims, though the behaviour may appear 'irrational' to those with different expectations. Immersion in a crowd itself identified with a sporting victor gives status to an individual who otherwise lacks it. This is a psychological, and the most common, example of deprivation. The behaviour is 'irrational' not because it has no reason but because it offers no permanent solution of the problem. Even if the fan is not himself killed or maimed in a football riot, he runs the risk of arrest and punishment, with its further lowering of social status. To the respectable world he emerges as a gaol-bird or a convict financially poorer; to his mates, as a fool for getting caught. Often he is looped in a circle from which he cannot extricate himself. It is here that society must intervene.

From his earliest years it is important to find something that he can do well, something from which he can derive a sense of achievement, something which will give him status. It may seem pointless for people to row across the Atlantic when they can take an aeroplane or a liner, to sail round the world when they already know it is round, to step on the moon before setting foot on Africa. Compared, however, with crusades and colonization, these harmless responses to challenges are merely the more spectacular ways in which man can satisfy his restless energies. From the Apollo mission a spin-off of improved communications, micro-miniaturization and navigational knowledge has already resulted. To many it may seem that it has been expensively won; that the cost of the entire project would have transformed the lunarscape of the slums and the ghettos into a New Jerusalem. But if these sagas are, in mechanical terms, a waste of time and money, if they even seem a neglect of moral responsibilities, they may turn out to have a moral function. They may be part of a great process of aggression-sublimation so that we do not turn upon ourselves with that ferocity previously directed against animal predators in the once-dominant jungle, or, like the legendary Alexander the Great, weep because we have no more worlds to conquer. Money snatched from the American space programme would have gone into the Vietnamese War, not into the slums. Wilhelm Reich[1] has suggested that wars are outlets for sexual energy; Norman Walter,[2] that they are blown-up sexual acts, cross-fertilization on the grand scale. If this is so, there should be more opportunities for individual sex, or peaceful sublimations of it and of international 'sex'. Human solidarity must partly be transferred from the football team to the whole species. If the Martians do not exist it may be necessary to invent them.

Lessons are never learned without experience. The baby does not master walking without falling over; the toddler, language without solecisms; the child, morality without collisions that set limits to his options. Today the magnitude of our dangers alarms us. But the magnitude of the alarm may be more effective than rational argument in obliging us to try new solutions. In some respects the demands of society will always conflict with the wishes of individuals, especially those that are stronger and more aggressive. As well as appealing to their common sense we must offer them harmless means of satisfying their physical and psychological needs. As well as adventure playgrounds and Outward Bound voyages, we must be willing to try new ways of maximizing satisfaction while minimizing real harm to society. Nature will out. We must help it along social lines, or at least lines that are not actively antisocial. It is pointless to tell Johnny to remember he is a 'little gentleman', when he is neither little nor a gentleman. Instead he should be given the fullest information about life and the likely consequences of his actions in the hope that he will 'choose' wisely, and provided with a number of relatively harmless opportunities in case he should 'choose' what more sophisticated people would call foolishly. For, short of radical biochemical intervention, we are not, just as he is not, able to change his basic nature. Repressive secondary or tertiary programmes may curb him for a bit, all the while charging up tension, but some time there is likely to be a short-circuit blowing all the fuses in his system.

From the work of Alfred Adler we know that anyone of normal sexuality without genius powers of sublimation must 'frig, fuck, bugger or bust'; that deprivation does not lead, as the moralists suggest, to spirituality but to aggression. There is, among the population at large, much less capacity for creative sublimation than intellectuals who are inverted snobs are ready to admit. Preoccupation with sex is seldom connected with getting too much of it, but too little of it. Instead of fulminations against permissiveness, society should be providing 'adventure playgrounds' for the amorous, with full facilities for hygiene and contraceptive slot-machines, and medically inspected brothels. If and when young people settled down into accepted relationships in the parental home or student hall of residence, these commercial or municipal undertakings would decline rather than prosper. For personal reasons some will find physical sex difficult or impossible, and should have full access to vicarious sex through pornographic books, films and other media. The

Danish experience suggests that if this is a 'morbid preoccupation', it is one which flourishes in a climate of repression and is eroded by a flood of freedom.

There will be other aggressive impulses arising from the frustrations of life, and here too society will do well to provide innocuous outlets. It is a pity to employ professional breakers of sub-standard china and abandoned cars when the aggressions of amateurs could profitably be unleashed. In this light, 'moronic' one-armed bandits and shooting galleries that are fast adding to the garishness of city centres may be seen to be serving some of the functions of 'war games' for American intellectuals in think-tanks. Though the latter are primarily for the purpose of establishing military and diplomatic options and the strategy of 'flexible response', they are clearly satisfying emotional needs in their practitioners.[3] Those of low I.Q. need more practical outlets.

These provisions are simple and obvious and rely on free participation by individuals – though none the less controversial for that. If we are trusted and have facts sympathetically explained to us, we may not become more rational in any intellectual sense but tend to behave more sensibly. In this way maximal co-operation with minimal controls may be achieved. And, however determined by subtle physical and mental processes, we will keep the illusion of free choice. Thereby we prize our achievements. But achievements will never be prized if they constantly fall short of our personal expectations. Especially is this true in the moral sphere. It is most important for educationists to forget the moralists when suggesting moral 'aims' for their pupils. For 'clean living and right thinking' as normally interpreted are an impossible ideal, the pursuit of which will lead to intolerable disappointment. Yet even if we have reasonable expectations of ourselves, some of us will still fail society. When this happens it is entitled to protect itself.

Without awaiting dramatic neurophysiological discoveries that seem to be approaching, it already has the knowledge to treat individual aggression. This can be done not by curbing its expression but by the infinitely more satisfactory way of preventing its formation. Individuals will then be peaceful not because they are shackled but because they are peaceable.

Nardil[4] is in regular psychiatric use for disturbed children. New 'anti-hostility agents'[5] are known but not in use. It has been suggested that, if no other preventive of war turns up, they could be applied, like fluoride for dental caries, to drinking water. In human beings, as in animals, aggression centres have been located in the brain and neutralized by carefully implanted electrodes. Less specific operations have achieved the same effects. Sex criminals can be cured or at least stabilized by hormone therapy, without recourse to castration. For the rest of us there are contraceptive pills for women, with those for men on the way, and sterilization operations, some of them reversible, for both; so that sexual intercourse can be enjoyed without conception. At present most of these techniques are applied voluntarily. If demographic disaster should ever suggest compulsion, society's intervention would be involuntary in one of two ways. Either we would not notice it at all (agents in drinking water) or there would be a once-and-for-all operation to be followed by personal freedom of choice. But we must all be watchful, suspicious, democratically questioning before we advance. Persomorality has no patron saints.

Hitherto we have been thinking of aggression directed outwards by extroverts. There is here likely to be unanimous agreement that the action is immoral. In the past it was usual to give – as many still do today – this label to aggression inwardly directed by introverts. Suicide is the extreme case. In Britain it was a crime (or the attempt was a crime) till 1961, and it is illegal in many countries today. Depression and certain forms of drug addiction are other examples. Though the one is usually treated as an illness, the other is often thought a crime. Modern medicine has brought many dehabituation techniques, and implantation of radioactive yttrium-90 in the emotional centres of the brain has been claimed as a simple cure. Research in this field is usually on the assumption that drug-taking is an illness from which the victim seeks release; and with the present nature of both society and addictive drugs this is often true. But centred on cannabis, L.S.D.-25 and later variants like S.T.P.[6] and D.M.T.,[7] there is a growing cult which sees drugs as a means of liberation and not of bondage. In its estimation they foster love instead of hate and tranquillity instead of aggression.

For those with little appetite to explore outer space in rowing boats or rockets, they provide the limitless challenge of J. G. Ballard's 'inner space'.[8] Personal responsibilities would not be abandoned for none would be undertaken. If moropractice dissolved in dreams so too would moromalpractice. So long as enough energy for metabolism was provided the individual would tick over in a moral vacuum. For there would be no activities to designate as *mores* or *immores*. Short of startling biochemical changes such a prospect is unlikely to be everybody's cup of 'tea', but in suitable circumstances it could be not only be a fount of pleasure but a reservoir that would save us all from extinction by human aggression.

There are those who will protest that extinction would be better than a future 'debased' in the ways set out in this book: a future of dirt, doubt and disbelief;[9] of smut, sex and sedition; of candour, chaos or compulsion. So they will call it. They will cry out for the forsaken myths and the abandoned birch. They will set themselves up as the champions of 'freedom' in the great issues of life while they continue to be repressive even in the small. While still brainwashing with tarnished superstitions, they now complain of conditioning by chromium-plated progressivism. Already they denounce the permissive society as the 'new decadence', and they will be outraged at any attempt to extend it and justify it on philosophical and moral grounds. Let them protest as they will. They are entitled to do so. Out of the dialectic of project and protest society advances. I would merely have them ask, as the first fever of choler subsides, what is free or elevated about the spawning of half-starved millions, the slaughter and maiming of idealistic factions, the regimentation of military cohorts and monastic penitentiaries, the shockwaves of guilt in urban neurotics. If it is debased to seek a way out of these, I am freely on the side of decadence.

Appendix 1

Empiricism, the belief that the world can be understood by observation of how it functions, flowered in the physical sciences in the seventeenth century. Gradually it pollinated biological, sociological and psychological disciplines, so that the magical has yielded to the logical interpretation even of man's dreams. More and more departments of life have come under the domain of descriptive and predictive laws, operating on causal principles. Even the neurophysiology of man. It would be surprising if in the whole deterministic universe his will had somehow escaped. To counter this conclusion the notion of causality has itself been challenged. Certainly it is a metaphysical assumption, as Hume long ago pointed out. All we really observe is an association of two events in time and space. If one comes before the other we say it caused it, but this is just a matter of linguistic convenience. Nevertheless it is convenient and we all know what it means. But, it has been argued more recently, quantum mechanics demonstrates that at the level of subatomic particles we cannot explain what is happening. Particulate behaviour is 'uncertain' and 'indeterminate'. From this the concept of non-causality arose. It has little to recommend it. Sub-atomic particles are themselves inferences or models of reality rather than anything which is directly observed. But let us suppose that they exist.

As our instruments are insufficiently refined to allow full observation, and the mere act of investigation alters the position or velocity of our material, we are 'uncertain' what these particles are doing. To us their behaviour is 'indeterminate'. But the statistical average of this behaviour is regular and predictable. Otherwise atomic power stations would not function – or only when the particles were in the mood. In the aggregate, particulate free will would lead to macroscopic events that were irregular and unpredictable. (Unless one were to argue, as a mere word game, that particles were 'free' to act as they liked but they always 'chose' to follow deterministic laws.) A similar analysis is true of human behaviour. Those who are perennially amazed at the – to them – incomprehensibilities of such behaviour have studied neither general social conditions nor individual psychology.

Appendix 2

The political effects of war are well known: the rise and fall of empires, the occupation and cession of territories, the domestic *coups d'état* and revolutions that fructify when armies are engaged abroad. The technological effects of war are often overlooked but are equally important. Not simply, as the Swedish inventor John Ericsson said to Abraham Lincoln during the American Civil War, that 'the time has come . . . when our cause will have to be sustained not by numbers but by superior weapons . . . if you apply our mechanical resources to the fullest extent you can destroy the enemy without enlisting another man';[1] that is, that wars are won by those who chance to have technical military superiority. More fundamentally, the planning for and waging of wars pose problems and release energies that fire inventors, technologists and the governments that support them. Nor is this only a feature of the last hundred or so years. 'War has always given an important incentive to technological development.'[2]

Soldiers in the field gain advantages from the surprise element as well as from the enhanced lethalness or safety in use of new weapons. In some cases, far from home in enemy territory, they need sophisticated communications, supply lines and transport. If they are successful they will impose new methods of technology, law and government on a subject people, and perhaps find useful techniques or arts to assimilate into their own culture. While they are away fighting, their countrymen at home face the problem of producing more goods, military and civil, with a depleted labour force. So sections of the population not hitherto productive are made so, leading to social changes which may be irreversible after the war, while mechanization and automation are encouraged. Years or even centuries later, the techniques which proved so powerful in war are found to be no less mighty in peace.

It is conjectural whether flints were first developed for war or peace, but metallurgy, and especially the use of iron from the Assyrians on, has owed so much to war that the 'father of history', Herodotus, in the fifth century B.C. lamented that 'iron had been sent us for our woe',[3] and much the same has been said of nickel and antimony steels in the intercontinental ballistic missiles of our own day. The fact that a mixture of saltpetre, sulphur and charcoal is explosive seems first to

284

have been discovered in China for aesthetic purposes: fireworks displays. But its rediscovery in Europe about A.D. 1300 was connected with warfare. 'Gunpowder' replaced the incendiary 'Greek fire' of the time of Herodotus, while its projectile powers led to the invention of the cannon and the mathematics of trajectories, just as astronomy was fostered by navigation, military or exploratory. It was not till the second half of the seventeenth century, first in France and then in Britain, that gunpowder was used for such civil purposes as blasting tunnels and mines. Since then the military, followed by the peaceful, use of new inventions has accelerated.

The War of American Independence (1775–83) stimulated the manufacture of cast-iron cannons in America and carronades in Britain. From the French Revolution, Revolutionary and Napoleonic Wars emerged far-reaching political and social change. But scientific developments, despite the guillotining of Antoine Lavoisier, were no less marked. At home the French advanced chemical engineering and established the Polytechnique and schools of civil engineering and mining, while communications with and the supply of a far-flung front line led to the use of observation balloons, telegraphy and food canning. Britain reacted by accelerating the enclosure system and improving the efficiency of her agriculture and industry to meet the war effort and increased trade. Steam power and machinery were introduced into the dockyards, textiles, iron and even, for a time, the riveting of boot soles, while tin-plating was invented for cans. Deprived of European imports, America developed her cotton-gin and cotton-spinning factories; then, when war broke out with Britain in 1812, she established woollen factories and evolved the clipper ship at Baltimore for privateering against the Royal Navy. To this Britain responded with a programme of frigate building.

Other wars of the nineteenth century similarly acted as scientific catalysts. During the Crimean War (1854–6) Russia developed the mine while Britain came up with Bessemer steel, breech-loading guns and, despite obstruction, modern nursing. The main stimulus to America's technological progress was the Civil War (1861–5). Victory came to the Union rather than to the Confederates, not by the triumph of manpower or moral urgency, but through the use of Whitworth's quick-firing gun, labour-saving devices like harvesters, sewing machines for leather, automatic screw-making lathes and the universal milling machine, observation balloons and Ericsson's gun-turret for a naval blockade of the South. Austria had the torpedo just before the land-based Austro-Prussian War (1866), which Prussia won with her breech-loading needle-gun. Five years later Prussia won the Franco-Prussian War (1870–1) with the aid of a railway network and the Krupp's iron and steel industry. During the Sudan War (1882) Britain successfully used the Kynoch cartridge case and during the Boer War (1899–1902) observation balloons (and concentration camps).

It took the First World War to demonstrate the value of the tank (forerunner of earth-moving and timber-clearing equipment), radio and the aeroplane, whose peaceful development came soon afterwards. Experiments by Ernest Rutherford before and during the war culminated in splitting the atom in 1919, but the Manhattan Project which produced the atomic bomb did not emerge till the end of the Second World War (1939–45) and the first commercial power station opened at Calder Hall in 1956. It was this second war which stimulated the exploitation of artificial fibres when nylon, discovered in 1932, demonstrated its virtues in parachutes. Similarly, jet engines, rockets and radar commended themselves in war before they were developed in peace. It is virtually certain that the 'space race', whose first success was the Russian sputnik in 1957, and from whose 'spin-off' we have gained such useful things as fat-free frying pans, micro-miniaturization in electronic computers and communications satellites, is a product of the Cold War, despite the camaraderie with which the Soviet Union and the United States have tried to invest it.

Notes to Nucleoethics

Introduction

1. *Oxford English Dictionary* (1933). Second meaning. Other meanings are 'mimicry' and 'character-formation'. The *OED* gives an interesting picture of the last generation's notion of all things ethical and moral.
2. Charles L. Stevenson's *Ethics and Language* (1944), p. 275.
3. In *The Permissive Morality* (1964) C. H. and Winifred M. Whiteley designate 1900.
4. It took the First and Second World Wars for the Second and Third Worlds respectively to achieve the more fundamental changes brought about in the First World by the French Revolution.
5. But a Gallup Poll (*Daily Telegraph*, 3 August 1970) found that 51 per cent of 2,158 adolescents aged 15 to 19 still talked problems over with and were helped by their fathers, and 68 per cent with their mothers, while a Harris Poll (*Daily Express*, 28 June 1971) found young people showed 'a sweeping display of confidence in the police (91 per cent), schoolteachers (86 per cent), parents (83 per cent), and the Royal Family (81 per cent)'.
6. 'Halt the Descent to Decadence' by J. W. Robertson in the Roman Catholic *Universe* (12 June 1970), aimed at 'extracting from candidates pledges' on a number of 'moral issues' ignored in the 1970 British general election.
7. Editorial in the Roman Catholic *Tablet*, 8 August 1970.
8. The hallucinogenic mushroom *Amanita muscaria*. See John M. Allegro's *The Sacred Mushroom and the Cross* (1970).
9. See chapter 15.
10. From a root meaning 'to go out' and stressing the role of will-power and creativity.
11. James Hemming's *Individual Morality* (1969), p. 26.
12. *ibid.*, p. 177. Anxious to avoid Christology yet sustain Christianity, many Christian writers now refer to 'self-transcendence' (see John Macquarrie's *Three Issues in Ethics* (1970), pp. 50–9). Similar views have been expressed by Sartre and by 'revisionist' Marxists like Roger Garaudy, Milan Prucha, Milan Machovec and Vitezslav Gardavsky (see *Slant*, January–February 1968).

Similar is Julian Huxley's 'Transhumanism' (*New Bottles for New Wine* (1957), pp. 13–17). Those humanists who stress this usually have strong Christian leftovers: cf. Hemming's themes of Christ the 'moral genius', the nobility of suffering, etc. (*op. cit.*, pp. 174 and 144).

13. From the statement of the Commune Movement as published in its journal *Communes*. See also 'Good Commune Guide' (*Sunday Times*, 5 September 1971).

14. One at the London School of Economics debated whether it ought to rush out and occupy the offices of the *Daily Express*. Nothing happened, not because anyone demonstrated the futility of the gesture but because after many hours the exhausted debate fizzled out. Nobody mentioned what would have been the first target of real revolutionaries: the BBC External Services at Bush House across the road.

15. It might uncharitably be said they tend to be of asthenic physique.

16. *Communes*, April 1970.

17. John Sparrow on 'Why do the young look like this?' (*Sunday Times*, 6 September 1970).

18. *Methodist Recorder*, 6 August 1970. The writer, Nicholas Timmins, rejects this simplistic approach, which is however typical of the religious Press (see reaction to the 'obscene' and 'blasphemous' *Council of Love* in, e.g., *ibid.*, 27 August 1970).

19. The mass youth movement – pop concerts and boutiques – is dominated by Hell's Angels as tough as any Chicago cop, the narrowest of peer pressures and tribal loyalties, and an obsessional respect for 'fashion'.

20. As set out in textbooks like Vernon J. Burke's *History of Ethics* (1968) and *Ethics; a textbook in moral philosophy* (1966), Carl Wellman's *The Language of Ethics* (1961) and Nicholai Hartmann's *Ethics* (Ger. 1926, Eng. tr. by Stanton Coit 1932). For a more personal account, see Albert Schweitzer's *Civilization and Ethics* (3rd edn, 1946), Joel J. Kupperman's *Ethical Knowledge* (1970) and H. J. McCloskey's *Meta-Ethics and Normative Ethics* (1969).

21. The most interesting of these is R. M. Hare's family tree of 'prescriptive language' in *The Language of Morals* (1952).

22. One of the charges hostile critics will bring is 'reductionism'.

23. A reaction, I suggest, against Nazism, Fascism, Stalinism, *Brave New World* and *1984*.

24. See B. F. Skinner's *The Behaviour of Organisms. An experimental analysis* (1938), *Science and Human Behaviour* (1953), *Verbal Behaviour* (1957), *The Analysis of Behaviour* (1961) and *Beyond Freedom and Dignity* (1972).

25. 'Immorality' could mean a repudiation of the conception of morality. Experience does not bear this out, as the most 'anti-social' have some moral code. Idiots may not recognize one but do not 'repudiate' the idea.

Chapter 1

1. Lyric from the film *It's a Mad, Mad, Mad, Mad World* (1963), directed by Stanley Kramer.
2. Author's transcript of broadcast, 23 October 1970; slightly different in wording from full report in the *Times* (24 October). Cf. Sir John Wolfenden's 'foul smell of anarchy, nihilism, destructiveness for their own sakes' (*Times*, 31 October 1970) and Richard Nixon's 'time to take the gloves off' against violent demonstrators and 'put the terrorists where they belong – not roaming around civil society, but behind bars' (*Sunday Telegraph*, 1 November 1970).
3. Dean Acheson to the US Military Academy at West Point, 5 December 1962 (*Keesing's Contemporary Archives* (1963–4), p. 19181).
4. Southey's *Essays, Moral and Political* (1832), p. 328.
5. *ibid.*, p. 335.
6. Henry Edward, Cardinal Manning on 'The True Story of the Vatican Council' (*Nineteenth Century*, March 1877).
7. Edward R. Pease's *The History of the Fabian Society* (1916), p. 18.
8. Opinion Research Centre (*Sunday Times*, 25 August 1968). Admittedly this coincided with the time of greatest dissatisfaction with Harold Wilson's Labour (but hardly Left) Government. But a more recent poll among secretarial students conducted by the Alfred Marks Staff Agency named Enoch Powell as the person most admired (*Sun*, 27 October 1970).
9. Dr Derek Miller, ex-chairman of Tavistock Clinic's adolescent unit, at the annual conference of the Headmasters' Association (*Times Educational Supplement*, 18 April 1969).
10. See, e.g., Monica Furlong's 'A crisis of authority – or a crisis of obedience?' (*Sunday Times*, 4 August 1968), Charles Davis's *A Question of Conscience* (1967), Gustav Husak's 'Speaking to our Soviet friends' (*Soviet Weekly*, 31 May 1969), *New Left May Day Manifesto* (1967) and *May Day Manifesto 1968*, edited by Raymond Williams.
11. Brief history, from the English viewpoint, of the Catholic–Marxist dialogue: 1960 – conference of the December Group; January 1964 – start of the Christian (largely Catholic) journal *Slant*, edited by A. C. Downing; May 1965 – Christians and Marxists met at Salzburg; March 1966 – John Lewis on 'Dialogue between Christianity and Marxism' (*Marxism Today*); September 1966 – Thomas Corbishley SJ spoke of 'common objectives' (*Marxism Today*); April 1967 – formal dialogue at Marienbad; March 1970 – *Slant* disappeared. See thirty issues of *Slant*, *Catholics and the Left* ('*Slant* Manifesto') (1966) by Adrian Cunningham, Terry Eagleton, Brian Wicker, Martin

Redfern and Laurence Bright OP, and *Dialogue of Christianity and Marxism* (1968), ed. by James Klugmann. Martin Shaw, at one time on the *Slant* board, became disillusioned with both the Vatican ('may have a conservative influence') and the Kremlin ('reabsorption . . . into the capitalist world market') and came to believe that all the dialogue really signified was 'an identity of interests between the ruling classes of East and West' (*Slant*, January–February 1968). On the philosophical level, at the Marienbad dialogue a Czech Marxist, Milan Prucha, said both Catholicism and Marxism are working 'towards establishing the ontological basis of man's historical immanence and transcendence' (*ibid.*).

12. *Times*, 7 April 1969.

13. Lenten Pastoral Letter (*Sunday Times*, 16 February 1969).

14. Article 'The Dictates of Rome' (*ibid.*, 6 October 1968). cf. *Authority in Crisis*, interview with Cardinal Suenens (BBC Radio 4, 30 October 1970).

15. 'Giving Youth Its Say' (*Soviet Weekly*, 5 April 1969).

16. See articles on the cultic implications of hippiedom in *Newsweek*, 9 May and 21 March 1966 and 21 April 1969. Apolitical 'dropping out' may be gentle and loving but it can be squalid (*Observer Magazine*, 14 February 1971, *Observer*, 15 August 1971, Peter Willey's report for the Anti-Slavery Society, 4 August 1971, and the Radio 4 series by Wilfred De'Ath on *Inside, Outside USA*, 10–14 January 1972), murderous ('Sharon Tate' ritual murders associated with Charles Manson and his hippie 'family') or cannibalistic (*Sunday Times*, 30 August 1970).

17. Mrs Jagmohan Joshi . See *The Black Man in Search of Power* (1968) by the *Times* News Team, p. 160.

18. Kenneth Leech's *Drug Subculture* (1969), p. 12.

19. *Quotations from Chairman Mao Tse-Tung* ('Little Red Book') (1967), pp. 59 and 63 (*Selected Works*, II, pp. 153 and 225).

20. See leader in *Times Educational Supplement*, 7 March 1969.

21. Raised by Frederick Wilder, president of the National Association of Head Teachers, at its 1969 conference (*Observer*, 25 May 1969).

22. See 'Computer dates for men only' (*Sunday Times*, 20 April 1969).

23. Launched in Britain by Germaine Greer (*OZ*, February 1970). Otherwise known as the Women's Liberation movement. Women's Lib began in America with Betty Friedan in 1963.

24. 'Naissance d'un Mouvement Étudiant' (*Le Monde*, 7 and 8 March 1968) quoted in *Student Power: Problems, Diagnosis, Action* (1969), ed. Alexander Cockburn and Robin Blackburn, p. 26.

25. *ibid.*, p. 29.

26. 'Universities and Violence' (*Survey*, October 1968).

27. 'Can the students see beyond their despair?' (*Tribune*, 23 May 1969).

28. Robin Blackburn in *Student Power*, p. 163.

29. *Paris: May 1968*, Solidarity Pamphlet No 30 (1968), p. 19.

30. *A Critique of Pure Tolerance* (US 1966, UK 1969), essays by Robert Paul Wolff, Barrington Moore Jr and Herbert Marcuse, p. 123.

31. See *Times Educational Supplement*, 16 February 1968, which describes the setting up of the Anti-University of London in Rivington Street, Shoreditch, four days before. I called there soon afterwards. People – mostly middle-class drop-outs or 'weekend hippies', and non-English (a lot of Americans) – were sitting around in groups in dreamy abstraction (? stoned) while one or two played guitars and recorders or argued in a mixture of hippie and Marxist jargon. A year or so later I called back and it had vanished without trace. Apparently some organic structure survived without a regular home; but 'anti doesn't mean anti any more. It means alternative' (*Sunday Telegraph*, 10 October 1971).

32. See H. J. N. Horsburgh's *Non-Violence and Aggression: A Study of Gandhi's Moral Equivalent of War* (1968), p. 64. Joan Bondurant says that those who claim to follow Gandhi practise obstructive *Duragraha*, which 'may end in alienation' (*Peace News*, 22 May 1970), and not creative *Satyagraha*. In America students have mostly turned from violence to the non-violence of expediency (see William Davis's 'Where Have All the Demos Gone?', *Evening News*, 19 November 1971).

33. *New Revolutionaries. Left Opposition* (1969), ed. Tariq Ali, p. 22.

34. ibid., p, 282.

35. Between *Tribune* 'evolutionary' MPs Michael Foot and Eric Heffer and *Black Dwarf* 'revolutionary' journalists Bob Rowthorne and Tariq Ali.

36. See Konrad Lorenz's *On Aggression* (1967), Robert Ardrey's *The Territorial Imperative. A Personal Inquiry into the Animal Origins of Property and Nations* (1967) and *African Genesis: A personal investigation into the animal origins and nature of man* (1967), Desmond Morris's *The Naked Ape: A Zoologist's Study of the Human Animal* (1967) and Anthony Storr's *Human Aggression* (1968).

37. John Lewis in 'Human Aggression: its Cause and Cure' (*Humanist*, June 1969). See also *Man and Aggression* (1968), ed. M. Ashley Montagu.

38. Katharine Whitehorn in 'I'm better for a change of mind' (*Observer*, 29 October 1967).

Chapter 2

1. (1912), V, p. 414.
2. (1909), V, p. 556.
3. From Vol. IV, beginning 4 November 1837. The journal was launched on 1 November 1834 and lasted till 1845.
4. From 'Morality' (6 January 1838), probably by the editor, George A. Fleming, who was more sympathetic to Christianity than most of his colleagues.
5. *Movement*, 6 November 1844.
6. *An Enquiry concerning the Principles of Morals* (1751), pp. 176–7.
7. *A Treatise of Human Nature: being An Attempt to introduce the experimental Method of Reasoning into Moral Subjects*, Vol. III *Of Morals* (1740), pp. 25–6. For further, and more accessible, reading see *Hume's Ethical Writings* (1965), ed. with introduction by Alasdair MacIntyre, and *Ethical Naturalism: New Studies in Ethics* (1970), ed. W. D. Hudson.
8. From stanza 4 of Rudyard Kipling's *Recessional*.
9. In his 1967 Reith Lectures (*A Runaway World?* (1968), p. 49) Edmund Leach identified this as the only universal tabu. On the other hand Morris Ginsberg believed that 'amidst variations moral codes everywhere exhibit striking similarities in essentials' (*On the Diversity of Morals* (1956), p. 110).
10. Inspired by the Vienna School of Moritz Schlick. Best-known popularizer is A. J. Ayer in his *Language, Truth and Logic* (1936). Logical positivism developed from Comtian positivism under the influence of Ernst Mach and his *Science of Mechanics* (1883).
11. The only book which appeared during his lifetime (1889–1951), *Tractatus Logico-Philosophicus* (1921), is more interested in logic than linguistic analysis.
12. Cited by A. F. M. Brierley in 'Philosophy and Humanism' (*Plain View*, Winter 1964).
13. Whose most famous book was *Principia Ethica* (1903).
14. Stevenson's *Ethics and Language*, p. vii.
15. See J. J. C. Smart's *Outline of a System of Utilitarian Ethics* (1961), p. 1.
16. R. M. Hare's *The Language of Morals* (1952), p. v.
17. John Wilson in *Introduction to Moral Education* (1967) by himself, Norman Williams and Barry Sugarman, p. 88.
18. e.g. R. M. Hare in *Freedom and Reason* (1963).
19. See Smart's *Outline*, Bertrand Russell and Paul Foulkes in *Wisdom of the West* (1959) and numerous papers by A. G. N. Flew on issues within normative ethics.
20. *Wisdom of the West*, p. 309.
21. *The Language of Morals*, p. 167 *et seq.*
22. *ibid.*, p. 160.

23. I am aware that the hard-core hippie can scarcely be said to have any political views at all and the hard-core anarchist is unlikely to be a drug-taker (other than tobacco and alcohol). But I think the two attitudes, personal and social, especially among young people today, tend to go together, if they are united by nothing but dislike of the 'fuzz', 'pigs' or whatever the groovy term for the police may be. In 1970 the Flower Children of California, who had previously wanted to opt out of politics, decided to combine politics with drugs and support the violence-oriented Black Panthers and Weathermen. At the same time, in the Netherlands the Provos (from *provokation*: confrontation) yielded to Roel van Duyn's Kabouters (Pixies), whose 'curious mixture of demonstration politics, direct action and campaigns against urban pollution' (*Idiot International*, July 1970) is mostly associated with the planting of flowers and trees.

24. Hare puts its evaluative use first.

25. *Language of Morals*, p. 91.

26. *ibid.*, p. 150.

27. See Matthew Arnold's *Culture and Anarchy: an essay in political and social criticism* (1869) and C. P. Snow's *The Two Cultures and the Scientific Revolution* (1959).

28. Awareness of this has become the basis of a new type of religious apologetics as exemplified by Eric Mascall's *Christian Theology and Natural Science. Some Questions on their relations* (1956) and Arthur Koestler's *The Ghost in the Machine* (1967).

29. *Ethics and Language*, p. vii.

30. Hare would probably say that 'social' is 'covertly evaluative' (*Language of Morals*, p. 92) or the framer of the sentence 'wishes to commend' something (p. 93). But this can to some degree be said of every statement. Personally I can regard the non-existence or painless extinction of the entire human species with as much equanimity as I regard a peach-tree (viz. depending on my mood at the time).

31. See *The Enforcement of Morals* (1965) by Patrick Devlin, p. vii.

32. I Corinthians 6, 19.

33. For a discussion of this theme, see Chapter 4 of *Towards a Quaker View of Sex* (1963), ed. Alastair Heron, Chapter 6 of John A. T. Robinson's *Honest to God* (1963), Douglas Rhymes's *No New Morality: Christian Personal Values and Sexual Morality* (1964), Joseph Fletcher's *Situation Ethics: the New Morality* (1966), James A. Pike's *You and the New Morality* (1967) and Chapter 2 of Macquarrie's *Three Issues in Ethics*.

34. See G. F. Woods on 'The Grounds of Christian Moral Judgements' (*Soundings: Essays Concerning Christian Understanding* (1962), ed. A. R. Vidler).

35. By mental processes described in Chapter 15.

36. Mark Woodnut, also an Isle of Wight County Councillor, who was shortly afterwards criticized in connection with concessions granted to his Bembridge Harbour Improvements Co.

37. Save, by convention, a parent, child, grandparent, etc.

38. In *The Silent Language* (1959) Edward T. Hall identifies ten kinds of message systems of which only one involves language.

39. As in the *Report of the Committee on Homosexual Offences and Prostitution* ('Wolfenden Report'), Cmnd 247 (1957), para. 13.

40. Patrick Devlin argues (*The Enforcement of Morals*, 1959 and 1965) that because 'corruption' is stated in the law the activity must be immoral. This is clearly the way the law has regarded these matters in the past but they need not remain so.

41. See D. and R. Morris on *Men and Snakes* (1965), *Men and Pandas* (1966) and *Men and Apes* (1966) and I. M. Marks and M. G. Gelder on 'Animal Phobias' (*Amer. J. Psychiatry*, July 1966). Appearances here, as elsewhere, may be deceptive and some strange-looking beasts have gentle manners and vice versa.

42. An abstraction whose meaning and dangers are discussed in later chapters.

Chapter 3

1. During the 1970 Congressional elections President Nixon said that 'the time had come for parents to exercise this responsibility to guide their children' (*Sunday Telegraph*, 1 November 1970).

2. 7 & 8 Geo. VI cap. 31, s. 7.

3. Leading to unkind innuendoes that its ancestors were the reactionary Oxford Movement (1833) and Oxford Group or Moral Re-Armament (1921) as well as the usual gibe about the 'home of lost causes'. More recently a Schools Council Moral Education Curriculum Unit has come to Oxford.

4. As individuals the members of the team have religious backgrounds. The director, John Wilson, was Professor of Religious Knowledge at Trinity College, Toronto, from 1961 to 1962. But in a private letter he tells me his personal religious views are 'don't know', he goes 'to church but also to Humanist meetings' and he 'shouldn't think' his colleagues had 'any single-minded active Christian adherence' (29 May 1970).

5. See Émile Durkheim's *Les Règles de la Méthode sociologique* (*The Rules of Sociological Method*) (1895).

6. A fact the more enthusiastic exponents of situation ethics overlook.

7. *Declaration of Independence*, 4 July 1776 (*The Constitution of the United States, ... the Declaration of Independence* (1791), p. 158. cf. Edmund Burke's 'The question with me is, not

whether you have a right to render your people miserable; but whether it is not your interest to make them happy' (speech in the Commons, 22 March 1775, *The Parliamentary History of England from the Earliest Period to the Year 1803* (1813), XVIII, p. 536).

8. See Mill's *Utilitarianism* (1863), reproduced from *Fraser's Magazine*. The word 'utilitarian' was derived from John Galt's *Annals of the Parish* (1821).

9. *A Fragment on Government and an Introduction to the Principles of Morals and Legislation* (1948), ed. Wilfrid Harrison, p. 125.

10. *ibid.*

11. Bentham's *Commonplace Book* (*Works*, X, p. 142): 'The greatest happiness of the greatest number is the foundation of morals and legislation.' In 1725 Francis Hutcheson the Elder had observed: 'That action is best which accomplishes the greatest happiness for the greatest numbers' (*An Inquiry into the Original of our Ideas of Beauty and Virtue* (1725), Treatise II *Concerning Moral Good and Evil*, p. 164).

12. Bentham's phrase. See Mill's *Utilitarianism*, p. 91.

13. See Richard Cumberland's *De Legibus Naturae Disquisitio Philosophica* (1672).

14. *Utilitarianism*, p. 9.

15. Smart's *Outline*, p. 4. The terminology 'act' and 'rule' was proposed by R. B. Brandt in *Ethical Theory* (1959). Smart subdivided it into 'actual' and 'possible'.

16. *The Metaphysics of Morals* (anon. 1st Eng. tr. 1799), I, p. xix. Earlier this is called the 'categorical imperative' (p. xviii).

17. *ibid.*, II, p. xxxii.

18. A rare exception is Smart, who simply appeals to the 'natural and widespread human sentiment . . . of generalized benevolence' (*Outline*, p. 4).

19. See *Principia Ethica* (1903) and *Ethics* (1912). Moore spoke of the 'greatest good' (agathistic or ideal utilitarianism) rather than 'greatest happiness' (hedonistic or eudaemonistic utilitarianism).

20. Normally human males have forty-six chromosomes in their cells, including an X and a Y. It is said, however, that some violent recidivists have two Y chromosomes.

21. *The History of England from the Accession of James the Second* (1858), I, p. 162.

22. Especially prominent in Christian literature; but also in Hemming's humanist *Individual Morality*, pp. 17 and 41.

23. In a *noto proprio* of 21 March 1969, *Paschalis Mysterii*, accompanying *The New Calendar* of the Sacred Congregation of Rites. Saints George, Christopher and Nicholas are among those whose very existence is questioned.

24. See Matthew 10, 39; 16, 25; Mark 8, 35; Luke 9, 24.

25. *Sunday Times Magazine*, 9 March 1969, concerning Pat Arrow-smith and the Committee of 100.
26. A survival of non-personal expiation is the doctrine of 'absolute liability' of a principal for his agents' actions in the law of torts.
27. *The Moral Judgement of the Child* (1932), p. 87.
28. *The Ethical Animal* (1960), p. 7.
29. The phrase is Julian Huxley's. See, e.g., American *Humanist*, January–February 1962.
30. Romans 10, 14.
31. *An Inquiry concerning Political Justice, and Its Influence on General Virtue and Happiness* (1793), p. 304. See also George Drysdale's *The Elements of Social Science, or Physical, Sexual, and Natural Religion* (7th enlarged edn, 1867), pp. 455–6, on 'causation' and 'motive'.
32. See Appendix I.
33. Advocated by some members of Radical Alternatives to Prison (1970).
34. *Encyclopaedia Britannica* (13th edn, 1926), III, p. 655.
35. Cf. H. J. Eysenck's *Crime and Personality* (1964) and the freedom of 'self-expression' he allowed his own children.
36. See Chapter 15.
37. Indian *yogi* are said to be able to do this. Perhaps with training one can induce an emotional state where the autonomic nervous system and endocrine glands together modify the natural rhythm of the heart muscle.

Chapter 4

1. Introduction to his *Critique of the Hegelian Philosophy of Right* (1844) (*Marx-Engels Gesamtausgabe* (1927), I, p. 607).
2. 'On the Influence of Authority in Matters of Opinion' (*Nineteenth Century*, March 1877).
3. *Epître à l'Auteur de Livre des Trois Imposteurs*, 10 November 1770; based on Ovid's *Ars Amatoria*, I, 637.
4. Matthew 7, 7; Luke 11, 9.
5. Alfred Lord Tennyson's *In Memoriam* (1850), LIV, lines 1–2.
6. See John 14, 23.
7. See Matthew 19, 17; Luke 19, 27; John 8, 51.
8. Alexander Pope's *An Essay on Man* (1732–4), Epistle I, line 294.
9. The centre of his moral teaching, inspired by the doctrine of attunement which came from Pythagoras and Heraclitus.
10. I don't know who originated this apposite phrase; perhaps Harold Loukes.
11. 'Historicism' was invented by (Sir) Karl Popper to censure some historians' belief in 'laws of history which enable them to pro-phesy the course of historical necessity' (*The Open Society and*

its Enemies (1945), I, p. 3). See also his *The Poverty of Historicism* (1944–5). 'Scientism' is used by William H. Whyte in *The Organization Man* (1956), Friedrich von Hayek in *The Counter-Revolution of Science: Studies on the Abuse of Reason* (1952) and Eric Voegelin in *Social Research*, December 1948, to describe the extension of scientific findings to areas where they do not apply.

12. Terry Eagleton in 'Why I oppose the Pope's ruling and stay in the church' (*Tribune*, 23 August 1968).

13. *La Pensée Sauvage* (*The Savage Mind*) (1966) by Claude Lévi-Strauss, p. 97.

14. *ibid.*, p. 214.

15. A moiety is always endogamous; a caste, usually. A clan may be simple (containing one totem-group) or complex (more than one).

16. *ibid.*, p. 221.

17. *ibid.*, p. 166.

18. Though the aborigines may persist in corroborees, mission life has undermined the religious beliefs and dependence on hunting (aided by the magic of hunt-corroborees) which gave relevance to them and status to adult males. Though they do not fully accept Western social life, they grow dissatisfied with their own and, now rootless, often seek consolation in alcohol, gambling and the like. Wearing unaccustomed clothes without attention to hygiene promotes rather than reduces disease. See Winifred M. Hilliard's *The People in Between: the Pitjantjatjara People of Ernabella* (1968) and *Records of the American-Australian Scientific Expedition to Arnhem Land*, II, *Anthropology and Nutrition* (1960), ed. Charles P. Mountford.

19. See Paul Fauconnet's *La Responsabilité. Étude de sociologie* (1920).

20. In Piaget's phrase, probably overstated.

21. B. Narayan at a congress in London on 'Not Bread Alone' (2 January 1969).

22. See the *Larousse Encyclopaedia of Mythology* (1959), pp. 378–84.

23. *Karma Yoga* is the path of work or action. But Hinduism is largely meditative and the Path of Attainment includes *Raja Yoga* (the path of will) and *Gnani Yoga* (the path of wisdom). Impregnating and 'transcending' them all is 'that which is known as *Bhakti Yogi*, or the *yoga* of devotion – the path of religious feeling' (Yogi Ramacharaka's *Advanced Course in Yogi Philosophy and Oriental Occultism* (n.d.), p. 102).

24. From scholastic definitions of 'substance' the physical universe can be deduced as being all-embracing, self-justifying and infinite. Theological premises lead to the same conclusion about God. Therefore the universe and God are identical.

25. Gandhi, assassinated by a Hindu fanatic, is regarded by the Indian atheist Gora, who knew him well, as more of a religious

sceptic than was generally believed (see *Freethinker*, 18 December 1971). Nehru was widely known to be an agnostic. Giving seats in parliament to the lowest caste has given their politicians a vested interest in maintaining the caste system.

26. *Encyclopaedia of Religion and Ethics*, V, p. 447.
27. In Zen Buddhism enlightenment is called *satori*.
28. *Dharma* in Sanskrit, *Dhamma* in Pali. Theravada, the sole surviving sect of *Hinayana* (small or lesser vehicle) Buddhism, places more emphasis on moral rigour than *Mahayana* (large or greater vehicle) Buddhism, some sects of which deify Gautama (Gotama) and rely on his divine aid. For the great complexity of Buddhist schools and attempts to unify Buddhist teachings see Christmas Humphreys's *Buddhism* (1951), especially pp. 71–6.
29. *Dhammapada*, verse 183. The title means 'path of virtue' or 'scriptural texts'. See notes to (Sir) Sarvépalli Radhakrishnan's *Dhammapada* (1950).
30. The major ones are set out in the Five Precepts (*Pancha Sila*): injuring living things, stealing, sexual immorality, falsehood and liquors which engender slothfulness.
31. *Encyclopaedia of Religion and Ethics*, V, p. 466.
32. e.g. Hsün Ching.
33. See James Legge's *The Chinese Classics* (1861, 3rd revised 1893), I, p. 357.
34. *Analects*, xii, 22.
35. *ibid.*, xii, 2; xv, 23.
36. *ibid.*, xiv, 36.
37. The Maoist party in Britain is called the Communist Party of Britain (Marxist–Leninist).
38. A plural word.
39. It survives in parts of Persia and among the Parsees in the Bombay area. I have devoted no sub-chapter to it as, save in so far as elements are incorporated in other religions, it is now isolated and uninfluential.
40. Called the *lex talionis* (Exodus 21, 23–5).
41. Mostly used in Catholic circles but attributable to all Judaeo-Christianity.
42. See Isaiah 42, wrongly said by Christians to foretell Christ.
43. Hebrews 12, 6; Revelation 3, 19.
44. Originally in every large centre, but because of corruption ultimately restricted to that at Jerusalem.
45. According to a legend this was the answer given to a heathen who asked Hillel to expound the entire Torah while he was standing on one foot. Based on Leviticus 19, 18 and 34 and taken over by Akiba (*Sifra, Kedoshim* 4, 12).
46. This includes such fierce pedantry as 'whoever forgets one (single) word of his study, scripture accounts it unto him as if he had incurred guilt (expiable) by his life' (*Aboth* 3, 8). The

natural law was revered and the things which are 'unnameable' –
viz. swine, leprosy, idolatry and sodomy – are those thought to be
especially 'unnatural' (footnote to p. 367 of *Kethuboth* (1936)
in *The Babylonian Talmud*). In the index to the thirty-five
volumes of the *Talmud* there are 295 entries for the sabbath,
118 for sacrifice and 100 for offering compared with eight for
ethics and related words, though ethics is, of course, implicit
in many places elsewhere.

47. See Genesis 13, 15; 17, 19.
48. In his last public statement Bertrand Russell sadly saw Israel
    embracing 'the traditional role of the imperial power' and quoted
    I. F. Stone on 'the moral millstone around the neck of world
    Jewry' (*Freethinker*, 11 April 1970).
49. For varying views on why the whole Gospel story is a myth, see
    Robert Taylor's *The Diegesis; being a Discovery of the Origin,
    Evidences and Early History of Christianity* (1829), Gerald
    Massey's *The Historical Jesus and Mythical Christ* (1921), *A
    Book of the Beginnings* (1881) and *The Natural Genesis* (1883),
    Georges Ory's *An Analysis of Christian Origins* (1961), John
    M. Allegro's *The Sacred Mushroom and the Cross: a study of the
    nature and origins of Christianity within the fertility cults of the
    ancient Near East* (1970) and G. A. Wells's *The Jesus of the
    Early Christians* (1971).
50. John 18, 36.
51. The biblical canon was not fixed till the Council of Carthage,
    A.D. 397.
52. e.g. Mark 9, 47.
53. Akiba, e.g., said that the utmost punishment in Gehenna (hell)
    would be twelve months.
54. John 13, 34. Previously found in Confucius, Epicurus and Leviti-
    cus 19, 18.
55. Matthew 5, 39.
56. Luke 6, 27–9. See also Matthew 5, 39–44.
57. e.g. Romans 8, 29; 9, 11; Ephesians 1, 5.
58. I Corinthians 9, 22.
59. John 3, 16.
60. Edvard Lehmann in the *Encyclopaedia of Religion and Ethics*, V,
    p. 513. The name of the angel Aša Vahišta means both 'the Best
    Righteousness' and 'Paradise'.
61. Matthew 28, 19.
62. 10 March 1933.
63. A phrase whose origin I have been unable to trace. See the
    Whiteleys' *Permissive Morality, The Permissive Society* (1969)
    based on a *Guardian* Inquiry (10 to 25 October 1967), David
    Tribe's *Humanism, Christianity and Sex* (1968), John A. T.
    Robinson's *Christian Freedom in a Permissive Society* (1970),
    Maurice Hill and Michael Lloyd-Jones's *Sex Education: the*

Erroneous Zone (1970), articles and letters in the *Methodist Recorder* (23 July to 13 August 1970), and *The Arts in a Permissive Society* (1971), ed. Christopher Macy. Alistair Cooke has dated the 'permissive society' to John Dewey's *The School and Society* (1899).

64. *Christianity: The Debit Account* (1965).
65. Matthew 26, 41; Mark 14, 38.
66. *The Book of Common Prayer* version, verses 1 and 2.
67. ibid., verse 41.
68. Luke 19, 27.
69. Galatians 1, 8.
70. James 2, 20.
71. Ephesians 2, 8–9. The authorship of this epistle has been disputed. See also Romans 11.
72. The Antinomi, supporters of antinomianism (1535).
73. I Corinthians 6, 12.
74. Matthew 5, 44; Luke 6, 27 and 35.
75. Matthew 5, 3–11; Luke 6, 27 and 35.
76. Matthew 19, 30; Mark 10, 31; Luke 13, 30.
77. Ephesians 6, 5.
78. Matthew 16, 18–19.
79. See H. D. Longbottom's *Rome's responsibility for Juvenile crime* (1944), Emmett McLoughlin's *Crime and Immorality in the Catholic Church* (1962), Adrian Pigott's *Vatican Versus Mankind* (1964), Chapter 17 of H. W. Crittenden's *Behind the Black Curtain* (n.d.) and numerous books by Avro Manhattan. The above works inevitably present a one-sided view of Catholicism but quote official criminal statistics and admissions by Catholics themselves.
80. See Michael Argyle's *Religious Behaviour* (1958), p. 100.
81. Preface to *The Cenci* (1820).
82. Well described in Whyte's *Organization Man*.
83. *The Oracle of Reason*, 27 November 1841.
84. Letter to Melanchthon.
85. Cited in Henry Varley's pamphlet *Lecture to Men* (1883).
86. Letter by John Wren-Lewis in *Observer* (20 November 1966).
87. O. Fielding Clarke's *For Christ's Sake* (1963), p. 20.
88. See L. E. Elliott-Binns on *English Thought, 1860–1900. The theological aspect* (1956), Chapters 1, 10, 15 and 16.
89. Reginald John Campbell's *The New Theology* (1907). His title was not original as it had been used before by Richard Harte (1894) and John Smart (1863).
90. 1927.
91. See *Letters and Papers from Prison* (1953), ed. Eberhard Bethge, especially a letter to a friend, 30 April 1944.
92. See 'New Testament and Mythology' in *Kerygma and Myth* (1953), ed. H. W. Bartsch, I, pp. 1–44.

93. See *The Shaking of the Foundations* (1949), Chapter 7.
94. Notably Thomas J. J. Altizer, William Hamilton and Paul Van Buren.
95. John Robinson in *Observer* (17 March 1963 and 14 March 1965) and *The New Reformation?* (1965).
96. Letter by John Biggs-Davison in *Observer* (13 April 1969).
97. Mark 12, 17; Matthew 22, 21; Luke 20, 25.
98. *The Quest of the Historical Jesus: a critical study of its progress from Reimarus to Wrede* (tr. W. Montgomery 1910).
99. *The Reports of Sir Peyton Ventris Kt* (1696), p. 293, relating to *King v. Taylor*. Taylor had not only said religion was a cheat but had called Christ a bastard and whoremonger. cf. Edward Gibbon's 'The various modes of worship which prevailed in the Roman world were all considered . . . by the magistrates as equally useful' (*The History of the Decline and Fall of the Roman Empire*, (1926 edn. by J. B. Bury), I, p. 31.
100. *Times*, 7 March 1812. Case of *King v. Daniel Isaac Eaton*.
101. Blasphemy Act 1697.
102. (1765–9), IV, pp. 43–4.
103. Conservative MP Sir Henry Wolff (*Daily News*, 22 May 1880).
104. e.g. the Divorce Bill in the Italian Parliament during 1970.
105. US Constitution, First (originally third) Amendment (*Constitutions* (1791), p. 175).
106. Some later changes were the 1936 Tithe Act and repeal of sections of the Acts of Uniformity by the Criminal Law Act 1967.
107. *Tribune*, 30 May 1969.
108. 30 per cent.
109. The mystical system was Sufism, which influenced the great Persian poets like Omar Khayyám. The main rationalist schools were Mu'tazilism, Falásifah and Reformism. Modernist writings appear in the *Islamic Review and Arab Affairs* (Lahore and Woking).
110. *Encyclopaedia of Religion and Ethics*, V, p. 503, and *The Encyclopaedia of Islam* (1913), I, p. 302.
111. *ibid.* In *The Thousand and One Nights* (of obscure Persian or Indian origin but given a Muslim flavour in the eighth century) appeals are made on the basis that Allah will deal with each person in the way he deals with others.
112. See the films of Akira Kurosawa.

Chapter 5

1. See Bryan Wilson's *Religion in Secular Society. A sociological comment* (1966), Alasdair MacIntyre's *Secularization and Moral Change* (1967), Ronald Gregor Smith's *Secular Christianity* (1966), D. L. Munby's *The Idea of a Secular Society and its*

Significance for Christians (1963) and Harvey Cox's *The Secular City. Secularization and urbanization in theological perspective* (1965).

2. Macquarrie says that 'some theologians, especially of the secularizing sort' are guilty of 'brash optimism . . . hardly to be distinguished from old-fashioned theories of progress' (*Three Issues in Ethics*, p. 142). Leading 'secular theologians' are Cox, R. G. Smith, Cornelius Van Peursen and Arend Th. Van Leeuwen.

3. First applied by G. J. Holyoake to Richard Carlile (*The Life and Character of R. Carlile* (1849), p. 29) and now used for the former Bishop of Woolwich (John Robinson) and the Death of God school in America.

4. Review of *The Humanist Outlook* (1968), ed. A. J. Ayer, in *Observer* (5 January 1969).

5. *Humanism* (1965), p. 9.

6. *Pragmatism. A New Name for Some Old Ways of Thinking* (1907), p. 12.

7. See Hector Hawton's *The Humanist Alternative* (1963).

8. *The Years of Protest: The Autobiography of Bertrand Russell*, III, 1944–67 (1969), p. 220.

9. Francis Huxley in (Sir) Julian Huxley's *The Humanist Frame* (1961), p. 177.

10. *An Autobiography* (1893), p. 89.

11. *ibid.*, p. 153.

12. *ibid.*, p. 263, and *The Christian Commonwealth*, 10 December 1913.

13. See Margaret Knight's *Morals without Religion* (1955).

14. Herbert T. Rosenfeld's *American Humanism: Can It Grasp Its Opportunities?* (1962), pp. 2 and 22.

15. In a *Perspective* symposium on 'Post-Christian Man' republished as 'The Coming New Religion of Humanism' (American *Humanist*, January–February 1962).

16. *The Phenomenon of Man* (Fr. 1955, tr. Bernard Wall 1959), p. 182.

17. Ronald Hepburn in 'A Critique of Humanist Theology' (*Objections to Humanism* (1963), pp. 29–54).

18. A. F. M. Brierley in 'Philosophy and Humanism' (*The Plain View*, Winter 1964).

19. cf. letter by Edward D. Cheshire: 'I think we should keep Humanism as a positive affirmation of man and ignore questions of God' (*Humanist News*, January 1969).

20. H. J. Blackham's review of Hemming's *Individual Morality* (*Humanist News*, May–June 1969). See John Dewey's *Common Faith* (1934).

21. Letter from Colin B. Campbell on 'The Humanist Tradition' (*Humanist*, October 1968).

22. See *Republican*, 13 October 1820. In 1826 Robert Taylor opened a deistic chapel where, in episcopal robes, he preached blasphemous 'sermons'.

23. *Republican*, 28 March 1823.

24. In, respectively, his *Critique of Pure Reason* (1781) and *Critique of Practical Reason* (1788).

25. In a review of Arthur Koestler's *Drinkers of Infinity* (1968) in *Observer* (8 September 1968).

26. The 1887 congress of the International Federation of Freethinkers resolved that 'Freethought cannot be indifferent to the question of social amelioration, but that it should not be identified with a Socialist or anti-Socialist solution' (*National Reformer*, 18 September 1887).

27. *Secularist*, 15 February 1876.

28. *Autobiography: Memories and Experiences of Moncure D. Conway* (1904), II, p. 363.

29. *Secular Review*, 21 January 1877.

30. *A New View of Society: or, Essays on the Principle of the Formation of the Human Character, and the Application of the Principle to Practice* (1813), p. 5.

31. *Mr Owen's Address: Delivered at the adjourned meeting of the City of London Tavern, August 21st, 1817* (1817), pp. 58–9.

32. A word coined by George Mudie in 1821 (see R. G. Garnett's *Ideology of the Early Co-operative Movement* (1966), p. 7).

33. (1840), title page. This became the motto of his Association of All Classes of All Nations (*New Moral World*, 4 July 1840).

34. 'Address to Social Missionaries' (see Lloyd Jones's *The Life, Times and Labours of Robert Owen* (1889–90), II, p. 94).

35. Preface to Vol. I (1842), p. ii. The journal ran from 6 November 1841 to 2 December 1843.

36. *Movement and Anti-Persecution Gazette*, 1 January 1845.

37. Letter to Edward John Trelawny (*The Necessity of Atheism* (facsimile of 1817 edn, 1950), p. 33).

38. See *Red Republican*, 20 July 1850.

39. Lloyd Jones, p. 326.

40. Of *The City of Dreadful Night* (1874), not of *The Seasons* (1726–30).

41. Letter from J. G. Crawford to W. J. Linton, 6 March 1863 (Bradlaugh Collection of the National Secular Society).

42. Presentation, initiation, admission, destination, marriage, maturity, retirement, transformation and incorporation.

43. See *The Sacraments of the Religion of Humanity, as administered at the Church of Humanity, 19 Chapel Street, Lamb's Conduit Street, WC* (1893) by Richard Congreve.

44. For a description, see William Kent's *London for Heretics* (1932), pp. 99–105.

45. Auguste Comte's *A General View of Positivism; or Summary Exposition of the System of Thought and Life, adapted to the Great Western Republic, formed of the five advanced nations, the French, Italian, Spanish, British, and German, which, since the time of Charlemagne, have always constituted a political whole* (Fr. 1848 and 1851, tr. J. H. Bridges 1880), p. 67.

46. *Discours sur l'esprit positif* (1844), p. 57.

47. I Corinthians 13, 13.

48. *A General View of Positivism*, p. 67.

49. *ibid.*, p. 112.

50. *ibid.*, p. 33.

51. *Collected Essays* (1893–4), I, p. 156.

52. *Reason and Revolution: Hegel and the Rise of Social Theory* (2nd edn, 1955), p. 342.

53. *National Reformer*, 20 August 1865. Edward Royle, a Holyoake specialist, believes however that W. H. Ashurst, a lawyer and publisher, was the real inspirer of secularism.

54. *The Principles of Secularism Illustrated* (3rd revised 1871), p. 11.

55. *Secular Review*, 6 August 1876.

56. *Reasoner and Secular Gazette*, 6 January 1858.

57. *Principles of Secularism Illustrated*, p. 7.

58. *ibid.*, p. 27.

59. Preface to *Verbatim Report*, p. v.

60. *Investigator*, 1 April 1854.

61. Preface to *Verbatim Report*, p. vii.

62. *National Secular Society's Almanack* (1870), p. 15.

63. *Verbatim Report*, pp. 44–5. cf. with letter to Bradlaugh from an early secularist, Joseph Barker, 10 November 1860 (Bradlaugh Collection).

64. *ibid.*, p. 21. See also *Reasoner*, 13 January 1858.

65. *Reasoner*, 8 January 1854.

66. *Verbatim Report*, p. 3.

67. *Chambers's Encyclopaedia. A Dictionary of Universal Knowledge for the People* (1866), VIII, p. 597.

68. Rev. William Nassau Molesworth's *History of England* (1856), II, pp. 304–6.

69. R. G. Ingersoll in *Freethinker*, 4 April 1897, and a scroll given to Bradlaugh by the Freethinkers of India at Bombay, December 1889.

70. See Annie Besant's *The Secular Song and Hymn Book* (1875).

71. *National Reformer*, 24 August 1861.

72. Dr John Cookson in *ibid.*, 1 June 1861.

73. Joseph Barker in *ibid.*, 20 July 1861. See also *ibid.*, 24 August 1861; *Barker's Review of Politics, Literature, Religion, and Morality*, 7 September 1861 to 1 August 1863; *Secular Review, Secularist* and *Secular Review and Secularist* for 1877.

74. Press release by David Tribe, ratified by the executive of the National Secular Society (*Freethinker*, 4 April 1970). See Tribe on 'oecumenical moralizings' (*ibid.*, 6 June 1970) and on James Hemming and Howard Marratt's *Humanism and Christianity: the Common Ground of Moral Education* (1969) (*ibid.*, 25 October, 22 November and 27 December 1969).

75. *English Republic*, 26 March 1853.

76. *An Ethical Philosophy of Life* (1918), pp. 59 and 60.

77. Sir John Seeley in *The Ethical Message*, November and December 1917, Special Number, p. 28.

78. *Ethical Philosophy of Life*, p. 352.

79. *Ethical Message*, p. 13.

80. William Mackintire Salter, author of *Ethical Religion* (1889) (*ibid.*).

81. After his death it was, symbolically, sold to the Roman Catholics.

82. *ibid.*, p. 4.

83. *Ethics*, 2 September 1905.

84. See *Ethical Union Minute Book*, 31 March 1910, and *Freethinker*, 8 January 1905.

85. Statements of Principle and Method, X, VIII and XII (*Ethical Message*, pp. 33–4).

86. *Ethics*, 29 July 1905.

87. R. C. K. Ensor on 'The Centenary of Bradlaugh' (*Spectator*, 29 September 1933).

88. *Ethical World*, 15 December 1908.

89. H. J. Blackham's *Humanism* (1968), p. 132.

90. *Ethical Message*, p. 10.

91. 1896 and 1897 respectively.

92. Core of the Principles of the Ethical Church (*Ethical Message*, p. 31).

93. Principle 2 (*ibid.*).

94. From the Sunday-school chorus 'Jesus Bids Us Shine'.

95. *Ethics*, 21 October 1905.

96. See *The International Humanist and Ethical Union and Its Member Organizations* (1959), p. 7.

97. See note 95.

98. W. T. Harris in Preface to Adler's *Moral Instruction of Children* (1892), p. v. 'Instruction' was, till recently, preferred by ethicists to 'education', just as 'religious instruction' was preferred to 'religious education'.

99. Blackham in Memorandum, 13 January 1950 (*Ethical Union Minute Book*).

100. Advertisement inserted by H. G. Knight, former secretary of South Place Ethical Society (*Psychic News*, 18 January 1969).

101. *The Philosophical Works of Descartes* (tr. Elizabeth S. Haldane and G. R. T. Ross 1934), I, p. 221.

102. *Theologische Jugendschriften* (ed. H. Nohl 1907), p. 89.
103. *Ethical Message*, p. 31.
104. A Gowans Whyte's *The Story of the RPA, 1899–1949* (1949), p. 36.
105. *Manifesto of Robert Owen the Discoverer and Founder of the National System of Society, and of the National Religion*, 2 February 1840, clause viii.
106. Peter Cadogan, now secretary of South Place Ethical Society and formerly active in many peace organizations, has described the movement's internal operations as 'constant war'.
107. Circular, August 1910.
108. p. 69.
109. Published 1914.
110. Letter from Robert Young, proprietor of the *Japan Chronicle*, to Hypatia Bradlaugh Bonner, 24 April 1918 (Bradlaugh Collection).
111. *Letter to the Members and Friends of the Rationalist Peace Society*, January 1916.
112. Circular letter from its chairman, H. B. Bonner, December 1917.
113. Published 1945. In his optimistic *The Outline of History, Being a Plain History of Life and Mankind* (1920) he had warned that 'human history becomes more and more a race between education and catastrophe' (II, p. 608).
114. *The Autobiography of Bertrand Russell*, III, p. 154.
115. See the writings of Jean Piaget, Lawrence Kohlberg and John Wilson.
116. *Introduction to Moral Education* (1967), pp. 54–5.
117. ibid., p. 61.
118. ibid., p. 77.
119. ibid., p. 90.
120. ibid., p. 88.
121. For those with a Binet IQ over 148 (the top 2 per cent of the population). An election for its international executive was in 1967–8 run by the Electoral Reform Society, whose general secretary described the campaign leaflets as 'irrelevant, personal and vituperative' and needing to be 'purged' (*Sunday Times*, 4 February 1968). Mensa's founder, Victor Serebriakoff, was defeated and withdrew. Little has been heard of the solutions to world problems that its egghead members were said to be producing.
122. *Pensées de M. Pascal sur la Religion et sur Quelques Autres Sujets* (1670), p. 267.
123. Matthew 5, 27–8.
124. *Fragment 1*.
125. Objects of South Place Ethical Society.
126. As in the Friendship Liberal League and National Liberal League (1876).

127. Introduced by German immigrants. In 1900 at the 75th annual meeting of the American Unitarian Association the International Association for Liberal Christianity and Religious Freedom was formed.

128. Letter from Edwin H. Wilson, executive secretary and treasure of the American Humanist Association, to Charles Bradlaugh Bonner, secretary (later president) of the World Union of Free-thinkers, 15 July 1946 (Bradlaugh Collection).

129. Phrase of Maurice Cranston, reviewing Blackham's *Humanism* in the *Sunday Times*, 7 April 1968.

130. A word coined by J. B. Priestley and Jacquetta Hawkes in *Journey Down a Rainbow* (1955), p. 51. The British Humanist Association has declared humanists to be 'squarely for humanity', 'actively humane', 'for humanity' and 'for it . . . if it's good for you' (advertisements in *Observer* in 1970).

131. Blackham's *Humanism*, p. 137.

132. Topic for BHA summer school, August 1969.

133. *Humanist News*, April 1969.

134. Letter by Colin B. Campbell (*Humanist*, October 1968).

135. Letter by A. Barraclough (*Humanist News*, May–June 1969).

136. Letter by Edward Cheshire (*Humanist News*, January 1969).

137. Blackham's *Humanism*, p. 13.

138. *ibid.*, p. 16.

139. *ibid.*, p. 80.

140. *ibid.*, p. 62.

141. *ibid.*, p. 54. The phrase 'open society' comes from Henri Bergson's *The Two Sources of Morality and Religion* (Fr. 1932, Eng. tr. by R. Ashley Audra, Cloudesley Brereton and W. Horsfall Carter 1935) and is defined on pp. 229–30 to connote a world outlook. In a different guise it was popularized in Karl Popper's *Open Society and its Enemies* to define a liberal society 'which sets free the critical powers of man' (I, p. 1). This usage is found in Hemming's *Individual Morality*, pp. 20, 26, 28, 32, 57, 110, 179, 181, 196, 199, 200 and 201. For a criticism of the BHA's attempt to idealize the concept and then make it a goal for action, see David Tribe's *The Open Society and its Friends* (1971).

142. Letter by H. J. Blackham (*Humanist*, April 1967).

143. I'm not sure who originated this phrase; perhaps Julian Huxley or Harold Blackham.

144. Blackham's *Humanism*, pp. 65 and 96.

145. Symbol of the BHA.

146. The International Humanist and Ethical Union has engaged in 'dialogue', like the Marxist–Catholic dialogue, with the Vatican Secretariat for Non-Believers at Amersfoort, Brussels and elsewhere. Other schools of freethought have not risen to this bait.

147. Blackham's *Humanism*, pp. 80–1.

148. Letter by Arthur Francis (*Humanist News*, October 1968).

149. *System of Economical Contradictions: or, the Philosophy of Misery* (Fr. 1846, tr. Benjamin R. Tucker 1888), pp. 464–6.
150. A. C. in 'A Journey from Christianity to Freethought' (*National Reformer*, 29 April 1866).
151. Baroness Wootton over the 'social clause'.
152. Letter by Paul Rom (*Humanist News*, April 1969).
153. Peter Draper (*Humanist News*, March 1969).
154. News item of 11 August 1965, beautifully satirized in the following *New York Times* by Russell Baker.
155. Evelyn Scott-Brown in *Humanist*, December 1968.
156. *Sunday Telegraph*, 27 November 1966.
157. Blackham's *Humanism*, p. 81; Galatians 5, 22; Ephesians 5, 9.

Chapter 6

1. Ludwig Feuerbach in *Blätter für Literarische Unterhaltung*, 12 November 1850.
2. See his *Leviathan: Or the Matter, Forme, and Power of a Common-Wealth Ecclesiasticall and Civill* (1651).
3. *On the Principles of Political Economy, and Taxation* (1817), p. vi.
4. *Jerusalem* (1804–20), p. 55.
5. *Tractatus Politicus* (*Opera Posthuma* (1677, eds J. van Vloten and J. P. N. Land 1914), II, p. 14).
6. *Nouveaux principes d'économie politique* (1827), I, p. 313.
7. See his *De L'Esprit: or, Essays on the Mind, and its Several Faculties* (1759), Essays 2 and 3.
8. See David Tribe's 'From El Dorado to Utopia' (*Twentieth Century*, No. 1035, 1967–8).
9. Speech of Bismarck in the Prussian Chamber, 18 December 1863.
10. See Geoffrey Bing's *Reap the Whirlwind* (1968), pp. 198–200, 313–14.
11. B. S. Phillpotts on 'Ethics and Morality (Teutonic)', V, p. 521.
12. See *The Spirit of Laws* by Charles de Secondat, Baron de Montesquieu, with *D'Alembert's Analysis* (tr. Thomas Nugent 1878), II, p. 110.
13. See his *An Enemy of the People* (1882).
14. Book by Vance Packard (1957).
15. See MacIntyre's *Secularization and Moral Change*.
16. *Manifesto of the Communist Party* (ed. Friedrich Engels, tr. Samuel Moore 1888), p. 9.
17. *ibid*.
18. Bertrand Russell and Paul Foulkes's *Wisdom of the West* (1959) p. 262.

19. *The Theory of Moral Sentiments* (1759), I, p. 339.
20. *An Inquiry into the Nature and Causes of the Wealth of Nations* (1776), I, p. 2.
21. *ibid.*, p. 17.
22. *Self-Help* (1859), p. v.
23. *On Liberty* (1859), p. 207.
24. The message of *Vivian Grey* (1826–7).
25. *Self-Help*, p. 1.
26. *Communist Manifesto*, p. 9.
27. *Self-Help*, p. v.
28. In *The Condition of the Working Class in England* (1845).
29. (1851–62).
30. I'm not sure who originated this phrase, common in Marxist literature.
31. J. A. R. Marriott's *The Life and Times of Lucius Cary, Viscount Falkland* (1907), p. 200.
32. The invitation to William of Orange was signed by three Tories and four Whigs.
33. *The Thoughts of a Private Person; about the Justice of the Gentlemen's Undertaking at York, November 1688* (1689), p. 7.
34. *ibid.*, p. 10.
35. *ibid.*, p. 26.
36. Eleanor Marx in 'A Reply to Ernest Radford' (*Progress*, December 1883).
37. I am informed by the Conservative Research Department that 'this quotation has never been pinned down' (letter 19 August 1970). See dubious correspondence in the *Times*, 27 January and 6 February 1969.
38. *The Primrose League. Its Rise, Progress, and Constitution* (1887), p. 23.
39. On the relations of business and morality, cf. Neil Wates, whose firm 'won't build in South Africa' (*Sunday Times*, 23 August 1970): 'Business exists to serve the customer, to serve the human needs of people which are expressed in monetary values. If you use your resources effectively to meet those human needs, then you must by definition be more profitable' ('The Ethics of Modern Business', *Financial Times*, 23 September 1970). See also 'Ethics and business not in conflict, say directors' (*ibid.*, 7 July 1970).
40. *Reflections on the Revolution in France, and on the Proceedings in Certain Societies in London relative to that Event* (1790), p. 75.
41. See Maurice Cranston's *Freedom. A new analysis* (1953), which sets progressive against romantic and rational against compulsory rational freedom.
42. Speech on 'The English Statesman the Protestant Oracle' by Anthony Ashley Cooper (first Earl of Shaftesbury) in the House of Lords, 25 March 1679 (*The History and Proceedings of the*

House of Lords, from the Restoration in 1660, to the Present Time (1742), I, p. 233).

43. First raised in May 1763 when Wilkes was released from the Tower of London after his arrest on a general warrant for seditious libel in No. 45 of the *North Briton* (23 April 1763).
44. Dated to Palmerston's Administration of 1855 (when the Peelites left) or 1859.
45. *The American Scholar, Self-Reliance, Compensation* (1893), p. 52.
46. Founded about 1840 by William Maccall. See his *The Elements of Individualism. A Series of Lectures* (1847) and *The Outlines of Individualism* (1853).
47. This and the London Liberty Club (St James's) had the Hon. Auberon Herbert as a prominent supporter. The Individualist Club was at 217 City Road.
48. Debate in 1881; Herbert for, Sir Wilfrid Lawson against.
49. Speech on the Early Closing Bill, 2 May 1888 (*Hansard* CCCXXV, 1129).
50. *The Universal Review*, 15 August 1890.
51. *De l'esprit des loix* (*lois*) (1748), I, p. 61.
52. *Self-Help*, p. 1. The philosophy is implicit in the Nixon Administration's policies and was formerly explicit in those of Edward Heath.
53. *On Liberty*, p. 153.
54. Echoed bitterly by the Owenites (*New Moral World*, 21 October 1837, 2 March 1839, 4 July 1840 and 27 March 1841).
55. Bradlaugh in *Will Socialism Benefit the English People?* (1884), his debate with the founder of the Social Democratic Federation, H. M. Hyndman, p. 16.
56. Reference to the Northampton Freehold Land Society, a forerunner of the Anglia Building Society (*National Reformer*, 14 May 1865).
57. *The Rise of the Meritocracy, 1870–2033. An essay on education and equality* (1958). Not to be taken too literally. I propose to write a book on *The Rise of the Mediocracy*. For nineteenth-century proposals on meritocratic franchise, see David Tribe's *President Charles Bradlaugh, MP* (1971), p. 89.
58. See *Philosophie der Geschichte* in *Sämtliche Werke* (1928), XI, pp. 563–4.
59. J. C. Léonard de Sismondi's *Nouveaux Principes d'Économie politique* (1819), pp. 21 and 52.
60. Franz Neumann's *The Democratic and the Authoritarian State. Essays in political and legal theory* (ed. Herbert Marcuse 1964), pp. 6–7.
61. *ibid.*, p. 264.
62. By the Chicago School of 'new monetarists'. See Milton Friedman's Wincott Memorial Lecture (*Financial Times*, 17 September

1970) and 'The New Monetarism' by Nicholas Kaldor in *Lloyds Bank Review* (July 1970). This theory is criticized by socialists as well as by Keynesians (see 'Who Runs Britain?' in *Tribune*, 16 May 1969).

63. 'On the state of Public Opinion, and the Political Reformers' (1816) in *Essays, Moral and Political* (1832), p. 353.

64. Preamble to US *Declaration of Independence* (*Constitutions* (1791), p. 158).

65. See editorial leader 'From Campus to Borstal' in *Daily Telegraph*, 16 April 1970.

66. *New Moral World*, 4 July 1840.

67. *The Co-operative Magazine and Monthly Herald* ran, with a slight change of title, from January 1826 to 1 March 1830.

68. George Jacob Holyoake's *The History of Co-operation* (1906 revised), I, p. 122.

69. *Political Unionist*, 30 June 1832. Henry Hetherington was chairman.

70. G. J. Holyoake's Fleet Street House (1853–61) was financed by a British Secular Institute of Communism and Propagandism. He used 'Communists' for supporters of communities: 'Onwards, Cummunists! to success or failure' (*Movement*, 6 November 1844).

71. Associated with John Malcolm Ludlow and liberal clergymen like Frederick Denison Maurice and Charles Kingsley from 1848. The term 'Christian Socialist' had earlier been favoured by some Owenites, e.g. John Finch and G. A. Fleming (*New Moral World*, 10 March 1838, 6 June and 18 July 1840 and 27 March 1841).

72. Address 'To the Peoples' of the Central European Democratic Committee (A. A. Ledru-Rollin, Giuseppe Mazzini, Albert Darasz and Arnold Ruge), London, 22 July 1850. See *Le Proscrit* (August 1850) and W. J. Linton's *The English Republic – God and the People* (December 1850).

73. Linton's comment on foregoing address (*ibid.*). *Vox populi, vox Dei* is attributed to Alcuin (about A.D. 800).

74. Edward R. Pease's *The History of the Fabian Society* (1916), p. 26.

75. Bradlaugh in *Will Socialism Benefit the English People?*, p. 16.

76. *Annie Besant. An Autobiography* (1893), p. 304.

77. *Mrs Besant's Socialism* (1886), p. 35.

78. *Capital. A Critique of Political Economy* (Kerr edn, 1906–15), I, p. 837.

79. Adopted 1918, attacked by Gaitskell, defended then effectively buried by Wilson (see Bernard Levin's *The Pendulum Years: Britain and the Sixties* (1970), p. 227).

80. *Tribune*, 7 June 1968.

81. As the vituperation intensifies or modifies. See the Maoist *Worker*, organ of the Communist Party of Britain (Marxist–Leninist).

82. Wang Ming's *China. Cultural Revolution or Counter-Revolutionary Coup?* (*Canadian Tribune*, 19 March 1969, and republished as a pamphlet by the official Novosti Press Agency Publishing House, Moscow).

83. Quoted *Tribune*, 19 July 1968. See his *Socialism Made Easy* (1917), Chapters 5 and 6. This view of the Soviet Union is held by the International Socialists (organ the *Socialist Worker*), Tony Cliff's *Russia : a marxist analysis* (1964) and the Socialist Party of Great Britain (advertisements in *Tribune*, 9 May 1969 and 27 November 1970).

84. Herbert Marcuse's *One Dimensional Man. Studies in the Ideology of Advanced Industrial Society* (1964), p. 47.

85. Letter by Ralph Miliband, author of *The state in capitalist society* (1969), in *Tribune* (23 May 1969). George Orwell had earlier used 'bourgeois reformism' (*New English Weekly*, July 1937).

86. *The British Road to Socialism : Programme of the Communist Party* (1968 edn), p. 71.

87. Slogan of the Great Proletarian Cultural Revolution of 1966 but implicit throughout Mao Tse-tung's writings, notably in 'Combat Liberalism', 7 September 1937 (*Selected Works*, II, p. 33), and 'On Coalition Government', 24 April 1945 (*ibid.*, III, p. 316), where he quotes the proverb 'Running water is never stale and a door-hinge is never worm-eaten'.

88. Perhaps first expressed in A. Bazard and B. P. Enfantin's *Religion Saint-Simonienne : Lettre à M. le Président de la Chambre des Députés* (1 October 1830): 'Chacun soit placé selon sa capacité, et retribué selon ses oeuvres.'

89. The cycle of permissiveness (P) and restriction (R), reflecting political changes, has been more or less as follows: 1917 (P); 1936 (R); 1944 (R); 1949 (R); 1955 (P); 1970 (R). In 1970 the Ministry of Justice (abolished 1956) was revived to combat slackers, drunkards and 'parasites', and the 1 per cent birth-rate revealed by the latest census put a premium on fertility. There is a special tax on the childless aged 18–60 and bonuses for settling in Siberia. These policies are chiefly directed at China.

90. 'Combat Liberalism' (*Selected Works*, II, p. 32).

91. The Brezhnev Doctrine.

92. George Orwell in his Preface to the Ukrainian edn of *Animal Farm* (1945), March 1947.

93. Said to the Australian novelist Frank Hardy (*Sunday Times*, 8 December 1968).

94. George Lukacs in the Budapest monthly *Kortars* (see *Tribune*, 28 March 1969).

95. Phrase popularized by Nikita Khrushchev.

96. *Manifesto of the Communist Party* (Engels edn, 1888), p. 15.

97. 'As Marx and Engels began to call it after the Paris Commune' (*The State and Revolution* (1951 edn) by V. I. Lenin, p. 40). See

also Marx's *Critique of the Gotha Programme* (1875) (*Karl Marx and Friedrich Engels Selected Works* (1949–50), II, p. 30). Mao Tse-tung has written ambiguously 'On the People's Democratic Dictatorship', 30 June 1949 (*Selected Works*, IV).

98. Article 10 of the *Constitution of the People's Republic of China*, adopted 20 September 1954 (1961 edn), p. 12.

99. *The State and Revolution*, p. 36.

100. John Ryan MP in *Tribune*, 9 May 1969.

101. e.g. New Lanark (1813–29), Spa Fields (1821–4), Orbiston (1825–8), New Harmony (1825–8), Rue Monsigny (1830), Ralahine (1831–3), Ménilmontant (1832), Versailles (1832), Manea Fen (1839–41), Queenwood (1839–45), Pant Glas (1840) and Conde-sur-Vesgres (1840). For the whole sad story see the *Co-operative World* (September 1826), *New Moral World* (2 March 1839, 4 April, 16 May, 30 May and 8 August 1840 and 20 February 1841), *Working Bee* (26 September 1840) and *Movement* (30 October and 6 November 1844).

102. *A New View of Society*, p. 13.

103. Quoted in the *Ukrainian Review*, Spring 1966.

104. In *The Practice and Theory of Bolshevism* (1920) he thought the mistakes were essentially practical, but he later decided that Bolshevism was simply Christian millenarianism given political nomenclature, e.g. dialectic (God), Marx (Christ) and the Revolution (Second Coming).

105. Frank Hardy's *The Heirs of Stalin* (1968), p. 25. See the *Sunday Times*, 8 December 1968.

106. Milovan Djilas's *The New Class. An Analysis of the Communist System* (1957).

107. *In Place of Fear* (1952), p. 13.

108. Quoted by Brian Walden MP in *Tribune*, 10 January 1969.

109. Anonymous correspondent in 'Russia' (*Sunday Times*, 12 January 1969).

110. e.g. abolition of capital punishment, penal reform, action against racial discrimination, abortion and homosexual law reform.

111. Bradlaugh claimed 'it nursed liberty on the continent when tyranny would have strangled it' (*National Reformer*, 15 February 1862).

112. *Today* (BBC Radio 4), 5 June 1969.

113. Acts 2, 44; 4, 32.

114. Including curiosities like the Priests of Jehovah (Process or the Church of the Final Judgment), till recently in Mayfair, now in North America.

115. *A Declaration of the Wel-affected in the County of Buckingham-shire* (1649) by Gerrard Winstanley, p. 8.

116. *The Works of Gerrard Winstanley* (ed. George H. Sabine, 1941), p. 343. Echoed by Henry George in *Land and People* (1888), p. 3: 'Since, then, all the Scottish people have the same equal

right to live, it follows that they must all have the same equal right to the land.'

117. The Owenites had mixed views on true communism and their communities were supported by both 'capitalists' and 'wage-slaves'. Saint-Simon wanted a 'community of goods'. In *Religion Saint-Simonienne* (1830) his disciples A. Bazard and B. P. Enfantin denied that Saint-Simonianism meant either this ('a manifest violation of the first of all the moral laws') or the 'community of women' ('a travesty'). But Bazard believed Enfantin really supported these institutions and seceded soon afterwards. Fourier's system was not strictly communist as he proposed dividing the rewards of production among capitalists (4 parts), labour (5) and talent (3) after basic requirements had been met.

118. In 'L'Organisation du travail' (*Revue du progrès, politique, social et littéraire*, 1 October 1841). G. A. Fleming put it: 'In return for the exertion of its powers and faculties ... each would be gratified to the extent of his wants and wishes' (*New Moral World*, 20 July 1839).

119. *The State and Revolution*, pp. 134–45, and F. Engels's *The Origin of the Family, Private Property, and the State* (Ger. 1884, Eng. 1888).

120. Cited in Samuel Kydd's *A Sketch of the Growth of Public Opinion. Its influence on the Constitution and Government* (1888), p. 4.

121. *Economic and Philosophic Manuscripts of 1844* (1959), p. 102.

122. *Grundlinien der Philosophie des Rechts* (*Sämtliche Werke*, VII, p. 328).

123. *The Origin of the Family, Private Property, and the State* (*Selected Works*, II, p. 288).

124. *The State and Revolution*, pp. 143–4.

125. 'Equal rights and duties' was a rule for the Communist League drawn up by Marx (see Eleanor Marx's 'Karl Marx' in *Progress*, May 1883). But he changed to say that people were not equal and equal reward for different work would lead to social injustice: *Critique of the Gotha Programme* (*Selected Works*, II, pp. 22–3).

126. *The State and Revolution*, p. 132.

127. *ibid*., p. 145.

Chapter 7

1. Francis Bacon's *De Heresibus* (*c.* 1626), based on Proverbs 24, 5.

2. John 8, 32.

3. L. Ron Hubbard in 'My Philosophy' (*Freedom. Scientology*, No. 7, 1968).

4. Written by A. D. White in 1896.

5. *Elements of Social Science* (1867 edn), p. 451.
6. 'The Path of Progress' (*The National Secular Society's Almanack for 1880*, p. 21).
7. *NSS's Almanack for 1888*, p. 18.
8. MacIntyre's *Secularization and Moral Change*, p. 75.
9. *The Ghost in the Machine*, pp. 326–7.
10. Hemming's *Individual Morality*, p. 230.
11. F. H. George's *Computers, Science and Society* (1970), p. 23.
12. John Wilson's *Reason and Morals* (1961), p. 152.
13. J. J. C. Smart's *Philosophy and Scientific Realism* (1963), p. 155.
14. Jacob Bronowski's *Science and Human Values* (1961), p. 72.
15. Bronowski at a conference on the social impact of biology (*Observer*, 29 November 1970).
16. Evidence given to the Scientific Committee of the World Federation of Mental Health (quoted in Barbara Wootton's 'Deviance, Criminal and Other', the 1970 Voltaire Lecture, *New Society*, 5 November 1970).
17. Barbara Wootton's *Social Science and Social Pathology* (1959), p. 337.
18. Basil Mitchell's *Law, Morality, and Religion in a Secular Society* (1970), p. 115.
19. Alec Comfort's *Barbarism and Sexual Freedom* (1948), p. 3.
20. *Freedom. Scientology*, No. 30, 1970.
21. *ibid.*, No. 7, 1968.
22. Hubbard used 'scientology' for a series of 'axioms' in 1936; his organization began in 1954 as the Church of Scientology, becoming the Church of Scientology of California in 1956. Up till 1966 it used to be called the Hubbard Association of Scientologists outside America. In some areas there is a sprinkling of 'pastors', 'bishops' and 'DDs'. Some members regard it as a religion, others as a science, others as a strengthener, like Subud, of other religions.
23. In forewords to *Scientology 8–8008. The Discovery and Increase of Life Energy* (1953) and *Scientology: Plan for World Peace* (1964).
24. *Scientology: The Fundamentals of Thought* (1967 edn), p. 11.
25. *Scientology Abridged Dictionary* (1970 edn), p. 16.
26. Hubbard's 'My Philosophy' (*Freedom. Scientology*, No. 7).
27. *Scientology: The Fundamentals of Thought*, p. 12.
28. 'Official Periodical of Scientology in the British Isles'.
29. *ibid.*, p. 128. 'By its application the sick become well, the insane sane and the sane much saner' (*The Key to Tomorrow. Scientology: its Contribution to Knowledge* (1955), compiled from Hubbard's works by U. Keith Gerry, p. 87).
30. *ibid.*, pp. 11 and 13.
31. *ibid.*, p. 47.

32. Originally called the Mathison Electropsychometer (*Electro-psychometric Auditing* (1953)), now the Hubbard Electrometer; said to measure the 'relative density of the body'.

33. Letter by David Gaimon, Scientology PRO, now English director, in *Observer*, 25 August 1968.

34. See *Science*, 17 January 1969.

35. Hence 'psychedelic'.

36. *Lyserg-Säure Diethylamid* (diethylamide of lysergic acid).

37. Introduction to King's *Life on the Planets* (1959). Aetherius describes King as 'not quite what he appears to be!' (*The Twelve Blessings. The Cosmic Concept* (1958), p. 12). How true!

38. *Life on the Planets*, pp. 2, 9, 18 and 22.

39. *ibid.*, p. 18.

40. *The Twelve Blessings*, p. 13.

41. Colin Bord in *Gandalf's Garden, Mystical Scene Magazine*, No. 4.

42. *Outline of History*, II, p. 608.

43. B. F. R. Skinner to John Davy (*Observer*, 27 April 1969).

44. Cyril Bibby in 'Towards Scientific Humanist Culture' (*The Humanist Outlook*, p. 17).

45. cf. the Vatican's inability to stop the 1970 Italian Divorce Bill from becoming law.

46. 'The Priest and the Acolyte' (*Chameleon*, December 1894). See H. Montgomery Hyde's *Famous Trials. Oscar Wilde* (1962 edn), p. 106.

47. *The Myth of Sisyphus* (tr. Justin O'Brien 1955), p. 23.

48. 'The view that scientists are objective, dispassionate, impartial and tolerant is a myth. They are just as prejudiced and emotional as any other group of people' (Sir Ernest Chain in 'Social Responsibility and the Scientist', *New Scientist*, 22 October 1970).

49. Originated at Pugwash, the Nova Scotia home of the Cleveland industrialist and farmer, Cyrus S. Eaton, in July 1957.

50. Formed in February 1969 to do what Pugwash failed to do.

51. *The Autobiography of Bertrand Russell*, III, p. 34.

52. Letter on Skinner to *Observer*, 11 May 1969.

53. *The Ethical Animal*, p. 206.

54. R. D. Laing in *The Politics of Experience* and *The Bird of Paradise* (1967), p. 24.

55. *Sanity, Madness and the Family* (1964), I, *Families of Schizophrenics* by Laing and A. Esterson, p. 5. See also David Cooper's *The Death of the Family* (1971).

56. Robert Phillips in the *Bulletin of the British Psychological Society*, April 1969.

57. By, e.g., Desmond Morris in *Wildlife Review* (31 December 1967) and *The Naked Ape*.

58. Herbert Marcuse's *Eros and Civilization. A Philosophical Inquiry into Freud* (1956), p. 4.

59. See Appendix 2.
60. Originally meant no detectible breath, pulse or heart-beat. Now defined in terms of electroencephalograms, capacity for independent functioning, cell metabolism and other specialist matters.
61. See David Tribe's 'Refrigeration Maybe, Heart Transplants Yes . . . but Head Transplants . . .?' (*Nova*, January 1969).
62. See *The Data Bank Society* (1970) by Malcolm Warner and Michael Stone.

Chapter 8

1. *The Myth of Sisyphus*, p. 55.
2. *Les Faux-monnayeurs* (*The Counterfeiters*) (Fr. 1925, Eng. 1928).
3. *Rebel without a Cause* (1955), directed by Nicholas Ray.
4. *What is Property? An Inquiry into the Principle of Right and of Government* (Fr. 1840, tr. Benjamin R. Tucker 1876) by P. J. Proudhon, p. 271.
5. *ibid.*, p. 277.
6. *Le Salariat* (*The Wage System*) (1889), p. 34.
7. *Subjects of the Day*, No. 2, August 1890 (from the *Universal Review*, VII, 25).
8. See Introduction.
9. *Der Einzige und sein Eigentum* (*The Ego and His Own*) (Ger. 1845, tr. Steven T. Byington 1912), p. 3.
10. *ibid.*, p. 62.
11. *ibid.*, p. 59.
12. *ibid.*, p. 490.
13. Founded by Jean-Pierre Schweitzer four years ago when he was living in London, and already moribund.
14. *Liber* LXXVII, IT/33, AL. II. 21.
15. *ibid.*, AL. I. 40 and 42–3.
16. *ibid.*, AL. I. 57.
17. *There is no god but man*, para. 5.
18. Founded in San Francisco in 1966 by Anton Szandor L. Vey.
19. *Daily Telegraph Magazine*, 31 July 1970. Other quotations on this theme are from the same source.
20. *The State and Revolution*, p. 166.
21. *The Ego and His Own*, p. 395.
22. See *The Open Society and its Enemies*, especially Chapters 5, 6, 7, 23 and 24.
23. Quoted by Edward (Lord) Boyle in 'Citadels of Privacy' (*Guardian*, 20 October 1967).
24. Kierkegaard's *Zur Kritik der Gegenwart* (1922 edn), p. 61.
25. *L'Existentialisme est un humanisme* (1946).

Chapter 9

1. See *The Will to Believe, and other essays in popular philosophy* (1897) by William James.
2. As in Exodus 20, 13, taken from the Code of Hammurabi, taken from . . .
3. James Boswell's *The Life of Samuel Johnson, LL.D.* (1791), I, p. 478.
4. Sir Keith Joseph, Secretary of State for the Social Services in the Heath Government, is impressed by the argument that £40 million spent on free contraception under the National Health Service should save £400 million in social services for unwanted pregnancies and children.

Chapter 10

1. By Jeff Nuttall, 1968.
2. cf. Mrs Jellyby in Dickens's *Bleak House* (1853).
3. Francis McCullagh's *With the Cossacks, being the story of an Irishman who rode with the Cossacks throughout the Russo-Japanese War* (1906), p. 178.
4. What an 'academic critic' said of John Dewey. Quoted in a paper by Sidney Hook (American *Humanist*, March–April 1969).
5. *Popular Science Monthly*, January 1878.
6. *Collected Papers of Charles Sanders Peirce* (eds Charles Hartshorne and Paul Weiss 1934), V, p. 464.
7. *ibid.*, pp. 306 and 282.
8. *ibid.*, p. 2.
9. Coined 1905.
10. A. J. Ayer in *The Origins of Pragmatism. Studies in the Philosophy of Charles Sanders Peirce and William James* (1968), p. 64.
11. James Mark Baldwin's *Dictionary of Philosophy and Psychology* (1901–5), II, p. 321.
12. See the American *Humanist*, March–April 1969. Dewey is the 'father of progressive education' and perhaps of the permissive society.
13. I Corinthians 6, 19.
14. Justice James Fitzjames Stephen said: 'If two persons are guilty of the very same act of negligence . . . it gratifies a natural public feeling to choose out for punishment the one who has actually caused great harm' (*A History of the Criminal Law of England* (1883), III, pp. 311–12). But in the calendar of criminal offences 'in order of gravity they are not arranged simply according to the harm done' (Lord Justice Patrick Devlin on *The Enforcement of Morals* (1965), p. 129).

15. Forty-four rungs (in Kahn's *On Escalation. Metaphors and Scenarios* (1965)).
16. Tricyano-aminopropene as a 'mental stabilizer' (*Man and Civilization. Control of the Mind* (1961), ed. by Semyour M. Farben and Roger H. Wilson, pp. 36–9, and Koestler's *Ghost in the Machine*, p. 327).

Chapter 11

1. *The Mechanical Bride. Folklore of Industrial Man* (1951), p. 34.
2. *ibid.*, p. 31.
3. Quoted in *A History of Metals* (1960) by Leslie Aitchison, I, p. 1.
4. See C. E. M. Hansel's paper on Rhine's assistants (*Journal of Parapsychology*, June 1961) and *ESP. A scientific evaluation* (1966), David Tribe's 'Parapsychology' (*Plain View*, Winter 1962) and John Scarne's *The Amazing World of John Scarne. A personal history* (1957).
5. i.e. ultimate purpose. Teleology as the study of functional purpose has been most useful in cybernetics.
6. *The Medium is the Massage* (1967), p. 8.
7. Peter Laurie in 'World in Danger' (*Sunday Times*, 17 November 1968).
8. Address in 1866 to the Academy of Sciences at Munich on *Die Entwicklung der Ideen in der Naturwissenschaft* (Eng. version *The Development of Science among Nations* (1867), p. 23).
9. Isaac Asimov, quoted in the *Radio Times*, 21 December 1967.
10. David Paterson's 'Computers and Society' (*Radio Times*, 22 May 1969).
11. Liam Hudson's *Frames of Mind. Ability, Perception and Self-Perception in the Arts and Sciences* (1968)
12. Vsevolod Perekalin (see *Progressive World*, December 1968).
13. *Mechanical Bride*, p. 31.

Chapter 12

1. Quoted by David Ogilvie in *Confessions of an Advertising Man* (1964), p. 147.
2. *The Distribution of Consumable Goods. An Economic Study* (1932) by Dorothea Braithwaite and S. P. Dobbs, pp. 43–5.
3. *Industry and Trade: a study of industrial techniques and business organization; and of their influences on the conditions of various classes and nations* (1919), p. 304.
4. Vatican Congregatio De Propaganda Fide.

5. Thomas M. Garrett, cited in *Advertising. A new Approach* (1960) by Walter Taplin, p. 129.
6. Ogilvie's *Confessions*, p. 148.
7. *ibid.*, p. 153.
8. *ibid.*
9. *Journey Down a Rainbow*, p. 51.
10. (UK 1958), p. 121.
11. John 3, 3 and 7; I Peter 1, 23.
12. Why the Church of England would not allow a BBC broadcast of the 1923 Armistice Day service (see Melville Dinwiddie's *Religion by Radio. Its Place in British Broadcasting* (1968), p. 20).
13. See age breakdown in *Colour and Citizenship. A Report on British Race Relations* (1969) by E. J. B. Rose, Nicholas Deakin *et al.*
14. Speech of Jaques in Shakespeare's *As You Like It*, Act 2, Scene 7.

Chapter 13

1. Respectively (1948) and (1956).
2. *The state in capitalist society* (1969).
3. Exposed by Wright Patman's Select Committee on Small Business (*Sunday Times*, 16 March 1969).
4. *The Managerial Revolution. What is happening in the world* (1941).
5. In *Political Parties: sociological study of the oligarchical tendencies of modern democracy* (1915).
6. (1956).
7. In *The Managing of Organizations. The administrative struggle* (1964).
8. *The Democratic and the Authoritarian State*, pp. 9 and 14.
9. *The State and Revolution*, p. 184.
10. *ibid.*, p. 95.
11. Frank Hardy (*Sunday Times*, 8 December 1968).
12. J. S. Mill's *On Liberty*, p. 200.
13. *Parkinson's Law; or the Pursuit of Progress* (UK 1961), p. 4. Reinforced by his 'Is the Civil Service Swallowing Britain?' (*Daily Telegraph Magazine*, 8 December 1967).
14. *Reason and Revolution: Hegel and the Rise of Social Theory* (1955), p. 437.
15. One sympathetic account of the British Civil Service, referring to its 'fertility of imagination' although 'understaffed and under-paid' (*The Queen's Government* (1967 edn) by Ivor Jennings, pp. 107 and 108), avoids these terms.
16. Max Nicholson in 'Elephantine Civil Service' (*Daily Telegraph Magazine*, 15 March 1968).

Chapter 14

1. C. H. McIlwain in *The Growth of Political Thought in the West from the Greeks to the End of the Middle Ages* (1932), p. 284.
2. Title earned by his *De Jure Belli et Pacis* (1625).
3. A very ancient concept clarified by the nationalist movements of the Reformation and expounded by Sir Robert Filmer in *Patriarcha: or the Natural Power of Kings* (1680).
4. Romans 2, 14–15.
5. *Constitutions* (1791), p. 158.
6. Or 'natural rights, inalienable and sacred to man' (*La Déclaration des Droits de l'Homme et des Citoyens*, 20–26 August 1789).
7. *Tractatus Politicus* (*Opera*, II, p. 6).
8. An idea to be found among the Greek Sophists (see Plato's *Republic*, Book 2, and *Gorgias*) and the Old Testament.
9. *The Political History of England*, VIII, 1660–1702 (1923) by Richard Lodge, p. 303.
10. Argument in his second *Discourse* (1755).
11. Introduction by G. D. H. Cole to Rousseau's *Social Contract – Discourses* (1955 edn), p. xiv.
12. *Inquiry concerning Political Justice*, p. 149. In law consent of the victim is no defence in assault cases except rape.
13. *Critique of Practical Reason* (1788).
14. Cole's Introduction to Rousseau, p. xvii.
15. Mill's *Utilitarianism*, p. 83.
16. Austin's *The Province of Jurisprudence Determined* (1832), p. vii.
17. *Commentaries on the Laws of England* (1765–9), I, p. 70.
18. Quoted by A. L. Goodhart in Alan Pryce-Jones's *The New Outline of Modern Knowledge* (1956), p. 581.
19. Peter Archer's *Communism and the Law. A Background Book* (1963), p. 16.
20. See note 18, p. 582, and Vyshinsky's *The Law of the Soviet State* (1948), p. 50.
21. Preamble, 10 December 1948.
22. W. T. Sherwin's *Republican*, No. 1, 1 March 1817.
23. See 'Justice concealed in trimmings' (*Times Educational Supplement*, 9 May 1969) and Frank Norman's 'Victims of the Law' (*Daily Telegraph Magazine*, 16 May 1969).
24. *Legal Education* (1969), Fabian Research Series 276, by a committee of the Society of Labour Lawyers under Michael Zander, p. 8.
25. Survival of the fittest in a social or political context.
26. *On Liberty*, pp. 29, 16 and 22.
27. *Liberty, Equality, Fraternity* (1873), pp. 134, 135 and 148. Mill died before he could reply. John Morley answered on his behalf (*Fortnightly Review*, 1 August 1873). Stephen replied to this in his second edition (1874).

28. 'Wolfenden Report', para. 61.
29. *ibid.*, para. 62.
30. Introduction to his collection *The Enforcement of Morals* (1965), pp. vi–vii.
31. Second Maccabean Lecture in Jurisprudence to the British Academy (1959), pp. 13, 17 and 15.
32. *The Morality of the Criminal Law* (1965), p. 35. His first answer was 'Immorality and Treason' (*Listener*, 30 July 1959), reprinted in *The Law as Literature* (1961), ed. L. J. Blom-Cooper.
33. *Law, Liberty and Morality* (1963), p. 79.
34. The latter point, he observed, 'has scarcely been adequately investigated yet' (*ibid.*, p. 1). This book attempts such an investigation.
35. Frederick Charles Shaw.
36. *Times* Law Report, 15 March 1961.
37. *Jones v. Randall* (Lofft. at p. 385).
38. (1961) 2 AER at p. 452; (1962) AC at p. 268. Lord Reid disagreed.
39. Stephen's *Liberty, Equality, Fraternity*.
40. BGB (*Bürgerliches Gesetzbuch*) is the German Code of Civil Law.
41. Law which modified the harshness of the common law, e.g. in torts. Until the Judicature Act 1873 there were special equity courts. Today equity operates mostly in the Chancery Division.
42. *Address* of Glanville Williams to 1965 AGM of the Euthanasia Society, now called the Voluntary Euthanasia Society.
43. Article by 'Caractacus' (W. E. Adams) in *National Reformer*, 10 November 1860. He referred to the Public Health Act 1848, Public Libraries Act 1850 and Adulteration of Food or Drink Act 1860. Between 1864 and 1877 the teetotal UK Alliance fought for a Permissive Bill making parish councils responsible for licensing pubs, in the expectation that some of them would refuse all licences (contrary to today's notion of the 'permissive society'). The 1967 National Health Service (Family Planning) Act is 'permissive' in this technical sense.
44. *On the Laws and Customs relating to Marriage* (1870), p. 29.
45. *Report* by the Working Party set up by a Conference on the Obscenity Laws convened by the Chairman of the Arts Council of Great Britain (May 1969), p. 18.
46. Sir Gerald Nabarro in the *Times*, 21 July 1969.
47. *News Release* of speech by Roy Jenkins to Abingdon Constituency Labour Party, 19 July 1969. He sponsored the 1959 Obscene Publications Act, which allowed literary merit or scholarly interest as a defence.
48. Leader, 21 July 1969.
49. cf. National Council for Civil Liberties' *Privacy under attack* (1968). Norman Marsh and Andrew Martin of the Law Commission privately believe it should be a new tort.

50. *The Enforcement of Morals* (1959), p. 25.
51. *ibid.* (1965), pp. 26 and 42.
52. *Report*, p. 17.
53. *ibid.*, A 27–8.
54. *Address* to Euthanasia Society (1965).
55. s. 1.
56. *Full Employment in a Free Society. A report* (1944), p. 248.
57. *Address*.
58. Lord Atkin in *Donoghue* (or *McAlister*) *v. Stevenson* (1932) (AC 562 at 580).
59. 'Humanism and the Future' (*The Humanist Outlook*, p. 272). See also his *Crime and Personality* (1964). Some of the Owenites rejected all punishment (*New Moral World*, 10 February 1838 and 25 July 1840) except 'Nature's rewards and punishments' (*ibid.*, 23 May 1835).
60. Following submissions by the Howard League for Penal Reform, National Secular Society and Prison Reform Council, conditions improved; but with recent signs of deterioration, mainly through overcrowding, Radical Alternatives to Prison (October 1970) became active.
61. Crimes are *mala in se*, offences are *mala prohibita* (like motoring offences, often purely technical).
62. Capital punishment remains for such crimes as treason and blowing up dockyards.
63. See his *Soviet Marxism: a critical analysis* (1958), Chapter 13.

Chapter 15

1. 'Machines, Robots and Minds' by R. Thomson and W. Sluckin (*Durham University Journal* 46 (1954), 122; reproduced in *Cybernetics* (1968), eds C. R. Evans and A. D. J. Robertson, p. 88). 'Cybernetics' (Greek *kybernétés*: steersman) was coined by Norbert Wiener in 1948.
2. *Cybernetics*, p. 78.
3. *National Physical Laboratory Report* (1948), pp. 1–20.
4. 'Computing Machinery and Intelligence' (*Mind*, October 1950).
5. The brain has been described as a continuous (but with discrete properties), controlling, universal (at birth B-type unorganized), partial decision, tightly-coupled, slow-learning (working on Selective Information Theory), non-specific, equipotential, conditional probability, servo-mechanistic, conative, cognitive, hysteretic, stochastic, redundant, random, diffuse, delocalized, integrative, replicated, diverse, heterogeneous, high relative entropy, efficient machine. For explanation of these terms see *Cybernetics* (1968), *International Dictionary of Physics and Electronics* (1961) and *Dorland's Illustrated Medical Dictionary* (1965).

6. When F. Wöhler synthesized it in the laboratory.
7. The 'hardware' is the physical assembly, the 'software' the package of basic programmes, dependent on the computer's potentialities and the chief needs of the purchaser, supplied by the manufacturer.
8. The most basic programming language which is valid for one particular model of computer only and which is its direct 'motivation'. See Peter C. Sanderson's *Computer Languages* (1970).
9. Intermediate programming languages common to families of computers, which the computer can itself translate into its machine code.
10. A reflex device operating on 'negative feed-back'.
11. *Cybernetics* (1968), p. 43.
12. A cyclical relay with intermediate units which feed back into the input and boost it.
13. Responsible for basic physiology like pulse rate, blood pressure, breathing and other mechanisms that are very sensitive to emotional reactions.
14. A computer is 'on-line' when its central processor is performing an operation, 'off-line' when it is not. Then the central memory store can be run off on to magnetic tape for permanent storage.
15. Christopher Evans and E. A. Newman in 1964; based on Eugene Aserinsky's discovery (1952) of the relation between rapid eye movements (REM) during sleep and dreaming (probably visual dreaming only) and William Dement's finding (1960) that 'when subjects were deprived of the opportunity to dream (as indicated by REM periods) for nights on end, behavioural and psychological disturbances began to show themselves' (Christopher Evans's 'The Stuff of Dreams' in *New Scientist*, 18 May 1967). I am very grateful to Dr Evans for kindly supplying reprints of his articles on this subject, including *Nature* (1 May 1965 and 28 February 1970), *New Worlds* (Vol. 51, No. 173) and *Trans-action* (December 1967).
16. i.e. recognizing and immediately destroying data in a memory store.
17. Evans and Newman's 'Dreaming: an analogy from computers' (*New Scientist*, 26 November 1964).
18. *ibid.*, 18 May 1967.
19. Chiefly sexual. See Sigmund Freud's *Die Traumdeutung* (1900).
20. Once thought, on the basis of electrode stimulation, to be localized on the surface of the cortex; now thought to be more random.
21. At the Department of Machine Intelligence and Perception under Professors Donald Michie (thinking), Christopher Longuet-Higgins (memory) and Richard Gregory (sense organs).

22. cf. Michael Davie's 'Futurology' (*Observer*, 3 and 10 January 1971) and Donald Schon's Reith Lectures for 1970 (*Change and Industrial Society*).
23. Emotional reaction to thought.
24. Judd Marmor (*Evening Standard*, 4 June 1969).

Chapter 16

1. *Times*, 25 July 1969.
2. *Daily Telegraph* (16 July 1969).
3. Pharmacologically 'narcotics' consist of ataractics (tranquillizers), sedatives and hypnotics. International law (based on American usage) includes stimulants like cocaine.

Chapter 17

1. See his *The Discovery of the Orgone* (tr. Theodore P. Wolfe 1942).
2. See his *The Sexual Cycle of Human Warfare. Being a New Theory of the Cause of War and an Inquiry into the Possibility of War-Prediction* (1950).
3. Note the boyish enthusiasm Herman Kahn (*On Thermonuclear War*, 1961) has for his work.
4. Nardil is the trade name for phenelzine sulphate, a stimulating anti-depressant.
5. K. E. Moyer of Pittsburg University to UNESCO conference on brain research.
6. Named after a petrol additive. It is really DOM (dimethoxy-methylamphetamine). Also said to mean 'serenity, tranquillity and peace' (Terence Jones's *Drugs and the Police* (1968), p. 31).
7. Dimethyltryptamine.
8. Contrasted with 'outer space'. Ballard is a science fiction writer.
9. The phrase used by Mary Whitehouse's National Viewers' and Listeners' Association when it was known as the Clean-Up TV Campaign.

Appendix 2

1. Letter, 2 August 1862, in W. C. Church's *The Life of John Ericsson* (1890), II, p. 34.
2. Quoted in *A Short History of Technology from the earliest times to A.D. 1900* (1960) by T. K. Derry and Trevor I. Williams, p. 278.
3. Quoted in *A History of Metals* (1960) by Leslie Aitchison, I, p. 1.

Select Bibliography

It would be pointless to repeat here the very many titles referred to in the text and the notes. Instead, I am making a rigorous selection of writers and works that seem to me to be seminal. Some were famous in their own day, some achieved fame later and some have scarcely gained it today. All these writers should be called philosophers, though some are better known under other labels. A few works are included because they are felicitous statements of particular world-views, not perhaps to be taken as definitively as their authors would have liked, but certainly presenting a side of this complex problem which should not be neglected. Other works have been influential not so much for the depth of their thought as for the breadth of their dissemination. For this reason I begin with the scriptures of the great world religions. With both these – which are largely anonymous or wrongly attributed – and the authenticated writings of individuals, I have concentrated on those whose moral implications are clearest and not necessarily on those by which they made their reputation for piety or profundity. In deference to the feelings of moral philosophers I have omitted the work of computer programmers.

For the sake of scholarly comparison I have quoted documented works in the form of their first editions, thus presenting a brief history of ideas which may be correlated with general history. For their own convenience readers will have no difficulty in finding modern edited translations where necessary. Most writings on ethics and morality down the years have appeared under the auspices of religion. These I have omitted, not because I reject the traditional view of religioethics but because few of the commentators, however rigorous and persuasive their presentations, have been as influential as the scriptures they echo and all of them are to some extent constrained by the demands of orthodoxy. Largely through a series of historical accidents the religion which has produced the most prolific literature is Christianity. Recent surveys of the scope and history of Christoethics are Otto A. Piper's *Christian Ethics* (1970) and N. H. G. Robinson's *The Groundwork of Christian Ethics* (1971). Religious organizations will themselves be happy to give further guidance.

Religious

HINDUISM: *Bhagavadgītā*.

BUDDHISM: *Dhammapada*.

ZOROASTRIANISM: *Zend-Avesta*.

CONFUCIANISM: *Analects*.

TAOISM: *Tao-te-ching*.

JUDAISM: *Talmud*.

CHRISTIANITY: *New Testament*, especially the four Gospels and the four undisputed Pauline Epistles, Romans, Corinthians I and II and Galatians.

ISLAM: *Qur'an*.

Secular

PROTAGORAS (*c.* 490–*c.* 420 B.C.): the morality of human pragmatism: *Fragment 1* on *Truth*.

SOCRATES (*c.* 470–399 B.C.): the morality of self-discipline: dubiously reported in Plato's *Apology* and Xenophen's *Memorabilia*.

PLATO (*c.* 428–*c.* 348 B.C.): the morality of social acceptance: *Republic* and *Gorgias*.

ARISTOTLE: (384–322 B.C.): the morality of the judicious mean: *Eudaemian Ethics* and *Nicomachean Ethics*.

THOMAS HOBBES (1588–1679): the morality of enlightened self-interest: *Leviathan: Or the Matter, Forme, and Power of a Common-Wealth Ecclesiasticall and Civill* (London 1651).

BENEDICT SPINOZA (1632–77): the morality of rational awareness: *Ethica* in *Opera posthuma* (Amsterdam 1677).

ANTHONY ASHLEY COOPER, 3rd Earl of Shaftesbury (1671–1713): the morality of the balance of power: *Characteristicks of Men, Manners, Opinions, Times* (London 1711).

FRANCIS HUTCHESON (1694–1746): the morality of utilitarianism: *An Inquiry into the Original of our Ideas of Beauty and Virtue* (London 1725) and *A System of Moral Philosophy* (Glasgow 1755).

DAVID HUME (1711–76): the morality of benevolent justice: *A Treatise of Human Nature: being An Attempt to introduce the experimental Method of Reasoning into Moral Subjects*, III, *Of Morals* (London 1740) and *An Enquiry concerning the Principles of Morals* (London 1751).

ADAM SMITH (1723–90): the morality of magnanimous competition: *The Theory of Moral Sentiments* (London 1759) and *An Inquiry into the Nature and Causes of the Wealth of Nations* (London 1776).

IMMANUEL KANT (1724–1804): the morality of universal duty: *Grundlegung zur Metaphysik der Sitten* (*Groundwork of the Metaphysic of Morals*) (Frankfurt and Leipzig 1785), *Critik der practischen Vernunft* (*Critique of Practical Reason*) (Riga 1788) and *Die Metaphysik der Sitten* (*The Metaphysic of Morals*) (Königsberg 1797).

WILLIAM GODWIN (1756–1836): the morality of radical determinism: *An Inquiry concerning Political Justice, and Its Influence on General Virtue and Happiness* (London 1793).

GEORG WILHELM FRIEDRICH HEGEL (1770–1831): the morality of law and order: *Grundlinien der Philosophie des Rechts* (*Naturrecht und Staatswissenschaft im Grundrisse*) (*Philosophy of Right*) (*Law*) (Berlin 1821).

MAX STIRNER (1806–56): the morality of anarchistic individualism: *Der Einzige und sein Eigenthum* (*The Ego and His Own*) (Leipzig 1845).

KARL MARX (1818–83): the morality of proletarian revolution: *Misère de la Philosophie. Réponse à la Philosophie de la Misère de M. Proudhon (The Poverty of Philosophy)* (Paris and Brussels 1847) and *Manifest der Kommunistischen Partei (Manifesto of the Communist Party*, with Friedrich Engels) (London 1848).

GEORGE EDWARD MOORE (1873–1958): the morality of non-rational intuition: *Principia Ethica* (Cambridge 1903) and *Ethics* (London 1912).

LUDWIG WITTGENSTEIN (1889–1951): the morality of inexplicable emotion. *Tractatus Logico-Philosophicus* (Vienna 1921).

JEAN PIAGET (b. 1896): the morality of careful education: *Le Jugement moral chez l'enfant (The Moral Judgement of the Child)* (Paris 1932).

Index

Index

333

334

341

343

344

Shamans, 181
Shaw, G. B., 91
Shelley, Mary, 219
Shelley, P. B., 120
Shinto, 108–9
Shylock, 248
Signalling, 53–4
Silent majority, 21, 147, 242
Simonds, Lord, 241
Sin, 72–3, 75, 81, 84, 87,
    90–1, 95, 129, 181, 184,
    212, 224, 244, 271
Sismondi, Léonard de, 149
Situation ethics, 25
Siva, 80
Slavery, 91, 93, 108, 151–3,
    158, 174, 218, 230
Sleep, 225, 260–2
Smiles, Samuel, 154, 158
Smith, Adam, 153–6
Smith, Ian, 137, 239
Smoking, 15, 270, 272
Sobriety, 96
Social class, *see* Class, social
Social contract, 235–8
Social Darwinism, 188, 239
Social Democratic Federation,
    164
Social Democratic Party, 230
Social engineering, 23, 276
Social justice, 13, 80, 116, 142,
    171, 201, 204, 239, 276
Social Morality Council, 127
Social Purity Alliance, 98
Social science, *see* Sociology
    and National Association
Social Security, 20, 158, 245,
    269
Social status, 16, 57, 152, 225,
    228, 248, 251, 277–8
Socialism, 18, 30, 32, 35, 121,
    147–8, 153, 159, 163–75,
    177, 182, 192–3, 195,
    222–3, 229–31, 238
Socialist Charter, 165
Socialist League, 164
Socialist realism, 166

Society of Equals, 174
Sociology, 18, 33, 39, 122–3,
    126, 131, 142, 153, 176,
    179, 183, 186, 188, 191, 229
Solidarity, 19
Solipsism, 49
Soper, Lord, 103
Sophists, 141
Sorbonne, 33
Soul, 17, 23, 49, 71, 80, 99,
    105, 129, 143, 180, 255
Southey, Robert, 30, 161
Southwell, Charles, 133
Soviet Union, 32, 165–6,
    168–9, 171–2, 174, 188, 220,
    222, 230, 237
Spartacus, 93
Specialism, 16, 188, 207, 231,
    257, 260
Spender, Stephen, 30
Spinoza, Benedict, 80, 149,
    235
Spiritualism, 17, 30, 120–1,
    164
Stability, 22, 56–7, 67, 78–9,
    84, 94, 109, 122, 149–50,
    152, 155–7, 160, 169, 184,
    205, 208–9, 228, 232–3,
    242, 250–1, 261, 263
Stahl, Friedrich, 123
Stalin, Josif, 19, 168
Stalinism, 34, 238
Stanley, Dean, 98
State, 123, 149, 165, 168–9,
    174–5, 190, 193, 195, 200,
    229–30, 235–40, 245–6
Statistics, 30, 50, 103, 110,
    171, 185, 268, 274
Stealing, 170, 208, 224, 226,
    228, 247, 271
Stephen, Sir James, 240, 250
Stephen, Sir Leslie, 130
Sterilization, 251, 281
Stirner, Max, 192–5
Stoicism, 87
Stokes, Lord, 173
Strikes, 19, 36, 173

349

351